```
946.08 Pri Ria        225855
Rial.
Revolution from above.
```

The Lorette Wilmot Library
Nazareth College of Rochester
WITHDRAWN

REVOLUTION
FROM
ABOVE

REVOLUTION FROM ABOVE

The Primo de Rivera Dictatorship in Spain, 1923–1930

JAMES H. RIAL

Fairfax: George Mason University Press
London and Toronto: Associated University Presses

© 1986 by Associated University Presses, Inc.

Associated University Presses
440 Forsgate Drive
Cranbury, NJ 08512

Associated University Presses
25 Sicilian Avenue
London WC1A 2QH, England

Associated University Presses
2133 Royal Windsor Drive
Unit 1
Mississauga, Ontario
Canada L5J 1K5

The paper used in this publication meets the minimum requirements of the American National Standard for Permanence of Paper for Printed Library Materials Z39.48-1984.

Library of Congress Cataloging-in-Publication Data

Rial, James H., 1946–
   Revolution from above.
   Bibliography: p.
   Includes index.
   1. Spain—Politics and government—1923–1930.
2. Primo de Rivera, Miguel, 1870–1930. 3. Spain—
Economic policy. 4. Spain—Social policy. I. Title.
DP247.R53   1986   946.08   84-72897
ISBN 0-913969-01-X

Printed in the United States of America

Contents

Acknowledgments	7
Introduction	9

PART ONE: Spain's Problems and the Dictatorship
1. Spain during the Last Years of the Constitutional Regime	17
2. The Regime	45

PART TWO: Political Reform
3. Local Government	79
4. Attempts at a New Compact	103

PART THREE: Economic Reform
5. Finances	133
6. Transportation and Energy	155
7. Industry, Agriculture, and the Dictatorship's Economic Legacy	169

PART FOUR: Social Reform
8. Palliatives	191
9. Corporate Labor Organization	205
10. Education	214
11. The Social Situation at the End of the Dictatorship	223

Conclusion	230
Bibliography	235
Index	252

Acknowledgments

It is a pleasure to acknowledge those who have contributed to this study. Edward Malefakis stimulated my initial interest when I was a graduate student in Spanish history, helped to start me on my research, and has been the source of valued suggestions ever since. At critical junctures Stanley Payne provided needed advice and encouragement. I am indebted as well to Juan Linz, Raymond Carr, James Sheehan, John Coverdale, Richard Herr, Vicente Pilapil, and Shannon Fleming for reading and commenting on earlier drafts. Help and advice were also received from Paul Preston, Herbert Southworth, Angel Viñas, Javier Tusell Gómez, Pedro Tedde de Lorca, Diego Mateo Peral, Enrique Moral Sandoval, María del Carmen Pescador del Hoyo, María del Carmen Salas, and María Jesús Cuesta. A special measure of gratitude is owed Joan Connelly Ullman. Her kindness and example have sustained the writing of this study while her deep understanding of Spain has helped shape its argument.

Much of the research for this study was made possible by the financial support of the National Endowment for the Humanities and the United States–Spanish Joint Committee for Educational and Cultural Affairs. I am also grateful to three unusually proficient typists: Gail Kralj, Louise Knoblow, and Kathleen Staab. In a more personal way, I have been thankful for the encouragement and interest of my parents, James and Lois Rial. In ways that only she can know, my wife, Ann Frontera-Rial, has borne the greatest burden in the completion of this book, and it is to her that I dedicate it.

Introduction

General Miguel Primo de Rivera y Orbaneja, the second marquis of Estella, was dictator in Spain from 13 September 1923 to 28 January 1930. Spain faced many problems in this period, and Primo was convinced that he could deal with them more effectively than the parliamentary government he overthrew. His reforms are the subject of this study.

The questions raised here have general importance. Spain's problems were shared by other countries in Southern and Eastern Europe in the years between the two world wars.[1] These latecomers to modernization lacked many social and economic resources needed for development. Their industries were frequently dependent on artificial supports. Modernization divided these countries initially more than it united them. They did not have either the internal unity or tradition of representative government required to support their imported parliamentary institutions. Reform legislation was needed to promote development and national integration. The problems these countries faced, however, militated against the formation of reform coalitions. The ineffectiveness of parliamentary government paved the way for authoritarianism in one country after another.

Regimes such as the royal dictatorships in Yugoslavia and Romania, the colonels in Poland, and Salazar in Portugal were presumably strong governments capable of forcing the sacrifices needed to further modernization, at the same time maintaining national integration through reforms, repression, and patriotic appeals. These authoritarian governments often fared little better than their parliamentary predecessors, however. Not only were they fallible, but the absence of a free press and loyal opposition meant that they often persisted in mistaken policies. More seriously, their policies were as badly skewed as those of elected governments by their ties to privileged groups. The difficulties they faced are shared by authoritarian governments in many parts of the world today. In the 1920s they were exemplified by Primo's dictatorship.

The fate of his regime, far removed from us in time and place, may become more, not less, relevant. Advanced countries have lately drifted toward a new realpolitik in their dealings with developing nations. In a hard and more threatening world, it is occasionally held that hard choices have to be made. The interests of the United States and other western countries may well be identified more strongly than in the recent past with friendly authoritarian regimes rather than with more popularly based, and occasionally unpredictable, governments. If authoritarianism, however, tends ultimately to be ineffective and fragile, westerners may in the end sacrifice their democratic principles without advancing their interests. Certainly the record of interwar authoritarianism, as exemplified in Primo's dictatorship, raises questions about the strength of strong men.

The major elements of this study are presented in Part One: Spain's problems as a developing nation and the dictatorship that sought to deal with them. Particular attention is given to the role played by World War I in aggravating social and economic difficulties and in discrediting parliamentary government. Primo's program and the composition and support for his dictatorship are then discussed.

Part Two treats political reform. Primo intended to bring a new elite to power at every level of government, from Madrid down to the smallest municipality. Local government reform and a national civic association were major parts of his program, and he looked to them to provide backing for his regime as well as to end the alienation of the nation from its political leadership. This effort was poorly conceived and produced few of its intended results.

Part Three discusses Primo's economic reforms. The dictatorship attempted far more than the parliamentary governments before it. Nonetheless, its programs were largely intensifications of mistaken policies begun before 1923. They contributed to a brief, narrowly based prosperity but did little to solve basic economic problems.

The final section, Part Four, deals with social reform. The dictatorship's program was premised on a belief that no radical changes were needed in the relationship between different groups in Spanish society. All that was attempted were small palliatives and a new labor arbitration system.

The dictatorship's ambition and energy provided much to admire. In almost every important area, however, Primo accomplished far less than he had set out to. The dictatorship's shortcomings and eventual collapse are partly attributable to political inexperience and ineptitude. But errors in Primo's conception of the country's problems and reform needs were decisive. With an essentially conservative political and social vision, he worked closely with established elites and developed policies in their interest. Those policies, however, were not in the long-term interest of the country and worked to perpetuate underdevelopment and exacerbate internal divisions. Spain has only recently begun to free itself from the consequences.

NOTE

1. Among the other countries in this area with authoritarian governments in the inter-war period were Portugal, Italy, Yugoslavia, Albania, Greece, Bulgaria, Romania, Hungary, Austria, Poland, Lithuania, Latvia, and Estonia. Czechoslovakia was the only exception to this trend in Southern and Eastern Europe.

REVOLUTION FROM ABOVE

Part One

SPAIN'S PROBLEMS AND THE DICTATORSHIP

1
Spain during the Last Years of the Constitutional Regime

The Old Order and Its Problems

A gap existed between political theory and practice under the Restoration regime that governed Spain for nearly half a century before Primo took power. The Constitution of 1876 established a parliamentary monarchy with "Don Alfonso XII, by the grace of God, constitutional king of Spain."[1] The king could not enact laws without parliament, the Cortes, but with ministerial approval he could issue decrees compatible with existing legislation. He had the right of ministerial appointment, although his ministers were subsequently responsible to the Cortes. The crown could prorogue the Cortes and call new elections. The king also had supreme command of the army and the navy.

The Cortes was bicameral. The Senate consisted of nobles, ex officio members, royally appointed life senators, and elected members. It was a select body. Even its elected members were chosen by a carefully circumscribed electorate and had to meet a number of preconditions. The Congress of Deputies was more democratic. After 1890 its members were elected by universal manhood suffrage. In general the system was a self-conscious adaptation of English institutions. The two parties that alternated in power were even called Liberal and Conservative.

If national politics was patterned on a British model, internal administration was structured along French lines. Administrative authority was vested in the cabinet, or council of ministers.[2] The president of the council was the country's premier. The interior minister was responsible for local government. He appointed the civil governors whose role in each of the fifty provinces was analogous to that of French prefects in their departments.

Provincial assembly members were elected directly from separate districts. The assembly did not have extensive legislative powers. Its authority was limited largely to advising the civil governor on how the province should meet the responsibilities mandated it by the central government. Assisting the governor in day to day administration was a separate provincial commission. The primary responsibilities of provincial government were public welfare, health, education, and highways. In meeting those obligations the provinces had to work with a small revenue base and limited taxation powers.[3] Most of their budget was met through compulsory municipal contributions.

The civil governor appointed municipal mayors who shared power with elected town councils.[4] Together each mayor and council were responsible for implementing the legislation of the national government. The concerns of municipal government included public safety, education, sanitation, and road maintenance. Mirroring the national government and provinces, each municipality's civil servants were patronage appointees. The low salary for these posts notwithstanding, there were always many more job seekers than positions available. If a municipal government failed to meet its mandated responsibilities, the civil governor could use his "tutelage" powers to remove local officeholders or carry out other necessary changes. Because the municipalities tended to be poorly administered and lacked adequate resources, this meant that they were almost always vulnerable to outside manipulation.[5] This circumstance reinforced the line of authority, which ran from the interior ministry through the provincial civil governor's office down to the smallest municipality.

The political system was neither as representative nor as efficient as the foreign models from which it derived. One difficulty was its excessive uniformity. The largest cities and smallest towns had virtually the same form of government—an artificial encumbrance for many smaller villages, but far too simple a mechanism for dealing with the social and political complexities of larger cities. The rise of regional separatism in Catalonia in northeastern Spain accentuated these problems as many Catalans came to believe that their region required special governmental structures of its own.

Overcentralization was a related concern. The Restoration continued an intrusion of the national government into local affairs that had begun half a century earlier. This usurpation of municipal and provincial autonomy obstructed development of local initiative. Grassroots apathy only facilitated further state intervention. Many *pueblos* regarded the representatives of the national government as an alien presence. As the state was not identified with local needs, it was handicapped in meeting them. Local resentment of the national government was sufficiently strong that it has been attributed a role in the spread of anarchism.[6]

Another problem was excessive fragmentation. There were more than 9,000 municipalities in Spain, each with its own mayor and town council.[7] That amounted to nearly one local government unit for every 2,500 people in the country. The administrative talent necessary to staff and to monitor so many offices was simply not available, particularly in the smaller municipalities.

Additional difficulties arose from the dual aspect of the civil governor's duties. The civil governor was the centerpiece of the electoral machinery of *caciquismo,* Spain's system of "boss" politics. Dealings with local power brokers over candidates, patronage, and government contracts required much of his time. As the French prefectorial corps was increasingly professionalized, the Spanish civil governor was reduced to a middle level political operative. This transformation had important consequences with the increased scale of government by the early twentieth century. The civil governor's immersion in day-to-day politics meant that when state ministries acquired new local responsibilities, the only way to meet them was to set up independent bureaucratic structures of their own. As a result, the civil governor began to lose his broad coordinative function, and local government itself was occasionally confused by a national administration whose right hand did not always know what its left hand was doing.

The most serious problems of government stemmed from grafting nominally liberal, democratic institutions onto a backward society. The Spanish Right long charged that liberalism was an exotic growth that survived only under artificially supported, hothouse conditions. The element of truth in this indictment lies in the fact that parliamentary government never acquired a wide popular base in the nineteenth century. It prevailed only because it was able to form new types of connective tissue between it and a largely apathetic country. One of these was the centralized and inherently authoritarian administrative hierarchy already outlined. Local autonomy was a potential danger when no consensus existed for liberalism. That freedom was considerably circumscribed as liberalism maintained itself through illiberal means.

Caciquismo was another type of connective tissue.[8] Most local residents had little interest in national affairs. Their traditional political reference points were community deference, dependence, and family ties. Similarly, the interest of most local elites in national government was limited to matters directly affecting their own well-being. In return for government patronage they used their influence to manufacture the majorities needed to elect a representative to the Cortes in Madrid.[9]

That representative's participation in one of the two national parties resulted, in turn, in new patronage opportunities further bolstering the hold of a particular elite group on local affairs. In some instances, a single family or group of families was sufficiently powerful to dominate an entire electoral district, making it their own pocket borough. Article 29 of the constitution took account of such circumstances by providing for the automatic election of unopposed candidates.

Most Cortes seats, however, were not firmly held by either party. In many districts several factions alternately competed and combined for advantage. Here the civil governor was important. By throwing the patronage and police powers of his office behind either the Liberal or the Conservative groups, he could assure their success at the polls. This support generally began by turning municipal government over to the supporters of the particular national party that had been designated to carry the district. The civil governor's maneuvering was frequently on behalf of candidates already selected by the interior minister and often not even known to the district. The rewards for supporting a successful candidacy, however, were no less great in that case. Some power brokers were so adept at adjusting to changing political tides that they never lost control of local government. When it was time, for example, to replace a Conservative deputy with a Liberal, they would dutifully help the civil governor manufacture a new majority.

Governments made elections, then, rather than elections producing governments. Once a particular political situation had been "exhausted," or a change of governments was required by either scandal or crisis, the government partly yielded to its opposition. The latter then used the electoral machinery of the interior ministry to install the civil governors necessary to produce election success in particular parliamentary districts. Since individual premiers might be the last to see the need for a change, the king played an important role in soliciting opinion from the government and the opposition. Here Spain's inability to sustain fully representative government extended the monarch's informal influence well beyond his by no means inconsiderable constitutional powers.

Until recently, *caciquismo* has been treated as a transitional phenomenon, similar to machine politics in certain North American cities and deference politics in an age of increasing formal democracy in England. Support for this view lies in the low levels of political mobilization under *caciquismo*. Once voting became a mass activity, the *caciques* lost their hold on urban areas.[10] Lately, however, there has been a new recognition of the system's ability to perpetuate itself.[11] Just as Giolitti in Italy was able to "attract" a wide variety of challengers from outside the system, the two *turno* parties in Spain were successful in their own way in coopting many republicans and reformists through safe seats or other favors. More important still was the system's virtual monopoly over patronage and coercion in rural areas. In a predominantly agricultural country that fact alone was sufficient to maintain it in power indefinitely.

The *turno* system only regulated the alternation in power of the Liberals and Conservatives. It did not eliminate differences between them.[12] The Conservatives were heirs of the mid-nineteenth century *Moderado* tradition with its commitment to parliamentary institutions directed by a stable, propertied elite. They drew much of their support from medium to large landowners in the central and southern provinces. By the early twentieth century they also attracted some backing from expanding industrial elites. The Conservatives were somewhat sympathetic to protectionism and stronger still in their support of the church, crown, and military. The Liberals, on the other hand, carried forward some of the old radical liberal *Progresista* traditions, but they were more amorphous. They tended toward anticlericalism and were less inclined to protectionism. They also showed more concern with civil liberties and were somewhat more interested in opening the political system to mass participation. The Liberals' principal sources of strength were medium-sized cereal producers in northern Spain and urban merchant and professional middle to lower middle classes, the *clases medias*.

These patterns, however, were far from uniform. Catholic peasant landowners gave the Conservatives important islands of strength in northern Liberal areas. At the same time, there were tightly controlled Liberal electoral districts in Conservative Andalusia, such as Niceto Alcalá Zamora's in the province of Córdoba and Santiago Alba's in the province of Cadiz. Moreover, despite their differences, Liberals and Conservatives alike remained elite parties without genuine mass support. Their roots and programs might vary, but their shared monopoly of power was ultimately sustained by electoral manipulation and characterized by a division between the governed and those who governed. In this sense, at least, there was more uniting than dividing them.

The dynastic parties' separation from the electorate handicapped them in meeting Spain's problems and left them vulnerable to increasing criticism in the late nineteenth and early twentieth centuries. The principal charge against the system they presided over was that it perpetuated the underdeveloped civic consciousness that was its own precondition. In the minds of many intellectuals the *turno* arrangement was closely associated with the country's backwardness. Today, of course, political corruption is no longer seen as incompatible with rapid economic development. Indeed, rapid economic growth has proven a spawning ground for political venality in a number of countries. But many regenerationists in Spain saw a different relationship. They held that there could be no progress until the old political bosses had been swept away by a new elite. Because *caciquismo* had its roots in local government, the process of reform would have to reach deep into provincial and municipal politics. These twin themes of "new men" and local government reform dominated the political reform movement.

No other issue, according to Tusell and Chacón, was the source of as much attention as local government.[13] Little, however, was accomplished before 1900. The reliance of Liberals and Conservatives alike on *caciquismo* meant that they approached the issue gingerly. There was, however, a more basic difficulty. In order to hand power over to the "people," there had to be a concerned, politically interested citizenry to receive and exercise that power. That element was long absent. Popular apathy, as much as the politicians, was responsibile for the reform movement's lack of vitality.

This situation began to change by the turn of the century. Defeat in 1898 gave impetus to reform. With the new century organized labor, regionalism, and anti-*turno* parties became more important. The anticlerical Radical party cultivated mass working-class backing in Barcelona, while the conservative, regionalist Lliga party attracted much support from Catalan property owners, both urban and rural. The mobilization of political energies they embodied largely drove the dynastic parties from Catalonia. Only by merging their separate party organizations did the Liberals and Conservatives manage to beat back a regionalist challenge in the Basque provinces. In Asturias the middle classes, especially intellectuals, gave increasing support to the moderately social democratic Reformist party. The Socialists elected their first deputy to the Cortes in 1909. The nineteenth century's neoabsolutist Carlists, though deeply fragmented, updated their program sufficiently to maintain a limited following among small and medium landowners, particularly in the northeast. Also appealing to conservative, religious landowners in the north was the clerical People's party (Partido Social Popular) born in the last days of the constitutional regime. Although not strong enough singly or together to dismount the *turno* system, these parties rallied political "outs" in many parts of the country and attracted a disproportionate share of the period's youthful idealists.

The dynastic parties were not indifferent to this challenge. In separate ways they sought to open the system to greater participation. The Conservatives, in particular, focused on local government. This emphasis was understandable given their belief that the country's rural municipalities provided a natural Conservative majority. To assure their dominance at this level, they proposed coupling administrative decentralization with extra representation for corporate interest groups on town councils. The Liberals also showed interest in local government, but their primary concern was in attracting the new, insurgent forces on the left. By aligning with the most rapidly expanding sectors of the electorate, they promoted their own political ascendancy. At the same time, by assimilating the monarchy's enemies, they could protect the political structure of privilege in which they had such a large stake.

Both parties, thus, reached out to the *neutra masa,* or silent majority, for a genuine base of popular support. Each saw itself motivated by the highest, nonpartisan principles. But each interpreted popular participation in the light most advantageous to its own fortunes. The threats involved in this situation were real. Once genuine electoral competition became a reality, neither party could regard public office as a sinecure guaranteed by private understandings. Since each party's interests were interwoven with its principles, it was difficult for either to compromise or to comprehend the other's position. Thus, the same forces that promoted political reform also made its realization problematic.

Catalan regionalism aggravated these difficulties. Political participation in local affairs was greater in Catalonia than in any other area outside the Basque provinces. Since the spearhead of the Catalan movement, the Lliga party, was dominated by conservative businessmen and since the Conservative party of Antonio Maura had shown some solicitude for industrial interests, the Liberals understandably feared an accommodation between the two groups. Limited autonomy for Catalonia in exchange for the support needed to pass Maura's local government reforms would have been disastrous to Liberal fortunes. But Catalonia's claim to a separate identity alienated many Conservative nationalists, particularly in the military, and that alliance never went beyond preliminary negotiations. Similarly, there was little sympathy for industrial Catalonia in Liberal, cereal producing central Spain. Since the Catalan issue could not be easily resolved by either party, it survived to bedevil them both. Catalan demands for partial autonomy greeted every effort to deal with local government. Spain's most modern and dynamic region became an obstacle to reform rather than an asset to it.

The persistence into the twentieth century of nineteenth-century issues also jeopardized political reform. Divisions between anticlericals and supporters of the church, and between monarchists and republicans, split the reform cause. Pursuit of basic constitutional changes wasted energies and talents that might have improved existing institutions. Moreover, the passions and fears aroused by these questions went well beyond those inspired by more mundane issues. Even though anticlericalism was only intermittently a central question, and the republican movement never dominated public attention, both were always present under the surface where they exacerbated and complicated the tensions aroused by other reform efforts.

The basic obstacle to political reform under the constitutional regime, however, continued to be the isolation of the Liberals and Conservatives from the electorate. Disagreement on how to meet demands for increased political participation produced splits over personalities, tactics, and programs. Since neither party had a firm base in the electorate, there was no final arbiter for those differences. As reform pressure increased, it could only lead to further fragmentation and inefficacy. This tendency was exacerbated by the burdens that working-class militancy and the Moroccan conflict placed on the system.

World War I brought these matters to a climax. Although Spain was neutral, the war produced economic dislocation and social tension. The inability of Liberal and Conservative politicians to deal with these problems diminished their public standing. Principal focal points of discontent were the working class, the army, and the Catalans. For a few brief months in 1917 it seemed that these groups might coalesce in a broad coalition with the republicans and middle-class reformers who stood outside the *turno* system.[14] In the end, however, the challengers were too few and too divided. The politicians in Madrid played one faction against the other. The army was coopted; the reform politicians and the Catalans were intimidated; and without allies a workers' general strike was easily quashed. The failure of this reform surge left the constitutional regime isolated from the country it sought to represent and govern. The decomposition of the two dynastic parties accelerated, and politics became more fluid. From 1917 to 1923 there were fifteen cabinets. The inefficacy of the politicians mattered because Spain was faced with serious social and economic problems.

A Backward Economy

Spain's principal economic problems were resource deficiencies and social inequality. The resource problem was evident in its mineral reserves. Spanish coal was low grade and difficult to mine. Transportation was also difficult because the principal deposits were in Asturias, far from the Basque steel industry and separated from the interior by the Cantabric Mountains. Other minerals were of higher quality and more easily exploited. But by 1900 many deposits were being exhausted that had made Spain a major mining exporter in the nineteenth century.[15]

Rough terrain hindered transportation and increased its cost. According to recent figures only 22% of Spanish rail track rests on level ground, and no more than 66% of it is without curves.[16] Over approximately 11,000 miles of track, there are 4,000 bridges, 1,165 tunnels, and 16,000 crossing points. Railroad development was also handicapped by a small and thinly spread population. There was a close correlation between Spain's low population density and its limited rail mileage.[17]

Georgraphic and social factors also hampered agriculture. Most rain fell in the North where the soil was least suitable for farming.[18] Depletion of forests and a cereal monoculture resulted in erosion, low water tables, and soil infertility. The social dimension of the agricultural problem was evident in southern latifundia provinces. Low peasant wages, not modern agricultural techniques, maintained the profits of large, absentee landlords.[19] Mechanization, crop experimentation, and irrigation were minimal. Indeed, by the early twentieth century, some landlords deliberately avoided increasing the productivity of their holdings for fear of enhancing their expropriation potential.

In northwest Spain the problem was almost the opposite.[20] Extreme overpopulation and poor soil resulted in a patchwork quilt of tiny farms, each striving for a meager self-sufficiency. There was disproportionate and reduplicative investment in buildings and work animals to the detriment of machinery and land.[21] The *foro,* a semifeudal land tenure system, aggravated these difficulties.[22] It produced endless conflict and contributed to the chronic indebtedness of agriculture in the region.

These problems gave Spain some of the lowest yields in Europe.[23] Low agricultural productivity had enormous implications for the rest of the economy. Malefakis has pointed out that more than half the population in forty-six of the country's fifty provinces were agricultural at the beginning of the century.[24] As late as 1924 agriculture produced nearly 43% of the nation's total income, compared with less than 35% from all extractive and manufacturing industries combined.[25] The poverty of such a large sector burdened economic development.

Low consumption limited production, which, in turn, pushed prices up and further constricted purchasing power. The hydroelectric industry illustrates this dilemma.[26] Spain pioneered in electric power in the 1870s and 1880s. By World War I, however, politicians, economists, and the electric companies themselves all expressed concern over the slow development of the industry.[27] The problem was that electrical production involves considerable economies of scale. Or, conversely, Spain was penalized for limited production. Since a large market did not exist, the first generating plants were small and inefficient. The high cost of their product discouraged consumption and retarded the industry's growth.

These circumstances were self-perpetuating and characterized many areas of the economy. There were several potential sources of stimulus capable of breaking through them: the world economy, the banks, and the state. Tourism and remittances from "guest workers" abroad were present in this period but lacked their recent importance as earners of foreign exchange for internal development. In the early twentieth century the principal sources of foreign capital were investment and trade. Foreign investment provided development funding that Spain could not generate easily itself, while trade provided needed capital goods that could not be efficiently produced at home. Nonetheless, Spain's very underdevelopment meant that its relationship with the world economy was weighted against it. Liberal concessions to foreign investors meant that Spain frequently lost as much as it gained by this means.[28] Since more foreign exchange was needed to pay for industrial imports than was earned through agricultural and mineral exports, trade was equally ineffective as a promoter of development.[29] Although one of the first imperial powers, Spain had slipped into a semicolonial economic relationship with more advanced nations well before the twentieth century.

The role of banks in mobilizing development capital was potentially important, because Spain had not industrialized early in the nineteenth century when the costs were small.[30] The banks were unequal to this challenge. In general, they remained small, family-run concerns, even after the arrival of such foreign bankers as the Rothschilds and the Pereires. After a brief flurry of government-encouraged railroad investment in the mid-nineteenth century, they preferred the safety of government securities or the high yields of short-term currency speculation to the uncertainties of industrial investment.

The failure of the banks and the world economy to break the circle of backwardness paved the way for state intervention. The regenerationist movement after 1898 and the international drift toward protectionism also promoted governmental activism. The state's poverty limited its help, however. The tax system was inelastic and regressive.[31] The

Spain during the Last Years of the Constitutional Regime 27

least advantaged social groups carried the heaviest burden. Commercial and industrial profits were taxed more heavily than agricultural wealth. Revenues were collected through tax farmers and other indirect means. Corruption was rife. Fraud and inefficiency reinforced each other.[32]

Partly as a result of these shortcomings, government economic aid consisted primarily of tariffs. In 1907, however, new legislation required government agencies to buy Spanish-made goods when possible.[33] The Commission for the Protection of National Production (Comisión Protectora de la Producción nacional) was established to implement that edict and to draft other economic measures. Railroads and shipping companies received subsidies and cash advances. Production bonuses benefited coal, textile, and sugar producers. Recipients of state aid were themselves urged, and occasionally required, to rely to some extent on domestic suppliers. Consumption of national coal was particularly encouraged.[34]

These programs did not constitute a totally autarkic policy.[35] Nonetheless, they did presume that Spain could attain a high degree of self-sufficiency and successfully generate growth from within. In the short term these measures encouraged industrial development. The fact remained, however, that many elements in production were produced domestically at high cost. Forcing small, inefficient producers to support each other ultimately perpetuated poverty rather than growth. In the process the state was transmuted from a catalyst for development to a crutch for producers too weak to stand on their own.

Policies of this sort compounded the basic problems of inadequate resources and social inequality. Particularly counterproductive was promotion of increased production without regard for consumption capacity. Clearly, capital concentrated in investment creates new wealth for consumption. Nonetheless, in capitalist economies a certain minimum balance between production and consumption capacities is desirable, even in the early stages of development. Preoccupation with productive capacity and infrastructure alone can be as self-defeating as the opposite policy of so dispersing wealth that no investment is possible.

Government policy in Spain inclined too far in the former direction. Overproduction resulted.[36] Cartels were formed in one sector of the economy after another to limit production and to maintain prices at artificially high levels. This course only further constricted purchasing power. Hypertrophy and backwardness existed side by side. The economy became topheavy while remaining underdeveloped. Antonio

Ramos Oliveira characterized this paradox as "the staggering circumstance that a nation of 25 million souls does not form a market capable of absorbing a production manifestly inferior to the national needs."[37]

The relationship between different sectors became less one of mutual support than of mutual draining. Industry was not pulled along by consumption from below but was an artificial and exotic growth. Its high-priced production, together with the tariffs and subsidies granted it, drained capital from the rest of the country.[38] At the same time, industrialists complained that agricultural protection raised the cost of food and, ultimately, of labor and manufactures. Demand was needed to integrate different sectors of the economy into self-sustaining growth. But the policies of the constitutional regime worked against that demand.

World War I and the postwar contraction complicated these problems.[39] The war disrupted Spain's shipping with foreign suppliers and customers at the same time that it produced virtually unlimited demand for Spanish products. The result was that Spain was paid more for fewer goods. Overall, export tonnage declined by 54% while export value increased by 22%.[40] The foreign-exchange influx reversed the trade deficit and boosted the peseta's value. It also produced high profits for many companies and reduced agricultural indebtedness.

The boom was brief and ephemeral, however. It peaked in some areas as early as 1916. The wealth it produced remained in few hands. Shortages of components and raw materials militated against industrial and commercial expansion. Moreover, the high prices and profits produced by this artificial sellers' market eroded the incentive to modernize. War profits went more into luxury spending, speculation, and a bloating of the banking and exchange systems than into sound reinvestment.[41]

These circumstances aggravated the postwar slump. Consumer demand was weak. No sooner had the wage-price lag of the war years begun to close, than an upturn in unemployment depressed purchasing power. Industry had grown accustomed to insatiable foreign demand. When foreign customers turned into competitors, Spanish producers lost their new markets and found themselves overpriced at home.[42] Industries that had sprung up as import substitutes during the war now clamored for protection. Production declined, and prices and profits fell precipitously. Agriculture had similar problems. Additional production capacity for the main export crops—oranges, olive oil, and wine—was achieved slowly and at high cost. By the time that expansion peaked, the contraction had begun.

Economic dislocation called for political action. The government established regulatory commissions, generally composed of government and producer representatives, for most major branches of industry and agriculture.[43] The commissions controlled the foreign trade, distribution, and price of different commodities. Widespread shortages and price rises testified to bureaucratic inability to implement such a far-reaching program.

The government was no more successful in promoting productivity. In particular, Lliga businessmen in Catalonia urged measures transforming the wartime boom into lasting competitiveness for Spain in foreign markets and self-sustaining growth at home.[44] But the rural roots of many Liberal and Conservative politicians inclined them to view the appeals of industrial Catalonia, and to a lesser extent those of the Basque provinces, as narrowly self-interested. They regarded Catalonia's request for a free port and export subsidies as threatening depopulation and industrial decline in the interior of the country. They did not see that regional separatism in those areas was at least partly due to feelings of being neglected by Madrid. Only after protracted footdragging on the politicians' part did Catalonia secure a commercial depository in 1916 and passage of an industrial development act in 1917. Both measures provided much less than Catalans had asked. Bureaucratic slowness and inefficiency lessened the value of even that aid. One year and two ministries later, in the wake of the revolutionary movement of 1917, Francesc Cambó of the Lliga occupied the development ministry in Antonio Maura's bipartisan national government. He was less interested in working with the watered-down programs he had inherited for industry than he was in drafting new legislation. But Cambó himself left office nine months later, before he could make much progress with his plans.

The political system's fragmentation and instability also precluded successful handling of finances. At the same time that the war produced an influx of foreign capital, Spain's Moroccan involvement required large state expenditures.[45] A flexible, efficient tax system could have brought these inflows and outflows together. This did not occur, despite an effort to improve revenue collection.[46] While the price of many agricultural products doubled during the war, for example, income from direct agricultural taxation remained nearly constant.[47] The lag in direct revenues forced additional reliance on indirect taxes.[48] In 1916 the Liberal finance minister from Castile, Santiago Alba, had proposed a wartime windfall-profits tax to increase revenues and lessen the regressive distortion of the tax system. Cambó expressed the opposition of Catalonia and the Basque provinces to this measure. He declared that it would fall more heavily on those industrial areas than on agriculture. Many Conservatives and Liberals also regarded the proposal as radical. After heated debate it was shelved, but not before it had enflamed separatist feeling in the two northern regions and had contributed to their support of the movement for a new constitutional order in 1917.

The failure of Alba's proposal increased the importance of finding a new way of financing the state's embarrassingly mounting deficits. Rather than continue to rely on the Bank of Spain to purchase new treasury issues, the government encouraged private banks to do so. New legislation in 1917 enabled them to use each state bond issue they purchased as security for borrowing capital from the Bank of Spain at interest charges below those paid by the bonds themselves.[49] This capital could be pyramided in still further debt purchases as well as invested in the private sector. In other words, by purchasing state bonds and using them as security for borrowing from the Bank of Spain, banks were simultaneously able to increase their profits, assets, and liquidity. This indirect monetization of the national debt increased the money supply from 2.4 billion pesetas in 1916 to 4.3 billion pesetas in 1920.[50] Bank deposits grew from 618 million pesetas to 2,610 million pesetas from 1915 to 1919. At the same time, new investment opportunities were created by the World War I belligerents' divesting many of their industrial and transportation investments in Spain. Bank investment portfolios increased from 565 million pesetas in 1915 to 1,484 million pesetas in 1919. These circumstances strengthened ties between the bankers and the government, and between the bankers and the business elite. The banks' presence became especially strong in railroads, shipbuilding, electric power, urban mass transit, and steel. The five largest banks benefited most.[51] Their present position as the pivot point for Spain's structure of privilege owes much to the fiscal expediency of government during these years.

The constitutional regime's shortcomings were evident in other economic matters. The war had aggravated the railroads' problems.[52] By 1920 many rail companies were forced to choose between reduced dividends and reduced service. Since lower dividends would cut off their credit, they let their equipment decline.[53] That decision only increased their long-term capital needs. The politicians temporized. They initiated several programs of cash advances between 1918 and 1921 but did nothing about the industry's costly fragmentation and duplication of service. The government established the Superior Railroad Council in 1922 to study the problem. But basic rail restructuring was complicated by the government's other competing concerns as well as by the substantial stake that leading financial institutions had acquired in the industry during the war.

The constitutional regime's lackluster economic record helped to discredit the system. Its failures raises the question of alternatives. Certainly there were no easy answers for Spain's difficulties. Crosscutting special interests, political instability, and bureaucratic shortcomings frustrated reform. Nonetheless, the constitutional regime's basic failure was one of approach, not of ability to pass or implement legislation. The politicians pursued development on a broad front with virtually every sector protected by high tariffs. Since Spain lacked the resources for a high degree of self-sufficiency, this policy hobbled the economy with high production costs and placed a continuing check on purchasing power.

A more productive approach would have been to support only limited sectors with a potential comparative advantage in the world economy. Such a program would have provided greater aid for lead sectors than a policy of blanket support allowed.[54] The wide discrepancy between domestic and international price levels would have been averted, and the problem of high-priced production components would have been obviated. A number of producers, in fact, argued for just this policy. The difficulty was political as much as economic. Whose interests were to be sacrificed for the common good? The contradictory claims of different interest groups pulled the constitutional regime in too many directions to allow a clear answer to that question. Worse, the temporizing and counterproductive precedents it established persisted long after it.

The constitutional regime would also have left a more positive legacy had it placed greater importance on the social dimension of economic development. In city and countryside alike an exceedingly uneven distribution of wealth militated against broad-based economic growth. Social reform was widely discussed in the last years of the constitutional regime and might have contributed to cutting through the self-perpetuating circle of mass poverty, social inequality, and small-scale, inefficient production.

A Divided Society

Spanish society was riven by deep cleavages. Class divisions were particularly strong in southern latifundia provinces. Land reform *(desamortización)* in the mid-nineteenth century eliminated the common lands on which many had depended. It also shifted property into the hands of a new "rural bourgeoisie" who were less paternalistic than either the church or the nobility. Although much new land was brought under cultivation, agricultural technology went essentially unchanged.[55] The importation of inexpensive American grain and an increase in rural population placed downward pressure on wages. These developments eroded the deference ties holding rural society together and contributed to the spread of anarchism.[56]

The gravity of this situation should not be overstated. Apart from Galicia, Spain did not suffer the extreme rural overpopulation of many Eastern European countries.[57] Nonetheless, agricultural daily wages were only one-third to one-half those of industry in the early 1900s.[58] This difference was only partly compensated by lower rural living costs. Worse, the agricultural work year was relatively short, ranging in different areas from 130 to 250 days.[59] A series of anarchist strikes in 1903 and 1904 revealed the depth of peasant discontent. Repression temporarily dulled millenarian hopes, but class antagonism remained deep. Wartime economic dislocation aggravated tensions. Since rural labor was not well organized, its grievances lacked a constructive outlet. Discontent slowly mounted until it exploded in three years of uncoordinated strikes and disorders, beginning in 1918.

A parallel social estrangement took place in the cities. The hardships of rural life produced large-scale migration to urban centers in the nineteenth century. The number of migrants exceeded available employment, housing, and educational opportunities. Worse, the church, which had long been the benefactor of the poor, was in decline. Local government lacked the resources to fill that void. By 1900 shanty towns had sprung up on the outskirts of many cities. There a motley group of beggars, bootblacks, street peddlers, and scavengers provided a seedbed for crime and revolution.

Only by comparison was the situation of many industrial workers better. Economic change produced a small industrial working class and capitalist middle class. But it was not powerful enough to generate the wealth needed for social peace between them. Labor relations had the same grim, hard-pressing quality of the industrial economy itself. Where economic conditions were particularly severe, anarchosyndicalism frequently gained its firmest supporters. This was the case with Barcelona's textile workers. Better paid crafts such as printing and industries organized in cartels or otherwise lacking competition, such as the railroads, were frequently Socialist strongholds. The greater size of the anarchosyndicalist movement testifies to the difficult position of labor in the early 1900s.[60]

Industrial expansion between 1900 and 1914 improved matters somewhat. Wages rose slightly, while the cost of living declined.[61] Nonetheless, working-class life remained hard. R. Joseph Harrison has summarized much of the available evidence on this question.[62] A 1909 study of diets expressed amazement that worker families managed to subsist at all.[63] Food adulteration was a major problem. Factory legislation was haphazardly enforced. Children under thirteen often worked thirteen or more hours a day, starting as early as three o'clock in the morning. Accidents were frequent and only rarely compensated.

In 1905 there were 438 buildings in Madrid with only a single source of water and a single toilet on each floor.[64] These buildings housed 52,521 persons. The conservative politician, the viscount of Eza, estimated that 270,000 of Madrid's 600,000 population lived in seriously substandard housing. Madrid was "the most crowded and disease-ridden capital in Europe."[65] From 1900 to 1905, 58,454 women died from tuberculosis alone in that city. The annual mortality rate in the Floridablanca area was 13 per 1,000.[66] In the shanty towns the rate ranged between 30 and 50 per 1,000.

The First World War brought additional hardship. Wages lagged well behind prices until 1920.[67] After that date the postwar contraction increased unemployment. These circumstances explain why the first quarter of the twentieth century was a time of growing labor consciousness and militancy.[68] Union membership peaked in 1919 and 1920. At 211,000, the Socialist UGT's membership had increased eightfold since 1900.[69] Few reliable figures exist for the anarchosyndicalist CNT. Membership estimates at the time of its December 1919 Congress range from 700,000 to nearly 1,300,000.[70] Strikes increased more than sixfold from 1915 to 1920. For most of this period the percentage won by labor also increased.[71]

By the end of the war employers were themselves combining to coordinate countermeasures. Employer resistance, an upsurge in unemployment, and labor's division over the Third International reversed the tide of working-class success in the postwar years. The percentage of totally unsuccessful strikes increased from 17% in 1919 to 43% in 1923.[72] Failure to make gains through strikes and negotiations inclined radical sectors of the working class, especially those affiliated with the CNT, in a violent, revolutionary direction. Social and political crimes rose rapidly as the number and success rate of strikes declined.

The violence peaked in the first nine months of 1923. Public opinion was particularly shocked by the murder of the moderate CNT leader, Salvador Seguí, in March and the retaliation assassination of the conservative Cardinal Soldevila less than three months later.[73] Calvo Sotelo claimed that 813 political crimes were committed from January through 13 September, when Primo took power.[74] Stanley Payne has estimated that incidents of that sort claimed 154 lives and 90 wounded over approximately the same period.[75]

Catalan regionalism also contributed to the downfall of the constitutional regime.[76] Catalanism drew support from several sources. Many in rural areas wished to preserve the Catalan language and tradition of local self-government from the encroachments of a centralizing state. Peasants upset over vineyard leasing conditions used Catalanism as a protest vehicle. Intellectuals protested Castilian cultural domination. By the late nineteenth century Catalonia's urban middle class had grown restive under a national government dominated by old-fashioned agrarian-based elites from the interior and the South. Catalan businessmen's dissatisfaction over the central government's indifference to their industrial region's special needs had led to the founding of the Lliga, which dominated Catalan politics during the century's first two decades.

In 1913 the Lliga extracted from Madrid the *mancomunidad,* a federation of the four Catalan provinces. Its limited home-rule powers were insufficient to satisfy regional aspirations. Worse, the central government's failure to deal with social unrest brought by World War I compounded the disillusionment engendered by debate over the windfall-profits tax and industrial-aid legislation. The working-class challenge, however, frightened many Lliga businessmen and made them dependent on the police powers of the central government. Their loss of zeal meant that leadership of the regional movement passed into radical hands.[77] In 1919 one militant group sought separate representation for Catalonia at the Paris Peace Conference. Catalan radicals encouraged Basque, Galician, and Valencian regionalists. They also expressed solidarity with Abd el-Krim, who led the fight against Spanish rule in Morocco. In early September 1923 the burning of a Spanish flag at a Catalan demonstration greatly offended nationalist feeling in the rest of the country.

The church was another source of division. Raymond Carr described this problem well:

> No convincing description of Spanish society at the turn of the century can be drawn exclusively in terms of the social conflicts common to western Europe. The survival after a hundred years of liberalism, of an officially Catholic state and a Catholic society meant that religion was the prism through which all other conflict was refracted; more than this, it meant that the claims of the Church on society were a primary source of division in themselves.[78]

With the clerical issue so interwoven with the period's other conflicts, the church's offensive against apostasy in the late nineteenth and early twentieth century could not be a matter of religion alone. Many in the vanguard of the Catholic revival saw winning lost souls for the church as part of a larger struggle against the church's enemies—liberalism, republicanism, and socialism. On the other hand, many liberals, republicans, and socialists feared that religious obscurantism would change the entire direction of national life. The church was only intermittently an issue in itself. More often it complicated the resolution of other problems, such as educational reform.

The military was a second institution that divided rather than united Spain.[79] Not large enough to hold together an empire in the nineteenth century, it was far too large for the small, poor country that remained after the loss of the colonies. The army was underpaid, undertrained, and underequipped. It was more a domestic and colonial police force than an instrument for foreign war. By the twentieth century it had become another inefficient government bureaucracy, albeit the most expensive.[80]

Defeat in 1898 discredited it. Since the army was the final guardian of public order and national unity, many of the attacks on it came from the Left and Catalonia. In 1905 military pressure resulted in a law making insults to the army subject to military trial. The army's problems increased in 1909. Fighting in Morocco made it difficult to reduce the army. However, existing troop levels left little money for the improved training and material needed to conclude that conflict. As the war dragged on, impatience with the army increased. Officers themselves grew hostile to politicians who charged them with fighting a war they lacked the resources to win. Inflation's impact on officers' salaries during World War I exacerbated military discontent. Beginning in 1917 many junior officers in the peninsula joined together in *juntas de defensa,* military syndicates demanding increased pay and promotions.

The politicians placated the military to survive that tumultuous year. Thereafter they lived at the sufferance of their soldiers. To undo the *junteros'* fears that their careers were not keeping up with those of combat officers in Africa, the politicians continued to maintain an oversized military establishment and pursued generous pay and promotion policies. To satisfy *africanista* officers in Morocco, successive governments persisted in the controversial war. These concessions did not win the military to support what they still regarded as corrupt and ineffectual politicians. Intraarmy rivalry between the *junteros* and *africanistas* did allow the government to abolish the *juntas* formally in

November 1922. But that step did not alter the basic pattern of military intimidation and hostility toward the politicians. *Juntero* officers continued to meet informally in the peninsula, while *africanistas* remained dissatisfied with the level of government support for the Moroccan effort.

Spain's social divisions ran deep. Their mutual reinforcement made reform coalitions difficult. The Lliga's domination by conservative business interests militated against cooperation between regionalists and labor. A similar situation existed in the Basque provinces. Discontented as the army was, it was more opposed than supportive of regionalist and working-class aspirations. The working class was itself divided between Socialists and anarchosyndicalist unions. These crosscutting pulls meant that movement for change was weaker than the sum of its parts.

Nonetheless, many politicians recognized the need for social reform. This was evident in the establishment of the Social Reform Institute in 1903 and the legislation of the next two decades. Laws were passed on women and child labor, industrial accidents, public housing, arbitration procedures, agrarian reform, retirement insurance, and the eight-hour day. This legislation had shortcomings. Most of it was directed to urban labor, while the most serious problems existed in the countryside. Both the retirement and agrarian acts were self-help measures, which were of little value to the very poor, who most needed assistance. Neither retirement nor accident benefits were particularly generous.

Still, this was not an unworthy body of legislation for a developing nation. What was lacking was enforcement. Reform-minded politicians could more easily pass a new law than secure funds for its implementation.[81] The state's poverty was a factor here. More basic, however, was the politicians' lack of a direct stake in reform. The Cortes's oligarchic elite ruled through electoral manipulation. Few parliamentarians felt direct responsibility to a working class constituency. Reform might be a matter of principle, and even of long-term self-interest, but in the short term it generally ran counter to the structure of privilege they presided over. Deputies from agricultural districts could support factory legislation, and deputies from industrial areas could support agrarian reform. But ultimately their ties to each other were stronger than their ties to their nominal constituencies.

Political instability also worked against social reform. In 1919, Ángel Ossorio was minister of development. He asked Pascual Carrión and other agronomists in Seville province to recommend solutions for the agrarian problem in northern Spain.[82] Before they could complete their work a new ministry was formed, and Carrión's study was left to gather dust in the archives. Public health also suffered from political shifts.[83] A creditable start had been made here at the beginning of the century, but the momentum was not maintained into the war years. The policy and personnel changes resulting from rapid ministerial turnover were no more conducive to social reform than they were to political or economic reform.

The Fall of the Old Order

The First World War and its aftermath clearly aggravated Spain's problems. The more serious these problems became, the more the politicians were divided over them. The more they divided, the more ineffective they became. Their failure produced disillusionment. Voter participation in large cities declined in the constitutional regime's last years.[84] The Reformist and People's parties, on the moderate left and right respectively, had arisen to join the Socialists, Traditionalists, Radicals, and regionalist parties in challenging the *turno* system, but none had been able to shake the dynastic parties' hold of *caciquismo's* electoral machinery. Many intellectuals detached themselves from politics.[85] The most influential journal of the war years had been politically concerned *España*. In 1923, José Ortega y Gasset began *Revista de Occidente,* which mirrored the elitism and political indifference of the 1920s. Interestingly, public disenchantment expressed itself more in apathy and cynicism than in extremism of left or right. Labor militancy certainly frightened employers and landowners, but the working class was not yet sufficiently large or well organized to produce a fascist counterresponse.[86] The regional problem was also serious, but a decade later, when it was far worse, Azaña was able to find a formula satisfying Catalan aspirations within the framework of the national state. Still more positively, the clerical issue was in temporary, if superficial, abeyance in the early 1920s. There were even indications that the personalistic factions of the Conservatives and, especially, the Liberals had begun to coalesce with some of the newer parties into broader, more responsive, and more modern political organizations. By 1923 the economy had also begun to recover from the postwar slump.

This is not to say that Spain was not passing through a difficult period. Strikes, labor violence, and other signs of discontent were on the increase in 1923. Worse, the politicians had almost totally discredited themselves. The fact remains, however, that public dissatisfaction was not yet extreme enough to prompt much discussion of alternatives to parliamentary government.[87] The constitutional regime was in trouble, but not on the brink of collapse.

The army was needed to overthrow it. The army had suffered an enormous defeat at Anual in July 1921.[88] Fewer than 3,000 Moors routed a Spanish force of more than 25,000. More than 8,000 Spanish soldiers died, nearly two-thirds of the total lost from 1919 to 1923. Generals Berenguer and Silvestre were responsible for the campaign. Both had been close to the king, and it was widely rumored that Alfonso had personally encouraged the fatal offensive. Anual was, then, not just a military disaster. It was a scandal that reached all the way to the crown and threatened the reputation of nearly every politician who had supported a forward policy in Morocco. Generals, politicians, and opponents of the Moroccan venture all blamed each other. Periodic disclosures of corruption and negligence kept their debate alive. By 1923 this criticism had become a serious affront to many officers. Many believed that the army's honor demanded a reversal of timid and defensive policies pursued in Morocco after Anual. A few even began to plot a military challenge to the politicians.

Adding fuel to the fire was the government of Manuel García Prieto. This last cabinet of the constitutional regime united the principal Liberal factions, promising proportional representation to lessen the *caciques'* power and challenging the religious monopoly of the church and the political prerogatives of the privileged represented in the Senate. The Government also promoted public works, land reform, and a liberal foreign trade policy. More disturbing to the military, in the face of an upturn in working-class terrorism and regional extremism in 1923, the government advocated a conciliatory social policy, including restoration of the civil liberties that had been abridged during the turmoil of the past several years. It appointed the first civilian civil governor in Barcelona in two years. In the face of an unyielding enemy in Morocco and French refusal to support Spanish military efforts, it also pursued a negotiated settlement to the North African war, notwithstanding the escalating demands of insurgent leader Abd el-Krim. Worse, the government promised vigorous investigation and prosecution of the officers responsible for the Anual disaster.

A new voter turnout low in the April 1923 parliamentary election indicated that the Liberal program had not reversed the country's increasing contempt for its politicians. But the Liberals did succeed in stirring elements in the army into action. Just as *junteros* were angry over the soft line toward working-class radicals and regionalists, the *africanistas* were upset by abandonment of a forward policy in

Morocco. For the senior and most political generals, closest to the government, there was almost as much cause for concern in the ministry's indifference to the military in making these departures as there was in the policies themselves. For many officers, then, the Liberals' reassertion of civilian supremacy over the military was doubly threatening for being coupled with national humiliation abroad and public disaster at home. The most important center of intrigue against the government was the "Quadrilateral," a group of four young generals in Madrid.[89] By the early summer this group had solicited the opinion of garrison commanders throughout the country. Few expressed opposition to its plans, but there was little enthusiastic support. If the conspiracy was to succeed it would need a senior general to lead it. By the end of the summer the Quadrilateral had their man—Miguel Primo de Rivera y Orbaneja, Captain General of the Barcelona military district.

NOTES

1. For the text of the 1876 constitution, see E. Tierno Galván, *Leyes políticas españolas fundamentales (1808–1936)* (Madrid: Editorial Tecnos, 1968), pp. 146–69.

2. The following sketch of local administration draws heavily on Javier Tusell Gómez and Diego Chacón Ortiz, *La reforma de la administración local en España, 1900–1936* (Madrid: Instituto de Estudios Administrativos, 1973), pp. 29–33; Eduardo García de Enterría, *La administración española* (Madrid: Alianza Editorial, 1972); and Kenneth Medhurst, *Government in Spain* (Oxford: Pergamon Press, 1973), pp. 119–23.

3. The Basque provinces and Navarre had a separate and more advantageous arrangement with Madrid; José Calvo Sotelo, "A Guisa de Prologo," *Anuario de la vida local/ 1925* (Madrid, 1925), 1:27–28.

4. The principal exceptions to the following pattern were Madrid and Barcelona, which were administered more directly by the national government.

5. On the problems of municipal government see Cirilio Martín-Retortillo, "Maura, municipalista," *Revista de Estudios de la Vida Local* 13, no. 73 (1954): 58; E.T.L. *Por pueblos y aldeas* (Editorial Católica Toledana, 1928), pp. 55–69; and José Tomás Valverde, *Memorias de un alcalde* (Madrid: Talleres Gráficos Escalier, 1961), pp. 16–35 passim.

6. J. A. Pitt-Rivers, *The People of the Sierra* (Chicago: University of Chicago Press, 1961), pp. 17–19, 220–23.

7. Tusell and Chacón, *La reforma,* p. 52, give a figure of 9,314. The exact total changed slightly from year to year and has undergone a general decline in the past quarter century. Today there are slightly more than 8,200 municipalities.

8. On *caciquismo* see Javier Tusell Gómez, "The Functioning of the Cacique System in Andalusia, 1890–1936" in *Politics and Society in Twentieth Century Spain,* ed. Stanley Payne (New York and London: New Viewpoints/Franklin Watts, 1976), pp. 1–28, and the same author's *Oligarquía y caciquismo en Andalucía* (Barcelona: Planeta, 1976). My description of the system draws heavily on his accounts. Also useful are Robert W. Kern, *Liberals, Reformers, and Caciques in Restoration Spain, 1875–1909* (Albuquerque: University of New Mexico Press, 1974), pp. 26–39; and José Varela Ortega, *Los amigos politicos* (Madrid: Alianza Editorial, 1977).

9. For local political minorities life under this arrangement could be difficult. In 1923

citizens in Murcia were still asking Madrid to take action on a land dispute, pending since 1880 against powerful local property owners; Archivo Histórico Nacional (Madrid), Sección de la Presidencia (hereafter AHN) Leg. 30, Exte. 542.

10. Voting trends in the last years of the constitutional regime are analyzed by Juan J. Linz, "The Party System of Spain: Past and Future," in *Party Systems and Voter Alignments*, ed. Seymour M. Lipset and Stein Rokkan (New York: The Free Press, 1967), pp. 210–16.

11. See, for example, Tusell, *Oligarquía y caciquismo*, pp. 524–29.

12. On the programs and support of the dynastic parties, see Stanley G. Payne, "Spanish Conservatism 1834–1923," *Journal of Contemporary History* 13 (1978): 777–79.

13. Tusell and Chacón, *La reforma*, p. 27.

14. The events of that year are described by Juan Antonio Lacomba Avellan, *La crisis española de 1917* (Madrid: Ciencia Nueva, 1970).

15. Banco Central, *Estudio económico/ 1956* (Madrid: Banco Central, 1956), p. 59.

16. Michael Perceval, *The Spaniards* (Devon: David and Charles, 1969), p. 152.

17. In 1900, Spain had 0.0423 miles of railroad track per square mile and a population density of 96 inhabitants per square mile. For other countries the respective figures are United Kingdom, 0.1806 and 340; Germany, 0.1532 and 270; France 0.1144 and 188; Austria-Hungary, 0.0914 and 188; Portugal, 0.0414 and 151; Romania, 0.0362 and 119. Arthur S. Banks, *Cross-Polity Time-Series Data* (Cambridge, Mass., and London: M.I.T. Press, 1971), pp. 15–132 passim.

18. R. M. Bofill Fransi, *Atlas de geografía de España* (Barcelona: Ediciones Jover, 1972), pp. c/2–c/3.

19. An outstanding analysis of this elite and its way of life is Edward E. Malefakis, *Agrarian Reform and Peasant Revolution in Spain* (New Haven and London: Yale University Press, 1970), pp. 11–34, 65–92.

20. Ibid., pp. 436–38.

21. The best breakdown of capital investments in Mediterranean dwarf farming during the interwar period has been done for Yugoslavia by Jozo Tomasevich, *Peasants, Politics and Economic Change in Yugoslavia* (Stanford: Stanford University Press, 1955), pp. 653–58. Dwarf farming predominated in northwest Spain but was not totally isolated to that region. Tendencies in this same direction have been identified for certain mountainous areas in Andalusia by Pitt-Rivers, *The People*, p. 46.

22. The *foro* system and its social and economic implications are discussed by J. A. Durán, *Historia de caciques, bandos, e ideologías en la Galicia no urbana* (Madrid: Siglo Veintiuno de España, 1972).

23. A yield index has been constructed for seven principal crops in selected European countries from 1931 to 1935 by Wilbert E. Moore, *Economic Demography of Eastern and Southern Europe* (Geneva: League of Nations, 1945), p. 193. If Europe generally has an index of 100, the index for individual countries is as follows: Denmark 178, Belgium 177, United Kingdom 143, Germany 134, Italy 108, France 105, Hungary 96, Yugoslavia 89, Poland 83, Spain 77, and Romania 67. The crops used to construct the index were wheat, barley, oats, maize, potatoes, rye, and sugar beets. The source of Moore's data was *Statistiches Jahrbuch für das Deutsches Reich, 1938*, pp. 42–45.

24. Malefakis, *Agrarian Reform*, p. 12.

25. Ibid., p. 11.

26. Juan Arespacochaga, "La política hidráulica en la decadencia económica española," *De Economía*, VII, Monografía III, pp. 162–63; F. F. Sintes Olives and F. Vidal Burdils, *La industria electrica en España* (Barcelona: Montaner y Simon, 1933), pp. 136–37; and Ramón Tamames, *Estructura económica de España*, 3d ed. (Madrid: Sociedad de Estudios y Publicaciones, 1965), pp. 248–49. Unless otherwise indicated, subsequent references to the latter work are to the fifth edition, published in 1970.

27. Carlos Serrano, "La racionalización de la industria de producción de energía eléctrica" *Revista Nacional de Economía* 30, no. 92 (July–August 1930): 4–5.

28. On foreign investment generally, see Manuel Campillo, *Las inversiones extran-*

jeras en España (Madrid: Graficas Manfer, 1963). Particularly useful for early twentieth century is Vergilio Sevillano Carbajal, *¿La España . . . de quien?* (Madrid: Graficás Sánchez, 1936). The role of foreign capital in building Spain's railroads is defended by Raymond Carr, *Spain: 1808–1939* (London: Oxford University Press, 1966), pp. 264–66. More critical is Jordi Nadal, "The Failure of the Industrial Revolution in Spain," in *The Emergence of Industrial Societies*, vol. 2, *The Fontana Economica History of Europe*, ed. Carlo M. Cipolla (London: Collins, 1973), pp. 549–53.

29. Instituto Nacional de Estadística (hereafter INE), *Principales actividades de la vida española en la primera mitad del siglo XX* (Madrid: Instituto Nacional de Estadística, 1952), p. 94, shows a steadily widening trade deficit in the first quarter of the twentieth century. Few Spanish statistics, however, are as unreliable as those for the cash value of imports and exports in this period. For this reason I have not quoted any specific figures here. Trade statistics are discussed by Valentín Andrés Alvarez, "Las balanzas de nuestro comercio exterior, *Revista de Economía Política* 1, no. 1 (January–March 1945), and "Historia y crítica de los valores de nuestra blanze de comercio," *Moneda y Crédito* 4 (March 1943): 11–25. Nonetheless, there is little question that Spain suffered from serious deficits in its balances of trade and payments, and that these imbalances, in turn, drained capital out of the country.

30. On Spanish banking, see Ramón Canosa, *Un siglo de la banca privada: 1845–1945* (Madrid: Nuevas Gráficas, 1945) and Gabriel Tortella-Casares, *Banking, Railraods, and Industry in Spain 1829–1874* (New York: Arno Press, 1977). For international perspective, see Rondo E. Cameron, ed., *Banking and Economic Development* (New York: Oxford University Press, 1972) and idem, ed., *Banking in the Early Stages of Industrialization* (New York: Oxford University Press, 1967).

31. On state finances are A. Bernard, *Taxation of Incomes, Corporations, and Inheritances in Canada, Great Britain, France, Italy, Belgium, and Spain*, U.S. Senate Document, no. 186, 8:8400 (Washington: U.S. Government Printing Office, 1925); Enrique Fuentes Quintana, "Reflexiones sobre el sistema tributario español," in *Lecturas de la economía española*, ed. Juan Velarde Fuertes (Madrid: Editorial Gredos, 1969), pp. 348–51; Carlos Ortega Grau and Juan Rafart Febrer, "Estudio sobre la deuda del estado español," *Cuadernos de Información Económómica y Sociológica*, no. 5 (December 1957): 141; and Isidro del Campo, *Lo que no ha dicho Romanones* (Madrid: Juan Pueyo, 1925), pp. 52–64, 82–134.

32. Since the declarations on which taxation was based were generally understated, the government had to raise tax rates themselves. With tax rates at an artificially high level, even the most civic minded hesitated before disclosing their full wealth. Taxation provided strange bedfellows. Landlords and tenants, for example, frequently understated rental payments since each faced a separate levy based on that amount; Miguel Royo Martínez, *El problema de la vivienda* (Seville: Editorial Edelce, 1953), pp. 4–5.

33. Tamames, *Estructura*, 3d ed., pp. 248–49.

34. Román Perpina Grau, "Notas históricas de la economía carbonera española," in *Lecturas*, ed. by Verlarde, pp. 348–51.

35. Nonetheless, as Carr has suggested, the break from free trade in 1891 was the first step toward extensive economic intervention and self-sufficiency; *Spain*, p. 395. Once begun, the process was difficult to reverse, and each additional step led to another. See, for example, John S. McGee, "Government Intervention in the Spanish Sugar Industry," *The Journal of Law and Economics* 8, no. 1 (October 1964): 121–74.

36. Electrical capacity, for example, increased from an index of 100 in 1901 to an index of 305 in 1913. During the same period consumption increased from an index of 100 to an index of 263; INE, *Principales actividades*, p. 84.

37. Antonio Ramos Oliveira, *Politics, Economics, and Men of Modern Spain* (London: Victor Gollancz, 1946), p. 238.

38. This process is placed in a larger historical context for a single *pueblo* in southern Spain by Pitt-Rivers, *The People*, pp. 53–55.

39. See Francisco Bernis, *Consecuencias económicas de la guerra* (Madrid: Imprenta

de Estanislao Maestre, 1923) and Santiago Roldán, José Luís García Delgado, and Juan Muñoz, *La formación de la sociedad capitalista en España 1914–1920* (Madrid: Confederación Española de Cajas de Ahorro, 1973). The paperback edition of the latter work is entitled *La consolidación del capitalismo en España*. Throughout the war the Social Reform Institute (Instituto de Reformas Sociales) also issued a number of studies of the effects of the conflict on the economy and labor relations. Among the principal titles are *Informe de los Inspectores de Trabajo sobre la influencia de la guerra europea en las industrias españolas* (Madrid, 1915), and *Informe de los Inspectores de Trabajo sobre la influencia de la guerra europea en las industrias españolas/1917–1918* (Madrid, 1918).

40. INE, *Principales actividades,* pp. 93–94.

41. Canosa, *Un siglo,* pp. 67–71, and Manuel Tuñón de Lara, *La España del siglo XX* (Paris: Librería Española, 1966), p. 22.

42. Coal illustrates this problem. Between 1913 and 1918, Spanish anthracite production increased 61.8% from 233,000 to 377,000 tons, with the value of that output increasing a still greater 433%. During the same period bituminous production increased 64.1% from 3,738,000 to 6,135,000 tons, while the value of that output rose 290%. By 1922, however, anthracite production had fallen to 256,000 tons and bituminous production to 4,180,000 tons. These declines of 32.1% and 31.9% respectively were exceeded by falls in value of 50.8% and 59.7% respectively. By way of comparison, imports of British coal fell from 3,098,000 tons in 1913 to 526,000 tons in 1918, but grew again to 1,696,500 tons by 1922. INE, *Principales actividades,* pp. 61–62, 96.

43. Bernis *Consecuencias económicas,* pp. 95–112.

44. Joseph Harrison, "Big Business and the Failure of Right-Wing Catalan Nationalism," *The Historical Journal* 19, no. 4 (1976): 910–11. On the Basque provinces in this period, see idem, "Big Business and the Rise of Basque Nationalism," *European Studies Review* 7 (1977): 371–91.

45. From fiscal year 1914 to fiscal year 1921–22 total state expenditures rose from 1,437,485,000 ptas. to 3,630,332,000 ptas., and the annual budgetary deficit rose from 174,487,000 ptas. to 1,101,441,000 ptas. Army, navy, and Moroccan budgets rose over the same period from 379,674,000 ptas. to 1,194,367,000 ptas.; INE, *Principales actividades,* pp. 124–25, and *Anuario estadístico 1925/26,* p. 370.

46. The state spent 37,931 ptas. on tax collection in 1908, 147,269,000 ptas. in 1913, and 247,108,000 ptas. in fiscal year 1919–20; INE, *Principales actividades,* p. 125.

47. Ibid., p. 127.

48. From fiscal year 1913 to fiscal year 1919–20, direct tax income rose 24.7% while indirect and state monopoly revenue rose 31.8%; ibid., p. 121. Corporate profits increased 114%, the money supply increased 124%, and the Bank of Spain's gold holdings increased from 670,000,000 ptas. to 2,540,000,000 ptas. from 1913 to 1920; Juan Sarda, *La intervención monetaria y el comercio de divisa en España* (Barcelona: Bosch, 1936), p. 207.

49. This arrangement is discussed by Juan Muñoz, *El poder de la banca en España* (Madrid: ZYX, 1969), pp. 13, 50–52.

50. On expansion of the money supply, see Santiago Roldan et al., *La formación,* 1:208; on bank investments during the war, see ibid. 2:231, 250–51, 260–65. On bank deposits, see Tuñón de Lara, *La España* 1:31.

51. The five were the Hispanic American Bank (Banco Hispano Americano), Spanish Credit Bank (Banco Español de Crédito), United Mine Credit Bank (Banco de Crédito de la Unión Minera), Bank of Bilbao (Banco de Bilbao), and Bank of Biscay (Banco de Vizcaya). Another important bank today, the Central Bank (Banco Central) was founded later and derived much of its rapid rise from the surfeit of capital produced by the war.

52. Salvador Canals, *La cuestión ferroviaria* (Madrid: Imprenta de "Alrededor del Mundo," 1923).

53. Francisco Wais San Martín, *Historia general de los ferrocarriles españoles: 1830–1941* (Madrid: Editora Nacional, 1967), pp. 329–30.

54. The importance of "leading industries" has been emphasized by W. W. Rostow. This concept is also central to F. Perroux, "Note on the Concept of Growth Poles," in

Economic Policy for Development, ed. I. Livingstone (Middlesex, England: Penguin Books, 1971), pp. 278–89. Perroux exemplifies the French thinking that has played an important role in Spanish economic planning in the 1960s and 1970s. Supporting evidence for this approach is provided by Nadal, "The Failure," p. 606.

55. David R. Ringrose, *Transportation and Economic Stagnation in Spain, 1750–1850* (Durham, N.C.: Duke University Press, 1970), pp. 136–38.

56. The evolution in rural consciousness is discussed by Richard Herr, *Spain* (Englewood Cliffs, N.J.: Prentice-Hall, 1974), pp. 267–83.

57. Rural overpopulation is complex and depends on soil fertility, effective use of existing resources, and an arbitrary standard of living measure as well as simple population density. These factors have been taken into account by Moore, *Economic Demography*, pp. 63–64. He concludes that Spain had a rural population surplus of 11.9% in 1930. Figures for other countries are Albania 77.7%, Yugoslavia 61.5%, Bulgaria 53.0%, Romania 51.4%, Poland 51.3%, Greece 50.3%, Portugal 46.9%, Italy 27.1%, and Hungary 22.4%. It should also be noted that Spain's population in towns of less than 5,000 was 3% greater in 1930 than in 1900; Jordi Nadal, *La población española* (Barcelona: Ediciones Ariel, 1971), p. 200.

58. Malefakis, *Agrarian Reform*, pp. 100–101.

59. Ibid.

60. The anarchosyndicalists were more a cause than an organization, oscillating between a mass following in revolutionary times and a small core after setbacks. The National Labor Confederation (CNT), their main trade union, was not established until 1910. Even after that date, membership figures are unreliable.

61. Manuel Tuñón de Lara, *Variaciones del nivel de vida en España* (Madrid: Ediciones Peninsula, 1965), pp. 30–42 passim.

62. R. Joseph Harrison, "The Beginnings of Social Legislation in Spain, 1900–1919," *Iberian Studies* 3, no. 1 (Spring 1974): 4–5, is the source for much of the information presented here.

63. Ibid., p. 5.

64. Early-twentieth-century social and housing conditions are discussed by Agustín Cotorruelo Sendagorta, *La poítica económica de la vivienda en España* (Madrid: Consejo Superior de Investigacions Clientificas, 1960), pp. 29–47.

65. Harrison, "The Beginnings," p. 4.

66. Ibid.

67. From 1913 through 1919 the wholesale price index rose from 100 to 180. The indices of men's and women's wages rose respectively from 100 to 147 and 135 over the same period; Stanley G. Payne, *The Spanish Revolution* (New York: W. W. Norton, 1970), p. 39.

68. On organized labor during the war and postwar years, see Gerald H. Meaker's definitive *The Revolutionary Left in Spain* (Stanford: Stanford University Press, 1974).

69. Payne, *The Spanish Revolution*, p. 65.

70. Ibid., p. 61.

71. The following strike information is taken from *Anuario estadístico/ 1930*, p. 552 and Fernanda Romeu Alfaro, *Las clases trabajadoras en España 1898–1930* (Madrid: Taurus Ediciones, 1970), Apendice Estadístico.

72. Strike activity in the first half of 1923 is described in Instituto de Reformas Sociales, *Avance estadístico de huelgas/correspondiente al primer semestre de 1923* (Madrid, 1924), pp. 11–13. There were 458 strikes involving 120,658 workers in 1923. Most of this activity took place before 13 September. These figures show an upturn from 1922 when there were 488 strikes involving 119,417 workers for the full years. Nonetheless, strike activity in 1923 was still less than in either 1917, when there were 895 strikes involving 178,496 workers, or 1920, when there were 1,060 strikes involving 244,689 workers; *Anuario estadístico 1930*, p. 552, and Romeu, *Las clases trabajadoras*, Apendice estadístico.

73. Middle-class opinion in this period is characterized by José G. Ceballos Teresi, *Historia económica, financiera y política de España en el siglo XX*, vol. 5 (Madrid:

Editorial El Financiero, 1931), pp. 105–7 and 114–23, and Francisco Cimadevilla, *El General Primo de Rivera* (Madrid: Afrodisio Agudo, 1944), pp. 26–34.

74. José Calvo Sotelo, *Mis servicios al Estado* (Madrid: Imprenta Clásica Española, 1931), p. 450. By way of comparison, Calvo Sotelo cites only 433 political crimes for the entire period from 1919 through 1922. Calvo Sotelo's participation in the dictatorship does not qualify him as a disinterested source. Nonetheless, his contention that social and political crimes reached a peak in the last months of the constitutional regime is generally accepted; see Payne, *The Spanish Revolution*, pp. 57–58. An insider's account of this period is Ángel Pestaña, *Terrorismo en Barcelona* (Barcelona: Editorial Planeta, 1979).

75. Payne, *The Spanish Revolution*, p. 57

76. Regional separatism in Spain was unusual in being spearheaded by a dynamic rather than backward region. Among those who have commented on this peculiarity are Salvador Giner, "The Structure of Spanish Society and the Process of Modernization," *Iberian Studies* 1, no. 2 (Fall 1972): 54, and Juan J. Linz and Amando de Miguel, "Within Nation Differences and Comparisons: The Eight Spains," in *Comparing Nations*, ed. Richard Merritt and Stein Rokkan (New Haven: Yale University Press, 1966), p. 278. The background for Catalan regionalism is discussed by Juan Reglá, *Historia de Cataluña* (Madrid: Alianza Editorial, 1978), pp. 183–215, and Edward C. Hansen, *Rural Catalonia under the Franco Regime* (Cambridge: Cambridge University Press, 1977), pp. 24–55.

77. Enrique Ucelay de Cal, "Estat Catala: The Strategies of Separation and Revolution of Catalan Radical Nationalism (1919–1933)" (Ph.D. diss., Columbia University, 1979), pp. 12–141.

78. Carr, *Spain*, pp. 463–64.

79. Basic sources for the military in this period are Stanley G. Payne, *Politics and the Military in Modern Spain* (Stanford: Stanford University Press, 1967), pp. 83–122, and Carolyn Patricia Boyd, "The Army and the Breakdown of Parliamentary Government in Spain, 1917–1923" (Ph.D. diss., University of Washington, 1974).

80. From 1908 to 1911 alone the army and navy's share of the national budget increased from 19.7% to 25.2%. Their share of the national income increased from 2.1% to 2.8%. The national income figures must be treated cautiously, however, since the methods used to derive them by the National Economic Council (Consejo de Economía Nacional) were crude and unsophisticated; INE, *Principales actividades*, pp. 124–25, 139.

81. Harrison, "The Beginnings," p. 3.

82. Manuel Tuñón de Lara, *Medio siglo de cultura española (1885–1936)* (Madrid: Editorial Tecnos, 1971), p. 216.

83. Carlos Rico Avello, *Notas para la historia de la sanidad española* (Madrid: Dirección General de Sanidad, 1955), pp. 15–20.

84. Juan J. Linz, "The Party System," p. 215.

85. The intellectual climate of these years in described by Tuñón de Lara, *Medio siglo*, pp. 145–239.

86. Stanley Payne, "Spanish Fascism in Comparative Perspective," *Iberian Studies* 2, no. 1 (Spring 1973): 5–6.

87. Payne, "Spanish Fascism," p. 5. There certainly was, however, a severe crisis of purpose and morale within the constitutional regime; Javier Tusell Gómez, *La crisis del caciquismo andaluz* (Madrid: Cupsa, 1977), pp. 16–23.

88. The Anual defeat and its political repercussions are discussed by James A. Chandler, "The Responsibilities for Anual," *Iberian Studies* 6, no. 2 (1977): 68–77.

89. The four were José Cavalcanti, Leopoldo Saro, Antonio Dabán, and Federico Berenguer. The latter was the brother of the former high commissioner in Morocco, who had been accused of partial responsibility for the Anual disaster; Payne, *Politics and the Military*, p. 192.

2
The Regime

Primo was not an obvious choice to lead the Quadrilateral's conspiracy.[1] During the past several years he had acquired a reputation as an *abandonista,* favoring withdrawal from Morocco. Primo was also something of an outsider and did not enjoy particularly close ties with most other generals. He was, however, ambitious, self-confident, and concerned about his country.

Primo was born into a large landowning family in 1870 in Jerez de la Frontera in Andalusia. His father was a retired colonel, and his uncle was a leading Liberal general who had helped restore the monarchy in 1874. From that uncle, the first marquis of Estella, Primo inherited a noble title. The Spanish aristocracy was increasingly cosmopolitan in the late nineteenth century. Primo's family, however, neither made extended travels abroad nor affected such English pastimes as polo and garden parties.[2] Primo entered the Military Academy in Toledo at age fourteen. He did not distinguish himself as a student. After graduation in 1888, however, his career advanced rapidly. He won several battlefield promotions and decorations, including the Cross of St. Ferdinand (First Class) for "conspicuous bravery" in Morocco. Critics later charged that his uncle's patronage had played a role in these honors and in his designation as commander by age twenty-five and his rise to general by age forty-two.[3]

Primo's detractors questioned his judgment, but seldom his patriotism. He was widely rumored to have shot General Margallo, his commanding officer in Morocco, in 1893. Margallo was believed to have incurred Primo's anger by selling weapons secretly to the Moors. Although this story is totally unsubstantiated,[4] it was a commentary on Primo that it could be told at all. Primo's emotional temperament was also evident when a republican Cortes deputy, Rodrigo Soriano, criticized his uncle in parliamentary debate. Primo challenged Soriano to a duel and wounded him.

Primo's wife died six years after their marriage. During that time the couple had five children. Primo was a conscientious father. Nonetheless, he maintained an active social life. He kept late hours and enjoyed the company of cabaret performers. Priding himself as a rake, or *mujeriego,* he moved from one romance to another. He was not discreet. As captain general in Valencia, his carrying on in a theater box with a chorus girl offended much of the audience.[5] In casinos he played for high stakes and occasionally overextended himself.[6] His countrymen later sang,

> Cards, women, and the bottle
> Are the coat of arms of the Marquis of Estella.[7]

These diversions and a military career were not enough for him. As a young man he had acquired a taste for politics and journalism. In 1898 he wrote for *El Guadalete* in Jerez, the first of several unsuccessful ventures as a political commentator.[8] He was also elected to the Senate from his native province of Cadiz. Primo was a more successful soldier than politician, but there was a parallel between the two careers. His family name, native talent, and driving ambition brought him close to the center of power. But he was too erratic, too flamboyant, and too much a gambler ever to win the confidence of his peers.[9]

Primo also exhibited an unaccustomed mix of naïveté and cynicism. He publicly criticized the Moroccan war early in 1917. His timing was significant, for the recently organized defense *juntas* generally opposed the war because it resulted in battlefield promotions discriminating against officers in the peninsula. No one could yet tell where the movement might lead, and Primo's remarks were interpreted as a bid to link his fortunes with the *junteros.*[10] Primo spoke against the war again in November 1921, four months after Anual, when the government was undertaking the controversial step of sending reinforcements across the straits. Once more his criticism was timed to give himself maximum publicity and the politicians maximum discomfort. But Primo was mistaken if he hoped to use Morocco to promote his own prospects. On each occasion the government suspended him from his command.

Primo said he was proud that he was an elected rather than ex officio member of the Senate. On the other hand, he did not campaign directly but arranged his election with party bosses and local *caciques.* He lacked party loyalty. His family had been associated with the Liberals, but he ran initially as a Conservative because of his close ties to that party's boss in Cadiz, the count of the Andes. Primo's statements on Morocco, however, cost him his chance to retain his seat in 1923 as a Conservative.

Santiago Alba headed the faction of the party to which the Liberals in Cadiz belonged. While publicly criticizing Alba for attempting to ransom the Anual prisoners held by the Moors, Primo had quietly praised that minister for his efforts in a February letter.[11] Neither Alba nor prime minister García Prieto, however, was willing to grant Primo's request for his party's backing. Insult was added to injury when Alba slated another general, with whom Primo had never gotten along, for a Senate seat in a neighboring province.[12] For the time being at least, Primo did not have a future in elective politics.

More than frustrated ambition led Primo to plot against the constitutional regime.[13] He thought one of the country's major problems was lack of discipline in the army, which he largely attributed to the politicians' weak and vacillating leadership on Morocco. Primo claimed that after his appointment as captain general of the Valencia military region in 1920, he realized that mishandling of these matters was symptomatic of a deeper malaise. Class conflict and labor violence were rife in Valencia. The politicians seemed helpless. When members of his own tertulia, or discussion group, expressed fears for their safety, he initiated a crackdown against local anarchosyndicalist militants. His success led him to believe that force alone might go far toward resolving the social problem.

Primo's disenchantment with the politicians increased after his appointment in fall 1922 as captain general in Barcelona.[14] His opposition to labor activists made him a hero to the city's propertied classes. In turn, he actively cultivated close ties with Lliga business interests and paid more than occasional lip service to regional aspirations.[15] Forebodings about this relationship prompted Salvador Seguí, the moderate leader of the anarchosyndicalist CNT, to propose that the union plan for a general strike in the event of a military takeover. Within a week the police arrested and shot Seguí to death in the act of "escaping."[16] Cambó had once described the Lliga as an elite that had been born to govern, but that had never had the opportunity. In 1923, Primo was also excluded from the system. In both their eyes, the ruling elite in Madrid was doubly damned: neither could it solve the country's problems, nor would it share power with those who felt they could.

Shortly after the May election in which he lost his Senate seat, Primo had an opportunity to upstage the Liberal government.[17] Months of bombings and violent labor conflict in Barcelona climaxed with a crippling transit strike. Attention focused on the liberal civil governor's unsuccessful efforts to negotiate a compromise agreement. Then Primo made a stunning announcement. Through secret meetings with the principals, concealed even from the government, he had settled the strike. Primo and the civil governor were summoned to Madrid, knowing that only one of them would return. Primo's success, however, prevented the embarrassed cabinet from moving publicly against him, and the general refused to help the government save face by accepting reassignment as head of the king's military household. A cheering throng of well-to-do supporters greeted Primo's returning train in Barcelona with "vivas" and shouts of "down with the government." More quietly, a new civil governor entered the city.

About this time, Primo began to test sentiment at other garrisons.[18] He found older, senior generals for the most part unwilling to move decisively against the constitutional regime.[19] He soon, however, crossed paths with the younger, more restive generals of the Quadrilateral. As with most other officers inclined to act against the Liberal ministry, the Quadrilateral looked to Gen. Francisco Aguilera for leadership. Aguilera was the senior lieutenant general and president of the Supreme Council of Military Justice. Known as a man of honesty and principle, he was thought acceptable to civilian as well as to army opinion. Primo himself urged him in a June meeting to assume leadership of the military movement.[20] But shortly thereafter a violent altercation in parliament involving Aguilera, over evidence for the investigation of Moroccan responsibilities, led to that general's public avowal of the supremacy of civilian authority and his disqualification as the dissidents' leader.

Primo's greatest problem in taking up Aguilera's mantle was that support for military intervention was strongest among officers favoring an aggressive Moroccan policy. Throughout the summer Primo attempted to live down his reputation as an *abandonista*. He declared that preservation of the army's dignity had to be the key to Moroccan policy.[21] Primo was also helped by the close ties he had enjoyed a decade earlier with General Cavalcanti, the dominant figure in the Quadrilateral.[22] No less decisive was the fact that no other general of Primo's rank had stepped forward to lead the dissent officers. By the end of the summer it was clear that, if there was a coup, Primo would lead it. How far the Catalans encouraged Primo is unclear. He did keep informed of his plans two of the region's greatest industrialists, the marquis of Comillas and the count of Güell.[23] By early July the first indirect word of Primo's plotting had already reached the government.[24] But the failure of the rumblings centered about the more prestigious Aguilera to produce an explosion lulled the cabinet into believing that Primo would not succeed in attracting significant military support.

Much has been speculated about Alfonso's role at this time.[25] It is unlikely that Cavalcanti and the other generals close to him would have conspired without his knowledge and tacit consent. It seems as well that Primo let Alfonso know of his ambitions at the end of July. At about the same time, Alfonso had confided to his minister of public instruction, Joaquín Salvatella y Gibert, that he was thinking of a short-term military government.[26] In August the king questioned Antonio Maura, the country's most prestigious Conservative, about his response to a military government, and on 6 September the king granted an hour-long interview to Primo and the Quadrilateral generals.[27] Alfonso had reason to be tempted by military intervention. Patronizing at best in his face-to-face dealings with most politicians, he spoke of them with increasing contempt behind their backs.[28] A special parliamentary report on Anual was also due after the reopening of the Cortes in mid September, and the subsequent debate might well have renewed questioning about the responsibility of the king and a number of senior generals for the disaster.

In any event, Alfonso had little room to maneuver. The dynastic parties were thoroughly discredited. Even with the military the Conservatives were almost as unpopular as the Liberals. Moreover, whatever his own wishes, he could not have readily replaced the former with the latter only five months after elections establishing the Liberals' parliamentary majority. Needing to disassociate himself from the politicians, and perhaps even a little fearful of being swept away with them, Alfonso was in no position to discourage the plotters. Nonetheless, it seems unlikely that he wanted a full military dictatorship. That course meant diminishment of his power as well as that of the Cortes. The Cavalcanti group, moreover, had originally intended to intimidate the politicians through a show of army solidarity, not to overthrow them altogether.

It would also have been unwise for the king to commit himself. The Quadrilateral's and Primo's soundings of army sentiment had revealed deep discontent with the government but less enthusiasm for a military takeover. Despite Primo's attempt to mend relations with the *africanistas,* he remained controversial with many officers and, especially, with senior generals. He could count on firm support only from his own garrison and that at Zaragoza. Captain General Zabalza at Valencia opposed a coup, while the country's five other captains general declined to commit themselves.

While Primo intrigued, the Liberals struggled to regain control of events. Lack of progress in enacting their reform program and the difficulties of dealing with a recalcitrant military had produced a cabinet shuffle on 3 September. Recognizing the impossibility of governing effectively against the wishes of *africanista* officers, García Prieto's new ministry adopted a more activist Moroccan policy. But the Liberals moved too late with too little, and they could not stem the flow of military sentiment away from them. Rumors of a coup circulated increasingly in the final week before Primo's 14 September date. Minister of State Alba urged the cabinet to take precautions. The war minister, General Aizpuru, had known of Primo's plans but had not shared his knowledge with the cabinet. Finally, on the evening of 12 September at García Prieto's direction, he formally ordered Primo by telephone from Madrid to desist from the coup. That order only made Primo advance his timetable by a day. Shortly before midnight that same evening he issued a manifesto declaring martial law and explaining his seizure of power. His action was in the tradition of the mid-nineteenth-century *pronunciamiento* by which a general simply declared his intent to assume power rather than used force to dislodge the government directly. He gave no offensive commands to the Barcelona garrison, only an order to stand by. The cabinet, however, did not resign but awaited the return of the king from his vacation in northern Spain. Worried, Primo told his confidantes, "if they come to fight us, we are lost."[29] Outwardly, though, he exhibited a sense of command. The day following his manifesto, he acted as the undisputed leader of a new military government as he opened a furniture exposition in Barcelona. Leading Catalan businessmen at the ceremony cheered him in that capacity.

On returning to Madrid on 14 September, Alfonso neither supported nor repudiated the rebellion. The first to yield in this war of nerves was García Prieto, who resigned the premiership when the king declined to relieve Primo from his command. Alfonso, however, was still not ready to turn the government over to him. He invited Primo to present plans for his consideration. Primo refused to submit to that procedure. And once Alfonso had let García Prieto go, he had no alternative to set against the general. On 15 September Primo arrived in Madrid with authority to govern in the king's name but without the full support of either the crown or the army. It was an anomalous position for a dictator, and Primo spent the next six and one-half years searching for firmer support.

Primo outlined his program in his manifesto and other public statements.[30] He saw politics at the heart of the country's problems, and he thought of politics primarily in terms of personalities and attitudes. He

The Regime

promised to deliver the country from "professional politicians . . . who, for one reason or another, offer us the spectacle of the misfortune and corruption which began in the year 1898 and which threaten Spain with an early end that will be both tragic and dishonorable."[31] The next step in his program was to summon "new men" to govern. He intended to establish

> a military Directorate of Supervision and Inspection, of a temporary character, charged with maintaining public order and insuring the working of the ministries and official bodies, requiring of the country that, in a short time, it offer us upright, wise, industrious, and honorable men, who can constitute a ministry under our auspices, but with complete independence of action, in order that we may offer them to the King if he sees fit to accept them.[32]

This leadership would "give the Spanish people a new political life, impelling them toward and helping them to understand it . . . by initiating them in a knowledge of the various functions of government and a true sense of their worth."[33] In other words, government was the catalyst for national regeneration. The old politicians had led the country into indiscipline and egotism. New, selfless patriots would set an example of sacrifice, unity, and order. Once the corrupt, enervating *cacique* system had been swept away, the Spanish people would work together in harmony for social and economic development.

For Primo this was not a partisan program. He declared,

> We are neither of the Right nor Left; we do not come in response to a social or political ideology; we represent simply a situation of force. We come to purify the air, to re-establish discipline, to destroy the closed cliques of the professional politicians, so that with the road cleared for them, civilians will be able to install a new politics.[34]

There was no question of principle here, only of character.

> This is a movement of men: let whoever is not fully masculine wait in a corner without interfering with the glorious future we are preparing for the country. Spaniards—long live Spain and long live the king![35]

Primo declared that within ninety days the process of reform would be sufficiently underway that he could withdraw from active government. Because he planned only a temporary political "parenthesis," he disclaimed the title dictator.

Even as self-serving statements for public consumption, Primo's analysis is superficial. He confused platitude with program. Only a diffuse "mentality," not a systematic ideology, held his thoughts together.[36] His reliance on rhetoric and moral example as agents of change was premised on a belief in the country's essential malleability. This simplistic view gave him confidence to seize power, but it had shortcomings as a guide to reform.

Primo's first concern after arriving in Madrid was staffing and organizing his government. He appointed the senior brigadier general from each of the eight captain generalcies, or military regions, as well as one rear admiral to serve on a ruling directory with him.[37] As a lietenant general serving as captain general of the Barcelona military region, Primo outranked his appointees. Primo did not envision the directory as a traditional cabinet, and indeed doubted its ability to function in that capacity.[38] He alone held ministerial status and swore an oath to office before the king. The other generals functioned as liaison officers to the ministries, not as supervisors of operations. Day-to-day administration of each ministry was entrusted to a senior bureaucrat.[39]

This arrangement was temporary. Primo planned to recruit prominent civilians as cabinet ministers serving under the directory. He believed he would have his pick of technical, political, and administrative talent. He hosted a gathering for a number of these individuals the same day he arrived in Madrid. However, Antonio Flores de Lemus, a leading economist and Primo's choice for finance minister, spoke for most when he said that the directory was far too risky an undertaking for someone of his stature to participate in.[40]

In his search for "new men," Primo drew extensively on the contacts his fellow officers had with younger, conservative politicians. José Calvo Sotelo was his most important discovery. Calvo Sotelo was born in 1892 as the son of a lower-court judge in a small Galician town.[41] Intelligence and hard work won him distinction as a law student and enabled him to place first in a competitive examination for an elite branch of the civil service. His career benefited from attracting the attention of Antonio Maura, the rallying symbol for young conservative regenerationists. After writing a book on Maura's relevance to the working classes, Calvo Sotelo served briefly as his secretary. Two years later, attesting to the sincerity of his interest in the working class, the prologue to his doctoral dissertation was written by Gumersindo de Azcárate, a republican social reformer and one-time head of the Institute of Social Reform.[42] By age 30, Calvo Sotelo was not yet nationally prominent but already had been elected to the Cortes and had served as a civil governor.

Calvo Sotelo was an acquaintance of General Cavalcanti, who recommended him to Primo. During two interviews, Primo expressed particular interest in Calvo Sotelo's ideas on local government.[43] Calvo Sotelo held, as reformers had for a generation, that the roots of *caciquismo* lay in local government and that a civil awakening at that level was necessary for the country's regeneration. Primo was sufficiently impressed by Calvo Sotelo to appoint him director general of local administration. Working briefly with Calvo Sotelo was José María Gil Robles, son of a former Carlist deputy, one of the founders of the abortive social Catholic People's party and later leader of the CEDA party (Confederación Española de Derechas Autónomas) during the republic.

Eduardo Aunós was recruited somewhat differently from Calvo Sotelo.[44] Born in 1894 into a Catalan landowning family with substantial business interests, Aunós was, like Calvo Sotelo, typical of the conservative activists who came of age in the second decade of the twentieth century.[45] Trained as a lawyer, he began his political career with the Catalan Lliga. He served as Cambó's secretary and represented the Lliga in the Cortes. Like Primo, however, he did not have strong party loyalty. In 1922 he joined Catholic reformers and *Mauristas* in seeking mass backing for conservative principles through the People's party. Shortly afterward, he affiliated with the Conservative Monarchist Union. Primo visited Catalonia in January 1924. During his stay, he attended a reception arranged by Emilio Barrera, his successor as captain general. Most of those invited with Aunós were supporters of either the Lliga or the Monarchist Union. Several questioned Primo sharply about the directory's anti-Catalan policies, but Aunós stood out in endorsing the government. Also helping his cause might have been substantial loans made by his father to Primo before the coup.[46] Primo asked to meet him the next day and again later in Madrid. The conversations centered on Aunós's interest in social problems. In early February Primo placed him in charge of labor matters. Similar in background to Aunós was the count of Vallellano. Intelligent, idealistic, a one-time Maurist deputy in the Cortes and later an activist in the People's party, he became Primo's mayor of Madrid.[47] Even for lower level positions, affiliation with conservative groups or the recommendation of prominent conservatives was useful.[48]

The nearly five months between the appointments of Calvo Sotelo and Aunós indicates Primo's difficulty in finding his "new men." Opportunities existed for job seekers with more ambition than ability and principle. Galo Ponte was one of these. Brashness and an ability to cajole politicians had substituted for prominent family and friends in advancing his judicial career.[49] Primo's arbitrary rule offended the legal sensibilities of many judges and lawyers, but Ponte had no such delicacy. As a judge eager to serve the new regime, he made a valuable collaborator. The directory enlisted him in one of its more sordid episodes, the *in absentia* prosecution on trumped-up charges of the dictator's nemesis, Santiago Alba.[50]

Ponte, Calvo Sotelo, and Aunós illustrate the combination of idealism and self-seeking inspired by the dictatorship in its first days. They are typical in another respect. They were not altogether "new men." Instead, they came from secondary political positions, lacking the right combination of age, social standing, and political patronage to propel them into the first rank under the constitutional regime. Primo's appointees also tended, as in the case of Calvo Sotelo and Aunós, to come from peripheral or radical conservative groups, such as the Traditionalists, Social Catholics, and Mauristas, which were years away, if ever, from taking power under the constitutional regime.[51]

Primo's difficulty in staffing top positions, despite reaching out to new pools of talent, meant that he and the directory generals assumed a more direct role in government than anticipated.[52] Primo turned to the military in other ways as well.[53] He replaced the fifty civil governors with military appointees, delaying a gradual return to civilian administration until 1925. He appointed junior officers as local governmental delegates to assist the governors and placed other officers in civilian bureaucratic posts. Military courts tried social and political crimes. To supervise the war ministry, Primo called on Gen. Luis Bermúdez de Castro, long associated with the Liberal party but alienated by its Moroccan policies. Primo entrusted Lt. Col. Gil Clemente with drafting railroad legislation, one of the directory's key economic concerns. More importantly and controversially, he placed Gen. Severiano Martínez Anido in charge of the interior ministry.[54] Martínez Anido was a strong monarchist with good relations with *africanista* officers. He was also notorious with the working classes for the brutal and frequently illegal methods he had used as governor in Barcelona against anarchosyndicalist militants from 1920 to 1922. He, in turn, appointed his assistant in Barcelona, Gen. Juan Arlegui, as director general of security, in charge of maintaining public order.

Public attention focused less on the staffing of the new government than on the stunning series of decrees issued in its first days. Voluble, spontaneous, and overflowing with energy, Primo dominated the public stage as no one before. Dissolving local governments and appointing military officers to oversee their affairs ignited a grass-roots anti-*cacique* hysteria. When Primo announced a crackdown on tax fraud, long lines of evaders quickly formed outside finance-ministry offices to make restitution. He declared that he would fire bureaucrats who treated their government posts as sinecures while working at second jobs elsewhere. So many civil servants returned to their offices in Madrid that there were rumors of a great shortage of desks. A decree on conflicts of interest *(incompatibilidades),* barring the constitutional regime's politicians from serving on the boards of firms with state contracts, sent brief, but strong, tremors through high business and political circles. Primo shocked Catalonia and cheered integral nationalists by restricting the Catalan language and outlawing that region's flag and local dance. Not all of Spain liked its iron surgeon, but few questioned that at last the country had a leader who got things done.

More than any other incident, the government's handling of a robbery in Tarrasa captured the public imagination.[55] On 20 September, six masked thieves stole 3,000 pesetas from a savings association in that town. Their getaway was foiled, but one member of Catalonia's volunteer militia, the Somatén, was killed in apprehending them. Because the country was under martial law, a military tribunal tried the case. Within twenty-four hours of the crime, that court returned its guilty verdict, and forty-eight hours later the two robbers sentenced to death were executed. The impression created by this incident was underscored by the ease with which the government suppressed a one-day general strike in Bilbao protesting Primo's takeover and the failure of an anarchosyndicalist call for a national general strike.

Such energetic display helped consolidate Primo's authority. Moderate newspapers had generally welcomed the coup.[56] Even papers associated with the ousted Liberal ministry reluctantly accepted the directory. García Prieto himself declared, "I have one more saint to commend myself to, Saint Miguel Primo de Rivera, because he has lifted the weight of government from my shoulders."[57] Future leaders of the republic, Manuel Azaña and Niceto Alcalá Zamora, though not effusive about the coup, recognized that the constitutional regime no longer had popular support. The Catholic newspaper *El Debate* was enthusiastic. Middle-class acceptance of the directory was also facilitated by the expectation that Primo would be true to his word in instituting only a short reform "parenthesis" before restoring parliamentary rule. Labor, weakened by several years of internal conflict and government repression, offered scant resistance, and Primo quickly reached out to the Socialists for cooperation. Successful floating of a bond issue, signifying support from the financial community, was an important milestone in October 1923. In November Melquiades Álvarez and the count of Romanones, presidents respectively of the lower and upper houses of the Cortes, asked Alfonso to fulfill his constitutional responsibility of reconvening parliament. The king brushed them aside, saying that the directory embodied the best prospects for the future and to oppose it was to oppose the welfare of the country itself.[58] Two weeks later a secure and confident dictator accompanied Alfonso on a previously planned royal visit to Italy. Alfonso introduced Primo to King Victor Emmanuel as "my Mussolini."

On returning to Spain Primo began the fundamental reforms he believed necessary for national regeneration. Legislation originated in the directory, with the generals meeting almost daily.[59] Once Primo decided on the desirability of a measure, he delegated its drafting to the responsible agency. These agencies and study panels multiplied greatly and carried out much of the directory's work. When an agency completed a proposal, Primo presided over the directory's deliberations on it. The generals rarely discussed even the most complex legislation for more than three days.[60] When they had approved a measure, they sent it to the palace for the king's signature.

Primo, however, was not constrained by set procedures. The dictator, who intended to restore discipline to national life, was the most undisciplined ruler since Queen Isabella II in the mid-nineteenth century. His diabetes repeatedly flared up because of his inability to stick to the diet prescribed by his doctor.[61] His hours were long but erratic. Well after midnight he might be found drafting public statements, writing so rapidly he had to use a pencil rather than a pen.[62] These declarations, trivial as well as important, were often intuitive bursts, released to the press without consultation with the directory or other government officials. Not all were written when he was sober.[63] He took pride in his prose. A mirror of his personality, his writing was overblown but not formal, unpolished but not clear and direct. Primo's highly personal style of government was also evident in the considerable time he spent dispensing favors and listening to individual complaints.[64] Even at meals Primo was frequently visible, taking the same table by a window at his club, the Peña, as he had before becoming a dictator.[65] Periodically for a break, Primo retreated with friends to a villa in the countryside for several days of wine, women, and song.[66]

The directory's most ambitious efforts were the Municipal Statute (Estatuto Municipal) and the Patriotic Union (Unión Patriótica).[67] Primo saw the statute as opening local government to the *neutra masa* and, thereby, as preparing that level of government to play a leading role in national life. He launched the Patriotic Union as a national civic association, a magnet for his "new men" and the heir to his dictatorship. He also reduced the independence of the judiciary, making it more subservient to the central government while attempting to insulate it from outside influences. He claimed that each of these efforts was necessary to cleanse the old politics of its vices and to prepare the way for rejuvenated parliamentary government.

The primacy of political reform and the demands made by the Moroccan war meant that Primo gave only secondary consideration to economic and social legislation. Claiming no expertise, Primo shared the economic nationalism that constituted the period's conventional wisdom.[68] He responded to the requests of the business community for support and protection by establishing an advisory National Economic Council (Consejo de Economía Nacional) and extending the Industrial Development Act of 1917. Coal mines, railroads, and shipping companies benefited from special studies, largely amplifications of the constitutional regime's programs. Believing labor productivity essential to national wealth, Primo exhorted workers to apply themselves to their jobs. He did not rescind the constitutional regime's eight-hour-day law, but neither did he enforce it vigorously. He thought "an hour taken away from the working day, at an average of 1.5 ptas. per hour of labor, boosts the costs of production three million ptas. per day."[69] He did recognize, however, a governmental social responsbility and amplified low-income housing legislation and raised teacher pay.

Most of this legislative flurry came during the first six months of 1924. During the same period Primo moved against an emergent but dispersed opposition. He imprisoned or drove into exile, among others, the philosopher Miguel Unamuno, the Conservative politician Ángel Ossorio y Gallardo, and the Liberal politician the marquis of Cortina. Primo even briefly considered arresting Antonio Maura for private criticisms of the regime. While extending the Somatén, a largely middle-class militia, from Catalonia to the rest of Spain, he curbed possession of guns in other hands.[70] By May 1924 he had largely driven the anarchosyndicalists and communists underground.

During the remainder of 1924 and 1925 the directory's activity slowed and was for the most part limited to amplifications of previous measures. The principal political reforms were the Provincial Statute, analogous to the earlier municipal act, and establishment of the Local Credit Bank to fund municipal and provincial borrowing. Primo also established a new lending agency for railroad companies, made modest improvements in agricultural credit, and began study of rural lease legislation.

Part of the slowdown derived from the directory's organization. The directory's generals insulated Primo from Calvo Sotelo, Aunós, and his other new men in the state administration. The only ministerial officials with direct access to him were fellow generals—Martínez Anido at the interior ministry and Bermúdez de Castro at the war ministry. Consequently, civil servants did not get the support needed to develop legislation, and Primo did not get the proposals needed to shape his nebulous reform aspirations.

More important, much of Primo's attention, and that of the country, focused on Morocco.[71] Primo angered *africanista* officers who had supported his coup by attempting initially to negotiate with Abd el-Krim—the same policy he had castigated Santiago Alba for pursuing. Against their objections and at the cost of heavy casualties, he withdrew Spanish forces from exposed positions in the Moroccan interior to the coast. But Primo quickly changed course when the French, fearful about the spread of the rebellion into their zone, proposed a joint military effort. In September 1925 a high-risk amphibious operation at the Bay of Alhucemas, overseen by Primo himself, broke the back of the rebellion. The war flickered on for two more years, but its outcome was never again in doubt.

No single event enhanced Primo's standing as much as that victory. His confidence was also boosted by the social peace brought by the directory and the general economic upturn that Spain shared with the rest of Europe in the mid-1920s. These developments increased Primo's prestige at the same time that they obscured his failure to achieve his original purpose—a new political compact between government and the governed. Neither his local government reforms, the governmental delegates, nor the Patriotic Union had produced the political leaders from the *neutra masa* to whom he could hand over power. No alternative yet existed to a return to the old politicians and the old parliament.[72] Primo never again enjoyed quite the sense of triumph he did in late 1925. But even at the height of his personal popularity, little support existed with the crown, military, or other significant sectors of opinion for the permanent institutionalization of his regime. The directory, moreover, had never been more than a temporary device. Its exceptional military character made it an anomaly after two years. Primo needed to reorganize his dictatorship and take it a step closer to his declared goal of political "normalcy." To do this he appointed the civil government on 3 December 1925.

For a self-proclaimed civilian government, the new cabinet had a strong military component. The two most important positions belonged to generals, with Primo as president of the council of ministers and Martínez Anido as vice-president and minister of the interior. Primo gave the army ministry to an old crony, General O'Donnell, the duke of Tetuan, while entrusting the secondary position of naval minister to a career officer, Admiral Cornejo.

The rest of the cabinet had the same conservative hue as the directory. Service and loyalty to the directory were important for designation to the civil government. Calvo Sotelo became minister of finance, moving from his previous post with local administration. Aunós, remaining at the labor ministry, was elevated to ministerial rank. Patriotic Union activists were prominently represented, as with Justice Minister Ponte, who had previously served as prosecutor for the supreme court. A founder of the Patriotic Union in Valladolid and a deeply Catholic law professor, Eduardo Callejo, became education minister, a position important to the church. Callejo had previously led a dogged, though unsuccessful, search for evidence of misdeeds by the old politicians.[73] Another Patriotic Union activist, Rafael Benjumea, the count of Guadalhorce, became minister of development after attracting Primo's attention as a member of the Madrid city council. Although Guadalhorce's family were Andalusian landowners, he had distinguished himself as a civil engineer. Also from the Andalusian landed elite was Primo's minister of state, José María Yanguas Messía, a law professor, author of several books, Spain's representative at the Hague Court, and a former Conservative Cortes deputy from Jaén.[74] No change in cabinet occurred until February 1927, when a foreign-policy disagreement caused Primo to take over the foreign ministry himself. Tetuan's death in November 1928 triggered a minor reshuffling, with Gen. Julio Ardanaz Crespo becoming the new army minister and Adm. Mateo García de los Reyes replacing Cornejo. At that same time, Primo appointed his old friend, Francisco Moreno Zulueta, the count of the Andes, to the new post of minister of the economy.[75]

The best of the civil government's second rank was Manuel Lorenzo Pardo.[76] An energetic and talented hydraulic engineer, he believed that the electric power and irrigation resulting from dam construction was the key to Spain's economic modernization. Although conservative, he had admired Costa and regarded public-works projects as apolitical. He later continued under the second republic the hydraulic development he oversaw for Primo.[77] César de Madariaga and Pedro Sangro y Ros de Olano at the labor ministry were also typical of the civil government's second echelon in coming from Catholic and Maurist circles. Several of the directory's generals received high-paying administrative posts under the civil government. Junior officers also frequently continued to exercise significant responsibilities under the new cabinet.[78]

In a confidential memorandum circulated to some of his future ministers in Fall 1925, Primo declared that he intended the civil government to be "decidedly radical and expeditious in its procedures," but "not inclining to the left or to the right."[79] Political regeneration would largely continue the work of the Patriotic Union and his earlier local government legislation. He wanted a public-works program, but he also sought to balance the budget by reducing expenses and reforming the tax system. He planned to update legal codes, simplify court procedures, reduce the size of the military, and subordinate it more effectively to the government. He saw little need for new labor legislation.

For Primo this melange was the blueprint for a technocratic, managerial government. Its inconsistencies and juxtaposition of the fundamental and the secondary suggests the dictator's difficulty in translating his platitudinous yearnings for national rebirth into specific programs. Primo relied heavily on his ministers for ideas and new legislation and allowed them considerable autonomy.[80] That delegation of authority, and the varied background of the cabinet, contributed to the appearance of a government at odds with itself. On occasion Primo's public musings differed significantly from policies planned or already instituted by his ministers. Members of the cabinet disagreed on future political institutions. After the collapse of the regime, Primo's ministers described their programs as constituting a systematic plan for national regeneration.[81] During the dictatorship, however, they frequently prided themselves on the "intuitive" basis of their efforts.[82] Primo claimed that the government's many "rectifications" showed sensitivity to "the continuing plebiscite of public opinion," but the cabinet's lack of internal coordination was mainly responsible.

The dictatorship also bore the characteristic liability of authoritarian government—censorship and lack of a loyal opposition.[83] Primo's attempts to mold opinion through mandatory insertion of government statements and sponsorship of *La Nación* as a progovernment daily only resulted in a journalism so dull that it lost many readers. Censorship was erratic. Neither did it eliminate some strong criticism of the government, especially in books, nor did it stop lively underground opposition journals. But it was sufficient to stymie the dialogue between government and country needed to correct policy mistakes before they were enacted into law.

Occasional missteps and cross-purposes notwithstanding, the civil government increased governmental activism. Calvo Sotelo, Aunós, and Guadalhorce as ministers, and energetic men such as Lorenzo Pardo in secondary posts, quickly embarked on major programs. The most ambitions was a ten-year public-works project announced in 1926 and funded primarily through a greatly increased national debt. The civil government also supported education, promoted modest improvements in social welfare, and, more significantly, instituted a national labor-management arbitration system.

These measures did not undo economic backwardness or deep-rooted social inequalities. They did, however, engender a financial crisis that led to major controversy over taxation in 1926 and that played a role in the nationalization of foreign oil interests in 1928. In a sense, the civil government had gambled that national wealth would increase so rapidly that conflicts over its distribution would fade. As early as 1927, however, some economic sectors faltered. By 1929 the dictatorship faced a hostile international financial community, the exchange rate of the peseta was falling, and the government had exhausted its capacity to borrow. Two international expositions planned for that year to celebrate the regime's triumphs constituted instead its denouement. No one connected with the regime seems to have understood what had gone wrong. Primo blamed many of Spain's economic problems on his countrymen's propensity to eat too much, while Calvo Sotelo accused a conspiratorial, international "monopoly of gold." Meanwhile, propertied groups declined to support social reforms that were, in any event, insufficient to satisfy working-class aspirations.

Against this background Primo's search for a new political formula acquired urgency. He had used a plebiscite in 1926 to demonstrate backing for his government and to support his controversial plan to convene a nonelective National Assembly (Asamblea Nacional) to advise him on legislative matters and write a new constitution. The Assembly did not meet until October 1927 and took two more years to draft its constitutional proposal. By then Primo had grown weary.[84] Opposition to his dictatorship had deepened and ranged from left to right. Students had challenged him openly in the streets for two years. Labor and regionalists were increasingly restive. Even the church, the king, and big business and landowners were turning from him. Dissident army officers had participated in a series of steadily more serious challenges to his authority.

Why had failure so quickly overtaken the self-styled iron surgeon? Part of the answer lies with Primo's personal shortcomings. Translating the dictator's inchoate and occasionally inconsistent aspirations into concrete programs challenged directory and civil government alike. Worse, Primo's political inexperience and clumsiness produced needless conflicts with virtually every sector of opinion. Confident of his own good intentions, he rode roughshod over the sensibilities of others. More basic still to Primo's failure was the society he had sought to transform. Under the constitutional regime, politicians far more adept than he had failed to weave between deeply divided and contending interests. In dealing with those divisions himself, Primo suffered from the contradictions of interwar Europe's "new right." He appealed inclusively to every social sector. But his emphasis on "new men" and a fresh spirit presupposed the essential soundness of established institutions—a position not compatible with the interests of the country's have-not majority. At the same time, his promise to turn government over to "new men" threatened the old political elite and the longstanding ties between government and prominent economic interests. Like Mussolini, Hitler, and some other rightist leaders, Primo affirmed the structure of society while introducing a jostling for position at its apex.[85]

Primo's bumbling and ambiguous social orientation meant that he had difficulty, despite his conservatism, in maintaining the support of established interests. He viewed the church as the embodiment of Spain's enduring values and harrassed the country's tiny Protestant minority. He courted the church with legislation on public morality, taxes, and education. His support of higher education even involved him in a major conflict with students and professors at the state universities, contributing to the downfall of his regime.

At first, through Catholic Action (Acción Católica) and the National Catholic Association of Propagandists (Asociación Católica Nacional de Propagandistas), the church supported Primo. But, notwithstanding the dictatorship's efforts, the church grew critical of what it charged was lax enforcement of public morality and inadequate financial support for the rural clergy. Restrictions on regional languages, urged on him by the military, led to a confrontation with the church hierarchy in Catalonia.[86] More seriously, his attempt to bridge the gulf between government and the more moderate working classes produced charges that the UGT was favored over the smaller Catholic trade unions.

Had the church been a status quo institution, Primo's task would have been simpler. But that institution shared the Right's new assertiveness.[87] Ángel Herrera, editor of *El Debate,* exemplified those looking to the regime to extend the church's influence. Cardinal Segura, primate of the Spanish church, typified those relying on the monarchy and dictatorship to mount a counter offensive against Catholicism's enemies. In exchange for the dictatorship's favors, however, the clerical establishment gave only limited support to Primo's search for a new political balance—one according the church many privileges but not fully realizing its outsized ambitions.

Few institutions were as important as the army to a general who had catapulted himself to power in a coup.[88] The values and concerns of

Primo's fellow officers were reflected in his early statements, from their emphasis on masculinity and the social responsibility of the elite to the need to defend a natural, militarylike hierarchy of society.[89] Primo's public-works programs were testimony to a soldier's regard for the technology of engineers, while his censorship evinced his suspicion for the free thought of intellectuals. Primo bowed to army sentiment on Catalonia, even at the cost of exacerbating regional sentiment there. Supportive of industry, he nonetheless heeded the army's occasional requests for foreign goods over the protectionist pleadings of manufacturers.

The army, however, continued as divided under the dictatorship as it had been under the constitutional regime. The junta-oriented Barcelona garrison had made Primo's coup possible, and Gen. Godofredo Nouvilas, the *juntero* leader, was secretary to the directory. Primo's initial policies catered, not surprisingly, to officers in the peninsula—well-paid government civilian positions for soldiers, no merit promotions benefiting *africanista* officers, and, especially, partial withdrawal from Morocco. The near rebellion of the *africanista* officers that contributed to a reversal of his Moroccan policy by 1925 also inclined Primo away from the narrow careerism of the peninsular officers toward the professionalism of the African army. Nouvilas found himself excluded from the directory's meetings.[90] Primo also established a common military academy for the three army branches and instituted merit promotions. The latter step precipitated the revolt of the aristocratic artillery corps.[91] Many artillery officers' fears were confirmed by Primo's use of promotions and honors to strengthen his military support, along with his removal of untrustworthy officers from sensitive commands.[92] That policy misfired badly, however, and not just with the artillery. *Junteros* and *africanistas* alike worried about Primo's subordination of the military to the government. Primo aggravated that discontent by attempting to prune the army's size. Senior generals, such as Francisco Aguilera and Valeriano Weyler, had their own complaints. They regarded Primo as an upstart and an illegal one at that. Resenting his failure to consult with them, they joined other restive military elements in efforts to overthrow the regime. By 1929, Primo could no longer shrug off those efforts. Among the many factors contributing to his fall, few would be more decisive than the army's withdrawal of support.

Primo preserved most outward signs of deference for the crown and was solicitous of Alfonso's business investments.[93] But Primo and Alfonso could not have been more opposite in temperament: the dictator garrulous and unaffected, the king suave and subtle. Nor did Alfonso's sense of importance and desire for the limelight reconcile him to having the center of the political stage preempted by Primo.[94] By Fall 1924, Alfonso had cooled on Primo and intrigued tentatively to remove. In Morocco, when the dictator heard of Alfonso's maneuverings, he said, "That gentlemen is not going to bourbonize me like the old politicians, and when I get to Madrid I'll settle that score. Let the king know that if I go, he'll go first."[95] The dictator and the king also disagreed about working with republicans and socialists. During a confrontation between Primo and the artillery corps, a rumor spread that the dictator had threatened to force Alfonso to abdicate if he supported the dissident military units.[96] In order to govern, Primo needed the king to sign his decrees. But Alfonso's fear of offending the old politicians delayed the edict convening the National Assembly for a year, during which time he against cast about charily for some alternative to the dictator.[97] In 1928, worried about the regime's declining popularity and about his own future in a post-Primo Spain, Alfonso embarked on a state tour to Sweden rather than remain in Madrid for the ceremonies celebrating the fifth anniversary of the coup.[98] The king also refused to discredit himself by allowing the embattled dictator to use a royal decree as a face-saving means of leaving office through establishment of a successor regime.

As a Spanish grandee himself, Primo could be expected to be sympathetic to wealthy nobles, and particularily to those from his native Andalusia. But if conservative aristocrats participated in the dictatorship, they were not as well represented as they had been in the Senate of the constitutional regime. Moreover, the dictatorship's technocratic orientation meant that old landed interests were slighted in favor of newer industrial and banking elites. The landed class especially resented Primo's attempt in 1926 to raise its taxes to fund his development program. The principal result of that effort, and of his later statements on agrarian reform, was to estrange many landowners from his government.[100]

Large industrialists and bankers, on the other hand, flourished under Primo and from the start were not reluctant in making their wishes known.[101] The dictatorship relied on the financial community to support its programs through bond purchases, and it rewarded financiers by paying high interest on those notes, leaving banks largely unregulated, and looking after their other needs. High tariffs and ambitious subsidy and public-works programs, along with attendant graft, cemented close ties between business and government. The present links between the Primo de Rivera and Urquijo families date from this period. In 1924,

Primo awarded the telephone monopoly to an ITT consortium associated with that banking family and certain Catalan interests, and Primo's twenty-one-year-old son, José Antonio, became a highly paid legal consultant to the new Telefónica.

Industrial and banking elites, however, were not unanimous in support of the dictatorship. Primo's advent brought opportunities for the ambitious. At the same time, because the dictatorship never shed its transitory quality, collaboration carried risks. Under these circumstances, in the maneuvering for political favor among economic elites, as among other social sectors, there were occasional changes in position. In Asturias prior to the dictatorship, the Conservative party had been split between the Herrero and Tartiere banking families. The Herrero interests were stronger economically and politically, but Ignacio Herrero's ties to José Sánchez Guerra, a leader of the national Conservative party and avowed enemy of Primo, meant that the road was clear for the Tartiere interests to develop a special relationship with the new regime.[102] Occasional turnabouts of that sort colored, but did not alter, the general pattern of government favor to industry and finance. Primo appointed so many businessmen to new advisory and regulatory agencies that Spain came close to government by special interest. Under the dictatorship, overall, the country's political center of gravity adjusted to the gradual shifting in economic importance away from the southern latifundia provinces to the northern and central manufacturing and banking zones.

Nonetheless, there was little sentiment in relations between the regime and banking and industrial leaders. In Catalonia assiduous campaigning had won Primo initial support from business elites. Elsewhere high business circles were more wary.[103] Their worries that Primo's reforming zeal might destroy the intimate relations between themselves and the government were seemingly confirmed by the directory's 12 October 1923 decree on conflicts of interest *(incompatibilidades).*[104] Primo himself said,

> Since that decree appeared certain elements of the rightist press that had previously looked on the directory benevolently and that had . . . declared they would not interfere with its work now see everything as black. . . . It is to be greatly lamented that neither among the conservative classes nor in their press has been found the disinterest shown by the working class, students, and active elements in society *(fuerzas vivas)* in whom so many hopes have been awakened by Spain's regenerating movement represented today by the military functioning in a civilain capacity.[105]

That decree and later conflict-of-interest legislation applied primarily to former government officials and was applied only partially even to them.[106] The new ties between the dictatorship and business elites were seldom more than marriages of convenience, with a measure of suspicion tempering the opportunism of both sides.

In this sense, Primo's relations with the business community paralled his involvement with the wealthy Mercedes Castellanos.[107] The daughter of a marquise, Castellanos attracted Primo with her charm much as financiers had with their money. Castellanos also had considerable business acumen and experience. No sooner was her betrothal to Primo announced in 1928 than she and financiers close to her used her new position to manipulate the stock market. The ensuing scandal left Primo sadder, Castellanos richer, and the engagement canceled. Though not tinged with romance, Primo's other dealings with big business and finance proved no more satisfactory in the end. By 1929 industrialists and bankers complained of overregulation and criticized the mounting debt that their own lavish spending recommendations had contributed to. Employers, too, had no more use than the church and the king for Primo's overtures to the Socialists.

Primo's difficulties with elites belie the contention that he was a simple tool of the privileged.[108] Indeed, his basic problem was that his purpose was less to serve the upper classes than to reach beyond them. He regarded society as much as an organism as a hierarchy. Its health required the full participation of its members at every level. Hence arose the dictatorship's attempt to awaken the *neutra masa,* or silent majority, and its increasing willingness to consider social reforms.

The rural *clases medias* supported this thrust of the dictatorship. Prior to rallying to Primo, many medium-sized landholders had supported Joaquín Costa, the regenerationist prophet of 1898, and had backed the conservative CNCA, the National Catholic Agrarian Confederation (Confederación Nacional Catolica Agraria). In Castile the rural *clases medias* had supported Maura, and in Aragon many subscribed to the traditional social and political values of Carlism. Primo regarded the rural *clases medias* as natural leaders of their communities. He legislated greater proportional representation for them in municipal and provincial government in much the same way that he looked to larger landlords and industrialists to participate in the National Assembly and National Economic Council. Similarly, while many leaders of the Patriotic Union and Somatén had noble titles, Primo relied on the rural *clases medias* for rank-and-file support for those organizations. Here above all was Primo's *neutra masa,* the conservative, religious, and patriotic group he most identified with. But even this constituency had misgivings about the dictator's flirtation with Socialists and republicans.

Less positive were the urban *clases medias*. Shopkeepers, professionals, and minor officials had been the backbone of radical, or *progresista,* liberalism in the mid-nineteenth century. The constitutional regime had assimilated many of them as low-level functionaries or dependents of political and economic elites. But that system provided what often seemed inadequate protection from a growing working-class challenge below while it perpetuated the rule of an oligarchic elite above. The ambiguities of the *clases medias'* position flowed into early-twentieth-century protests. This group was an important constituent in the meeting of chambers of commerce in Zaragoza in 1898, a tax strike in the early 1900s, the Assembly in Barcelona in 1917, various regional movements, and republican parties on the left and Maurism on the right. In 1923 many also supported Primo's call for an end to corruption and the establishment of careers open to talent in national life. The Patriotic Union initially attracted those committed to reform along with those seeking to advance their careers. For some, membership in the Somatén was a mark of status as well as a guarantee of public order. A decree against personal recommendations in hiring, though of little effect, appealed to this group.

However, the dictatorship's birth in industrial Catalonia and Primo's early advocacy of higher tariffs alarmed many merchants. The Madrid Mercantile and Industrial Directorate was typical in joining in Primo's condemnation of the old politicians, but also in deploring his resort to force to deal with the problem.[10] Its recommendations to the new government were very different from those of the economic elite. Large bankers and industrialists had endorsed protectionism and large-scale government spending funded by internal borrowing. The smaller Madrid manufacturers and merchants, on the other hand, proposed cutbacks in government spending, a stronger peseta, and a reduced cost of living—the latter presumably obtainable through lower tariffs. Primo's early commitment to the program of big business, and his increasing the tax burden of the urban *clases medias* to pay for that program, produced resentment.[110] Small manufacturers also complained that the dictatorship's regulatory machinery favored large companies at their expense. The Catalan *clases medias* opposed the regime after Primo turned his back on their regional aspirations. As the dictatorship stayed on, intellectuals and professionals were among those concerned about its ilegality and offended by its censorship and other civil-liberty enfringements.[111] These discontents drove many who were not direct beneficiaries of its patronage into the arms of the growing republican opposition.[112]

Primo's problems with the urban *clases medias* were not readily amenable to solution. Constraints from more privileged sectors of society tilted his policies against the interests of many in this group. But declining support from the urban *clases medias,* as evident in an atrophying Patriotic Union and Somatén, meant that Primo lacked not just mass support but the pivot point he needed to transcend the still larger division separating the working classes from the rest of the country.

The dictator's good will toward the working classes was genuine, but he was more reactive than self-initiating in meeting labor's needs. Seeing a butcher distraught and his wife crying as they were being evicted, Primo ordered his chauffeur to stop his car and help him restore the couple's possessions to their premises. Twice, believing his government had a budgetary surplus, he ordered that part of that money be used to redeem the pawned bedding of the poor. Even in his last months in power, embattled on every side, Primo took time to write the duke of Peñaranda, asking him to repair his farm buildings so his tenants' grain would not be ruined by rain.[114] But concern for the less fortunate did not mean that as a soldier he tolerated insubordination from workers who did not act in accord with their place in society. Nor did it free him from elite pressure against social reform.[115] He lent his support to reforms benefiting the working classes, but he in no way favored structural changes altering the essential balance between classes. His was a conservative purpose, inclined to strengthen the existing order rather than alter it fundamentally.

His pledge to labor in September 1923 had been to set an example of selflessness and hard work. In exchange for a modest increase in governmental paternalism, workers were expected to apply themselves diligently to their jobs, producing greater wealth for every social class to enjoy.[116] On this basis Primo suppressed the antisystemic anarchosyndicalists and communists and sought a working partnership with the Socialists.[117] The PSOE (Partido Socialista Obrero Español), the Socialist's political arm, had developed a commitment to parliamentary government under the constitutional regime. Its leading spokesmen, Indalecio Prieto and Fernando de los Ríos, did not welcome Primo's ban on political activity but were unwilling to risk destroying the wider Socialist movement by opposing the new regime. They did, however, draw the line at collaboration. The more numerous Socialist trade union, the UGT, on the other hand, was attracted by the benefits possible as the sole, legal working-class organization. Manuel Llaneza of the Socialist miners' union became the directory's principal working-class apologist, while Francisco Largo Caballero, originally a Madrid plasterer, accepted appointment to an advisory Council of State in 1924.[118] The union's greater weight in the fused Socialist leadership was also evident in the 1924 decision to participate in municipal councils and provincial deputations. UGT leaders used their positions within the regime to intervene on a number of issues relevant to workers.[119]

Seduction of Socialist leaders, however, did not alter rank-and-file perception of the dictatorship's conservatism. The maneuvering for position at the top of Spain's structure of privilege introduced by Primo did not change the working class's position at the bottom of the social pyramid. Indeed, in evaluating the dictatorship's social impact, few facts are as important as the Socialists' slow growth despite the regime's support. The rapid recovery, after the collapse of the dictatorship, of the more radical anarchosyndicalist organization, the CNT, also attests to the continuing alienation of the working classes.

Here Primo's political fate begins to come into focus. In retrospect, his tentative efforts to reach out to Spain's disadvantaged and to expand political participation can be faulted primarily for not having gone far enough, and indeed they largely failed to inspire enthusiasm or gratitude among their intended beneficiaries. Those same efforts, however, unsettled many privileged groups. As a result, Primo lacked firm support from either left or right, and his attempt to forge a new political middle ground foundered on the competing interests of a deeply divided society.

NOTES

1. Primo's biographers provide only cursory accounts of his family, education, and military career. Among the biographical sources are Anonymous, "Pillars of Government," *The Living Age* 325 no. 4220 (May 23, 1925): 405–10; Eduardo Aunós y Pérez, *Semblanza política del General Primo de Rivera* (Madrid: Gráfica Minerva, 1947) and *Soldado y Gobernante* (Madrid: Editorial Alhambra, 1944); Francisco Cambó, *Primo de Rivera* (Madrid: Editorial Reus, 1946); Jacinto Capella, *La verdad de Primo de Rivera* (Madrid: Hijos de T. Minuesa, 1933), Cimadevilla, *El general;* Julián Cortes Cavanillas, *La dictadura y el dictador* (Madrid: Talleres Tipográficos Velasco, 1929); Fernando C. Duarte, *España: Miguel Primo de Rivera y Orbaneja* (Madrid: Julián Espinosa, 1933); Manuel Gandarias, *Perfiles psíquicos del dictador Primo de Rivera y bosquejo razonado de su obra* (Cadiz: Escuelas Profesionales Salesianas, 1929); César González Ruano, *El General Primo de Rivera* (Madrid: Ediciones del Mocimiento, 1954), and *Miguel Primo de Rivera* (Madrid: Ediciones Nuestra Raza, n.d.); Lewis Haroc (pseud. for Lewis Rodríguez Aroca), *General Primo de Rivera* (Madrid: Editorial Dolar, n.d.); Dudley Heathcote, "Primo de Rivera and the New Spain," *The Fortnightly Review* 120 no. 719 (November 1926): pp. 593–603; Miguel Herrero García, *Primo de Rivera* (Madrid: Edito-

rial Durcalla, 1947); Miguel de Unamuno, "Primo de Rivera," *The Living Age* (September 1924); José Manuel Cuenca, "Miguel Primo de Rivera a la escala de historia," *Historia y Vida* 3, no. 22 (January 1970); and Rafael Salazar, "Perfil humano de Primo de Rivera," *Historia y Vida* 3, no. 22 (January 1970): 58–63.

2. Primo's father suffered a series of business reversals that might be partly responsible for the absence of such conspicuous consumption; González Ruano, *El General*, p. 23.

3. Cimadevilla, *El General*, pp. 16–25, is a sympathetic view of Primo's military career. More critical, especially of the role of family influence in his rapid advance, is Vicente Blasco Ibáñez, *Por España y contra el rey* (Paris: Editorial Excelsior, 1925), pp. 73–76.

4. Payne, *Politics and the Military*, p. 63.

5. Blasco Ibáñez, *Por España*, pp. 76–77.

6. On Primo's gambling, see ibid., pp. 76–78. On his debts, see *Hojas Libres*, April 1927, pp. 44–45, and January 1928, pp. 86–88.

7. Charles Petrie, *King Alfonso XIII and His Age* (London: Chapman & Hall, 1963), p. 180.

8. Primo's early journalistic ventures and his relationship with the press during the dictatorship are discussed by Dionisio Pérez, *La dictadura a través de sus notas oficiosas* (Madrid, Barcelona, and Buenos Aires; Compañía Ibero-Americana de Publicaciones, 1930), pp. 13–18.

9. The Conservative prime minister Allendesalazar had considered Primo to head the war ministry in his cabinet in 1920 but rejected him as "too dangerous;" Payne, *Politics and the Military*, p. 189. The original source for the quotation is José Gallo de Renovales, *Allendesalazar* (Madrid: Editorial Durcalla, 1946), p. 18.

10. There is reason to believe that he also opposed the war because he had been excluded from it; Boyd, "The Army," p. 806.

11. Ibid., p. 976.

12. Primo's political setbacks at this time are discussed by Gabriel Maura Gamazo, *Bosquejo histórico de la dictadura* (Madrid: Tipografía de Archivos, 1930), 1:22–24; and Eduardo Ortega ya Gasset, *España encadenada* (Paris: Juan Dura, 1925), pp. 177–79.

13. The dictator's version of the events leading up to the coup is contained in Miguel Primo de Rivera y Orbaneja, *La obra de la dictadura* (Madrid: Imprenta Sáez Hermanos, 1930), pp. 7–13.

14. Primo declared in a 1926 interview that he had thought about seizing power for nearly a year before the coup itself. Andrés Revesz, *Frente al dictador* (Madrid: Biblioteca Internacional, 1926), pp. 13–14.

15. Primo's ties with the Catalans antedate his appointment to that region. Cambó himself was instrumental in the Cortes's exempting Primo from inheritance taxes on his grandeeship in 1921; *Hojas Libres*, June 1927), pp. 60–66. In January 1923, Primo wrote Cambó, saying "no one can fail to recognize that Spain, and every other country, must transform their political composition, returning perhaps to the regionalism that was their origin"; Boyd, "The Army," p. 1002.

16. Payne, *Politics and the Military*, p. 190.

17. Boyd, "The Army," pp. 998–1002, and Ciges Áparicio, *España bajo la dinastía*, pp. 433–34.

18. Two accounts of Primo's coup are Payne, *Politics and the Military*, pp. 187–207, and Eduardo Ortega y Gasset, *España encadenada*, pp. 46–133.

19. Boyd, "The Army," p. 1004.

20. Ibid.

21. Payne, *Politics and the Military*, p. 194. Primo's evolving attitudes and subsequent policies on Morocco are discussed in greater detail in Shannon E. Fleming, "Primo de Rivera and Abd-el-Krim: The Spanish Struggle in Morocco, 1921–1927" (Ph.D. diss., University of Wisconsin, 1975) and Shannon E. Fleming and Ann K. Fleming, "Primo de Rivera and Spain's Moroccan Problem, 1923–1927," *Journal of Contemporary History*

12, no. 1 (1977): 85–89. See also J. A. Chandler, "Spain and her Moroccan Protectorate," *Journal of Contemporary History* 10, no. 2 (1975): 301–22.

22. That friendship is described in González Ruano, *El General*, pp. 55–56.

23. Maximiano García Venero, *Historia del nacionalismo catalán* (Madrid: Editora Nacional, 1967), 2:306–7.

24. Pabón, *Cambó* 2:446.

25. The difficulty of Alfonso's position is discussed by Maura Gomazo, *Bosquejo* 1:27–30. The official position of Alfonso and the dictatorship was that the king had no prior knowledge of the coup; Aunós, *Soldado*, pp. 52–57. The unlikelihood of Alfonso's having an active role is argued by Vicente R. Pilapil, *Alfonso XIII* (New York: Twayne, 1969), pp. 154–61.

26. Boyd, "The Army," p. 1017.

27. Payne, *Politics and the Military*, p. 195, and García Venero, *Historia del nacionalismo catalán* 2:307–8.

28. After their overthrow he became more vocal in public, declaring in an after dinner speech in Valencia, "Almost all my ministers were thieves, and all of them were, without question, incompetents and imbeciles;" Blasco Ibáñez, *Por España*, p. 92.

29. Payne, *Politics and the Military*, p. 200.

30. Primo's manifesto has been translated by Dillwyn F. Ratcliff, *Prelude to Franco* (New York: Las Americas Publishing Company, 1957), pp. 89–93.

31. Ibid., p. 89.

32. Ibid., p. 90.

33. These were the words Primo used on 22 October to announce the appointment of military delegates to supervise municipal government throughout the country; Maura Gamazo, *Bosquejo* 1:41.

34. Cortes Cavanillas, *La dictadura*, p. 143.

35. García-Nieto et al., *La dictadura*, p. 53.

36. Superficial as Primo's program might have been, even some of his strongest opponents recognized his sincerity. An underground journal edited by Miguel Unamuno and Eduardo Ortega y Gasset in France declared, "that talk of 90 days was then sincere. Primo was expecting that within that period the politicians would be vanquished and reconciled to the situation . . .;" *Hojas Libres*, June 1928, p. 3. On the distinction between mentality and ideology, see Juan J. Linz, "An Autoritarian Regime: Spain," pp. 253–83, in Erik Allardt and Stein Rokkan, eds., *Mass Politics* (New York: The Free Press, 1970).

37. The naval representative was Antonio Magaz y Pers, the Marquis of Magaz. The army representatives were Francisco Gómez-Jordana, Luis Hermosa y Kith, Antonio Mayandía y Gómez, Mario Muslera Planés, Luis Navarro y Alonso de Celado, Dalmiro Rodríguez Pedré, Francisco Ruiz del Portal y Martín, and Adolfo Vallespinosa y Vior; Ceballos Teresi *Historia económica* 5:133. The most striking feature of this group is its lack of distinction. Gen. Gómez-Jordana was the son of a former Moroccan high commissioner and later acquired a role in the Franco dictatorship. Gen. Muslera played a minor part in traditionalist politics during the second republic, for which he paid with his life when the civil war began. Adm. Magaz had been director of the naval academy and took Primo's place at the head of the government when the dictator was engaged in Morocco. Magaz was the only member of the directory to show much independence of thought. The others were nonentities in whom little was heard before or after the dictatorship. The relative standing of the directory's generals can be seen in Magaz' generally chairing its meetings in Primo's absence, Gómez-Jordana doing so to a lesser extent, Hermosa Kith only twice, and no other general doing so at all; Archivo General de Alcalá de Henares, Archivo de la Presidencia del Gobierno (hereafter PG), *Diario de Presidencia del Gobierno, 1924–1930*.

38. Ceballos Teresi, *Historida económica* 5:132–33.

39. Foreign Affairs was entrusted to Fernando Espinosa de los Monteros, Justice to Fernando Cadalso y Manzano, Finance to Eduardo de Illana, War to Gen. Luis Ber-

múdez Castro, Labor to García Martin, Development to Arche, Public instruction to Alfonso Pérez Gómez Nieva, and Interior to Millán de Priego, who was soon replaced by Gen. Severiano Martínez Anido. The ministries themselves were named secretariats during the directory. This designation was discontinued with the appointment of the civil government in December 1925; ibid. 5:134.

40. Ibid. 5:129.

41. Calvo Sotelo's youth and early career in politics are described by Aurelio Joaniquet, *Calvo Sotelo* (Madrid: Espasa-Calpe, 1939), pp. 15–52 passim.

42. Labor also valued Calvo Sotelo as a sympathetic official in the finance ministry; AHN, Leg. 33, Exte. 1848.

43. Calvo Sotelo, *Mis servicios,* pp. 1–11, describes the steps by which he joined Primo's government.

44. Aunós, *Soldado,* pp. 57–62, describes how he was recruited by Primo.

45. For a general European perspective on this phenomenon, see Robert Wohl, *The Generation of 1914* (Cambridge: Harvard University Press, 1979).

46. S. Cánovas Cervantés, *Apuntes históricos de "Solidaridad Obrera"* (Barcelona: Ediciones C.R.T., n.d.), p. 64.

47. Richard A. H. Robinson, *The Origins of Franco's Spain* (Pittsburgh: University of Pittsburgh Press, 1971), p. 27, and Bravo Morato, *Golpe,* p. 62.

48. In support of his successful application as a stock exchange broker in Barcelona, for example Leandro Negre Olivar claimed membership in the Monarchist Union and the backing of the governor of Barcelona, Joaquín Milans del Bosch; AHN Leg. 33. Exte. 2026.

49. Quintiliano Saldaña y García Rubio, *Al servicio de la justicia* (Madrid: Javier Morata, 1930), pp. 20–23.

50. Strongly disliked by the military and Catalan industrialists as well as by Primo personally, Alba made a convenient scapegoat for the abuses of the old regime. Primo directed five ministries and the prosecutor for the nation's highest court to search for financial improprieties committed by him; AHN Leg. 36, Exte. 3803. Some interpreted this effort as an attempt to intimidate the politicians into acquiescence of the dictatorship; *Hojas Libres,* July 1927, pp. 5–6. In fact, public pillorying of the self-exiled Alba had the opposite effect. Worse for Primo, by the standards of the constitutional regime, Alba was an honest politician, and the dictator could not make his charges stick; AHN Leg. 29, Exte. 143.

51. For more on the directory's appointments at different levels, see PG, *Acuerdos de los Consejos de Ministros,* pp. 92, 248, and 296–97; and PG, *Altos Cargos: 1925–1933.*

52. Their overlapping ministerial responsibilities are evident in their division of labor in preparation of the 1925–26 budget; AHN Leg. 1, Exte. 206 (12 November 1924).

53. Primo's reliance on the military for his office staff is evident in PG, *Altos Cargos: 1925–1933.* See also the executive order for the dissolution of the directory; AHN Leg. 41, Exte. 6638.

54. A critical view of Martínez Anido's record is provided by *Hojas Libres,* May 1927, pp. 80–86; June 1927, pp. 37–48; and August 1927, pp. 50–58. That same underground publication presented a strong circumstantial case that Martínez Anido, who had once faked an attempt on his own life, used *agents provocateurs* to stage an abortive insurrection against the directory on 7 November 1924 at Vera de Bidasoa; ibid., April 1927, pp. 16–27 and 77–81.

55. Bravo Morato, *Golpe,* pp. 117–18.

56. Tusell, *La Crisis,* pp. 31–36, reviews press reaction, especially in Andalusia, to Primo's seizure of power.

57. Gabriel Maura Gamazo and Melchor Fernández Almagro, *Por qué cayó Alfonso XIII* (Madrid: Ambos Mundos, 1948), p. 435.

58. Bravo Morato, *Golpe,* p. 121.

59. PG, *Diario de la Presidencia.*

60. Indeed, on only five occasions in two years did they even invite the ministerial officials responsible for a proposal to take part in their deliberations; ibid.

61. Brenan, *The Spanish Labyrinth*, p. 80.
62. Pabón, *Cambó* 2:471.
63. Brenan, *The Spanish Labyrinth*, p. 79 n. 1, and Payne, *Politics and the Military*, p. 249.
64. Appreciation for his accessibility is evident in correspondence directed to him. See, for example, AHN Leg. 138, Exte. 3.
65. Petrie, *King Alfonso*, p. 180.
66. Brenan, *The Spanish Labyrinth*, p. 80.
67. Even at the end of his dictatorship, Primo continued to view these early political reforms as of primary importance; Miguel Primo de Rivera, "Prólogo," p. ix in *Curso de Ciudadanía* (Madrid: Junta de Propaganda Patriótica y Ciudadana, 1929).
68. Economic thought in the period is summarized by Carlos Velasco Murviedro, "La política economica de la dictadura, cincuenta años después," pp. 157–79, in *Cuadernos Económicos de I.C.E.* 10 (1979).
69. García Nieto et al., *La dictadura*, p. 77.
70. Federico Bravo Morata, *La dictadura*, vol. 1 (Madrid: Fenicia, 1973), pp. 12 and 22–23.
71. From July 1924 until October 1925 Primo spent more than half his time in Morocco; personal letter from Shannon E. Fleming, 22 October 1978.
72. Primo's fear of the old politicians' return was clearly evident in an April 1926 banquet speech; Dionisio Pérez, *La dictadura a través de sus notas oficiosas* (Madrid: CIAP, 1930), p. 81.
73. *Hojas Libres*, June 1928, p. 3.
74. Yanguas's checkered relationship with Primo is described by Tusell, *La crisis*, pp. 142–45 passim.
75. Andes's appointment was typical of Primo's penchant for cronyism; *Hojas Libres*, January 1929, pp. 65–66.
76. The dictatorship's second rank is discussed by Manuel Tuñón de Lara, "La dictadura de Primo de Rivera como régimen político. Un intento de interpretación," pp. 28–31, in *Cuadernos Económicos de I.C.E.* 10 (1979).
77. Gabriel Jackson, *The Spanish Republic and the Civil War 1931–1939* (Princeton: Princeton University Press, 1965), pp. 81, 91–92, and 439. For his own perspective on his work for the dictatorship, see Manuel Lorenzo Pardo, *La conquista del Ebro* (Zaragoza: Heraldo de Aragón, 1931).
78. On the transition of military personnel from the directory to the civil government, see AHN Leg. 41, Exte. 6638.
79. Calvo Sotelo, *Mis servicios*, pp. 99 and 102.
80. Indicative of this delegation of authority is a comparison of the directory's meeting almost daily in 1924 and 1925 with the civil government's meeting less than twice each week on average from 1926 through 1929; PG, *Diario de la Presidencia del Gobierno 1924–1930*.
81. See, for example, the statement of Guadalhorce in Ceballos Teresi, *Historia económica* 7:20.
82. Pemartín, *Los valores*, p. 637.
83. The censorship is described in detail by one of the regime's operatives in Caledonio de la Iglesia, *La censura por dentro* (Madrid: Compañía Ibero-Americana de Publicaciones, 1930). Typical of the mild criticism permitted in books is Francisco Cambó, *La valoración de la peseta* (Madrid: Aguilar, n.d.) and idem, *Las dictaduras* (Madrid: Espasa-Calpe, 1929). The principal underground journals were *España con Honra* and *Hojas Libres*, the latter claiming a circulation of 7,000 in July 1927. Primo's attempt to influence the press extended beyond Spain to bribing *The Times* of London; *Hojas Libres*, April 1927, pp. 59–61, and Carr, *Spain*, p. 572 n. 3.
84. Indicative of the dictator's weariness was his increasing disinclination to call cabinet meetings. He convened the civil government 142 times in 1926, 80 times in 1927, 58 times in 1928, and 77 times in increasingly desperate 1929; PG, *Diario de la Presidencia del Gobierno, 1924–1930*.

85. See, for example, David Schoenbaum, *Hitler's Social Revolution* (Garden City, N.Y.: Doubleday & Company, 1967), pp. 275–88; H. Stuart Hughes, *The United States and Italy* (New York: W. W. Norton & Company, 1968), pp. 65–92; and Antony Polonsky, *Politics in Independent Poland 1921–1939* (Oxford, at the Clarendon Press, 1972), pp. 419–35.

86. Primo's discrimination against the Catalan church extended to taxation, as in his refusal to grant an exemption to the Bishop of Lerida in 1924 while ruling favorably on a similar request made by the Archbishop of Toledo in 1927; AHN Leg. 35, Exte. 3107, and Leg. 44, Exte. 7905.

87. Indicative of the church's resurgence was an increase in religious vocations in the 1920s; Jaime Vicens Vives, *Historia de España y America* (Barcelona: Editorial Vicens Vives, 1961), p. 148.

88. The military under the dictatorship is discussed by Payne, *Politics and the Military*, pp. 187–225, and Maura Gamazo, *Bosquejo* 1:42–43, and 2:225–38, 308–10, and 333–36. For the government's perspective, see Pemartín, *Los valores*, pp. 102–8.

89. Boyd, "The Army," p. 1047.

90. Pabón, *Cambó* 2:470–71.

91. Primo's conflict with artillery corps is discussed in *Hojas Libres*, September 1927, pp. 14–30 and 77–81.

92. Maura Gamazo, *Bosquejo* 2:97.

93. Standard sources on Alfonso are Pilapil, *Alfonso XIII*; Petrie, *King Alfonso XIII*; Álvaro Alcalá Galiano, *The Fall of a Throne* (London: Thornton Butterworth, 1933); and Carlos Seco Serrano, *Alfonso XIII y la crisis de la restauración* (Barcelona: Ediciones Ariel, 1969). On Alfonso's business dealings, see Blasco Ibáñez, *Por España*, pp. 53–54; *Hojas Libres*, December 1927, pp. 67–73, and June 1928, pp. 25–36; and Ciges Aparicio, *España bajo la dinastía*, pp. 446–47.

94. On the difficulty of Alfonso's position, see Calvo Sotelo, *Mis servicios*, pp. 112–21, and Maura Gamazo, *Bosquejo* 1:29›0, and 2:339–43. By 1929 association with the dictatorship badly tainted Alfonso, as was evident in the controversy in April at the Central University in Madrid over awarding him an honorary degree; *Hojas Libres*, June 1929, pp. 24–36.

95. Ciges Aparicio, *España bajo la dinastía*, p. 442.

96. *New York Times*, 17 September 1926, p. 5.

97. In 1927, Alfonso asked Gabriel Maura, son of the former Conservative leader, if he would be willing to head a transitional government, including Martínez Anido from the dictatorship as well as such noted liberal critics of the regime as Gregorio Marañon. However, support for such a compromise termination of the regime was lacking both within and outside government; *Hojas Libres*, August 1927, pp. 5–6.

98. Melchor Fernández Almagro, *Historia del reinado de Don Alfonso XIII* (Barcelona: Montaner y Simón, 1924), p. 516.

99. This point is made concerning aristocratic participation in the National Assembly by Juan J. Linz, "Spanish Cabinet and Parliamentary Elites: From the Restoration (1874) to Franco (1970)," paper prepared for a meeting at Bellagio, August 1970, pp. 97–99. On other aristocratic participation in the dictatorship, see PG, *Altos Cargos: 1925–1933*.

100. The temperamental affinity between the dictator and the lesser nobility was evident in firmer, more consistent support from that quarter; Antonio de Hoyos y Vinént, *El primer estado* (Madrid: Compañia Ibero-Americana de Publicaciones, 1931), p. 225.

101. Three weeks after Primo's takeover, for example, a large Madrid employers association issued a statement complaining about excessively high wages and social legislaton. Five weeks after the coup a royal commission headed by the wealthy Conservative Joaquín Sánchez de Toca concluded two years of consultation with leading business interests by calling for higher tariffs and subsidies. Prominent bankers presented Primo with their recommendations. No more reticent was the leading Catalan business association, the Fomento de Trabajo Nacional, with its economic policy suggestions in early 1924.

102. José Luis Gómez Navarro, María Teresa González Calbet, and Ernesto Por-

tuondo, "Aproximación al estudio de las élites políticas en la dictadura de Primo," *Cuadernos Económicos de I.C.E.* 10 (1979): 189–92.

103. Typical was the guarded reaction of *Las Finanzas* 3, no. 90 (18 September 1923): 1357–58.

104. The banking community's negative reaction was expressed in ibid. 3, no. 95 (23 October 1923): 1443–44.

105. Duarte, *España: Miguel Primo de Rivera,* pp. 72–73.

106. AHN Leg. 2, Exte. 1105, and Leg. 492, April 1924.

107. On Primo's aborted romance see Cánovas Cervantes, *Apuntes históricos,* pp. 68–69.

108. His son and political heir, José Antonio Primo de Rivera, was particularly bitter about the dictatorship's lack of support from elite groups; Gonzalo de Reparaz, *Las responsabilidades políticas de la dictadura* (Madrid: Galo Sáez, 1933), pp. 75–85.

109. *Las Finanzas,* 3, no. 90 (18 September 1923): 1358.

110. *Hojas Libres,* January 1928, p. 83.

111. The importance of the intellectuals is dealt with by Salvador Giner, "The Structure of Spanish Society and the Processes of Modernization," *Iberian Studies* 1, no. 2 (Fall 1972): 55. On Primo's conflict with intellectuals, see Juan Castrillo Santos, *¿Se ha redimido España?* (Madrid: Zoila Ascasibar, 1930), pp. 69–71. The most troublesome professional group was the Barcelona bar association; Javier Tusell, "Abogados catalanes contra la dictadura," *Historia 16* 4 (October 1979): 46–54; also on lawyers, see Santiago Alba, *Para la historia de España* (n.p., 1930), p. 30, and Ángel Ossorio y Gallardo, *Mis memorias* (Buenos Aires: Editorial Losada, 1946), pp. 146–50. The activities of the Human Rights League (Liga de Derechos del Hombre) are detailed in AHN Leg. 335, 31 July 1924.

112. The best discussion of the republican movement is Shlomo Ben-Ami, *The Origins of the Second Republic in Spain* (Oxford: Oxford University Press, 1978).

113. The essentials of Primo's social thought are contained in "Social and Labor Conditions: The Directorate's Manifestoes to Workmen and Employers," *The Economic Review* 8 (9 November 1923): 404–5; Eduardo Aunós y Pérez, *España en crisis: 1874–1936* (Buenos Aires: Librería del Colegio, 1942), pp. 289–90; Capella, *La verdad,* pp. 120–21; Calvo Sotelo, *Mis servicios,* pp. 252–55; Revesz, *Frente,* pp. 102–10; and Bruno Alonso, *El proletariado militante* (Mexico City: Casa Ramírez, 1957), pp. 43–56.

114. AHN Leg. 139, Exte. 450–451.

115. Those pressures are discussed by José Andrés Gallego, *El socialismo durante la dictadura* (Madrid: Tebas, 1977), pp. 50–53.

116. This recurrent theme of Primo's is evident in *Las Finanzas* 3, no. 92 (2 October 1923): 1392; Revesz, *Frente,* pp. 107–8; and *Unión Patriótica,* 1 July 1927, p. 8.

117. Primo's relationship with the Socialists is described by Paul Preston, *The Coming of the Spanish Civil War* (New York: Barnes & Noble, 1978), pp. 4–16.

118. Primo went to particular pains to win Llaneza's cooperation in 1923, appointing him to an important mining study commission and personally overseeing the paperwork providing the union leader with his expense money; AHN Leg. 30, Exte. 580.

119. Large Caballero was especially active in this capacity; AHN Leg. 355. Typical of the cases where collaboration produced small organizational benefits was the favorable ruling on a disputed tax claim of a Socialist railroad workers' cooperative; AHN Leg. 33, Exte. 1898.

Part Two

POLITICAL REFORM

3
Local Government

Primo's continuing priority during six and one-half years in power was a new political compact. Initially this meant breathing new life into the 1876 Constitution's version of parliamentary government. But Primo's thinking was too unsystematic to remain committed to any specific set of political institutions, especially as time and circumstance altered. What did not change was the powerful, if somewhat nebulous, purpose he attached to a new compact: the establishment of direct communication and identity of interests between government and governed to replace the rule of an isolated, self-interested oligarchy. A necessary part of such an arrangement was assimilation of Catalonia within the nation state. Toward these ends the directory began work in 1923 and early 1924 on reform of election procedures, the courts, and the Senate. But for Primo the key to national regeneration was local government. Through the governmental delegates and the municipal and provincial statutes he intended to awaken the *neutra masa* by granting it new powers of self-determination. Through these same devices he also sought to place local government more firmly in the hands of conservative, propertied interests.

The Governmental Delegates: "Pocket Iron Surgeons"[1]

In one of its first actions, the dictatorship purged those who held local office under the constitutional regime. On 20 September Primo announced the dismissal of all municipal council members and mayors. Their places were eventually taken by appointees of the regime's new military provincial governors. During the following months the newspapers were filled with stories of public officials and even entire city councils being sent to jail for corruption and negligence.[2] Even the mayor of Madrid did not escape. Mysterious fires destroyed the records of many towns, while a number of other officeholders, less benefited by providence, committed suicide before arrest and scandal could overtake them. The entire country seemed caught up in avenging hysteria, determined to root out every last vestige of *caciquismo*.

The regenerationist torrent unleashed by Primo's takeover complicated establishment of the new government's authority as well as orderly administration in general. Primo turned to the army for help. On 22 October he announced that he would use junior officers as governmental delegates, supervising municipal affairs.[3] There was to be one delegate for each judicial district *(partido judicial)*, generally comprising several municipalities. The size of these districts could range as large as 120 *pueblos* with as many as 200,000 people.

The October 1923 decree gave the delegates a wide-ranging mandate. It charged them with inculcating civic spirit and overseeing the affairs of municipal government. After the proclamation of the Municipal Statute the delegates were asked to hold meetings, with all citizens required to attend, so that the benefits of this new legislation could be explained. The delegates were also asked to seek out and put to use the best political talent locally. Sponsorship of the *Somatén* was another responsibility. They were to see that students had physical education and were to encourage their participation after school in the Explorer youth group.[4] Literacy and civic education programs were also established.

The purpose behind these scattered efforts was to take the management of public affairs from the old politicians and hand it to an aroused citizenry. Starting from this premise, any program that improved the social and economic condition of the people or their political awareness was a logical responsibility of the delegate. An amorphous and ill-defined task soon became all encompassing as Primo issued a continuing stream of new suggestions. Typical was an April 1924 memorandum urging the delegates to encourage gymnastics by "organizing public associations and clubs for that purpose that could engage in the sport, preferably as part of holiday observances."[5] The same memorandum suggested that the delegates sponsor "the raising of birds, bees, rabbits, and especially silk worms, so they can serve as the basis of an important national industry."

The core of the delegates' mission, however, remained the political awakening of Spain at the grass-roots level.[6] The first step here was the removal from office of the corrupt remnants of *cacique* politics. The edict announcing the arrival of a delegate asked that "each citizen within five days present to me his complaints and denunciations." The delegates generally spent their first days in office traveling throughout their district hearing these grievances. As might be expected, complaints ranged from unpaid government bills, high taxes, and unfair assessments to gossip about the personal lives of local officials. During this initial tour most delegates also examined municipal financial records and acquainted themselves with local office holders. The chronic abuses and mismanagement uncovered in this investigative foray confirmed their initial prejudices concerning the evils of *caciquismo*. Justice and sound administration alike demanded the punishment of those responsible. The wave of arrests and prosecutions that had begun with Primo's coup in September was thus sustained and carried into the first months of 1924 by the delegates.

More often than not, however, it was the low paid secretaries, mayors, and council members of small towns that were investigated. Few local elites or prominent politicians of the constitutional regime were directly implicated in the myriad of small vices and illegalities committed by local government. Moreover, in those instances where one faction of *cacique* politicians was prosecuted for misconduct in public office, the principal beneficiary of their fall was generally only a rival faction.

The source of this political failure was the great myth by which the dictatorship lived and died. Primo believed, as did the delegates and country generally, that *caciquismo* was a conspiracy perpetuated by the few against the many, not the political expression of a late modernizing society in which all were included. The delegate came hard against this problem in his search for Primo's "new men," that large pool of talent and energy presumably waiting to be rallied to the cause of the national regeneration. To find that group the delegate turned, not surprisingly, to "the civil guard, judges, mayors and ex-mayors, municipal secretaries, the clergy, doctors, pharmacists, veterinarians, teachers, larger taxpayers, heads of different political factions, presidents of clubs and casinos, and workers."[7] That is, he turned to the dominant social and economic elites, their operatives and dependents, and, where they existed, their local rivals. These groups, for their part, were well aware that they had much to gain through cooperation with the delegate. Typically, they greeted him with large welcoming ceremonies replete with music and ringing church bells.[8]

The national connections of some local elites created additional problems for the delegates. Not every one was adept at traversing the political minefield presented by assignment to an unfamiliar district. Acting on the usual hearsay evidence of denunciations and a hasty investigation, a delegate in Galicia arrested Mon y Landa as a *cacique*. Mon y Landa, however, belonged to an influential family and was a member of the Cortes. That same evening the delegate went personally to the prison to apologize and release him. But Mon y Landa refused to go until the morning when his friends could witness the event. Even less prominent local figures complained to Calvo Sotelo in Madrid about the delegates.[9]

Petitions of that sort, however, were infrequent because the delegate usually relied on social and economic elites for support and tended to look at local problems through their eyes. The delegate might move against the mayors, councilors, and municipal secretaries directly implicated in past fiscal mismanagement and election chicanery. But, seeing *caciqismo* as the disease and not the symptom, he seldom challenged the position of the larger landlords and notables who dominated rural life.

A partial exception to this pattern resulted from intraelite conflict, generally a carry-over from the competition between Liberal and Conservative factions under the constitutional regime. Each faction's interpretation of local problems, its ties to Madrid, and the delegate's own predispositions might lead to support for either the "ins" or the "outs." In one such instance, the delegate aligned himself with the Conservative faction, although a local minority, in the Andalusian district once controlled by a Liberal cabinet member, Niceto Alcalá Zamora. But Conservatives could not always count either on the delegate's support. That was evident in the government's attack on the interests of two former leaders of that party, José Sánchez Guerra and Ángel Ossorio y Gallardo, both of whom had run afoul of the military before Primo's coup.

As that example suggests, the delegates were not always powers unto themselves. Either the provincial governor, a military man in the dictatorship's early days, or even one of the directory's generals might have special personal or political interests in a particular area and the delegate became their instrument. Local officeholders might still be purged, but critics claimed, as a piece of doggerel suggested, that

> All Spain is played the fool
> Because she does not remember
> That the broom is dirtier
> Than that which it sweeps away.[10]

In any event, where there were divisions in a community, the delegate could not easily stand above them. As he began to cooperate more with one faction than another he lost his disinterested quality and frequently, without even realizing it, became inextricably enmeshed in local politics. In other words, he became a participant in the *caci-*

quismo that he originally had intended to abolish. As he did so, he lost much of his efficacy as an agent of reform.

The appeal for an apolitical, civic awakening stirred curiosity and interest among many in the beginning. Once the delegate became mired in local rivalries, however, he was reduced to the status of simply another alien intrusion of the central government in local affairs. Those who answered his call for participation in the Somatén and Patriotic Union were all too often only favor seekers, not selfless patriots.[11] His pronouncements on the need for education and improved sanitary practices seemed irrelevant to the traditional lives of many workers and peasants. Public apathy, backwardness and the delegate's own false assumptions about reform, defeated him in the end.[13]

The less idealistic did not worry about such matters. One delegate in Motril in Andalusia was even reported to have established his own *cacique* system.[14] But Primo could not disregard the fact that the delegates had proven dubious regenerators. Gradually, beginning in December 1924, he reduced their numbers and limited their functions to little more than organizing the Patriotic Union locally. An indication, however, of how quickly the delegates had put down roots was their general protest over this cutback—a complaint in which they were almost alone.

The Municipal Statute

Parallel with the changes in personnel and attitudes pursued by the delegates, the dictatorship sought changes in the structure and functioning of local government. This commitment was evident in public statements and private planning. Within two weeks of the coup Calvo Sotelo was charged with drawing up comprehensive local government legislation.[15] To assist him in preparing the Municipal Statute he recruited conservative academicians and politicians, such as Luis Jordana de Pozas, José María Gil Robles, Antonio Flores de Lemus, and the count of Vallellano. They drew on a variety of past precedents, especially Maura's proposals of 1907 and 1918.[16] Work proceeded quickly, for the directory wanted prompt action. In January 1924, Calvo Sotelo presented his draft.

The structural changes attempted were many and important.[17] Their basic premise, according to Calvo Sotelo, was that the municipalities existed not as administrative conveniences for the national state, but as instruments of the local communities themselves for their own self government. The artificial uniformity of nineteenth- and early-twentieth-century local government was abolished. Small rural municipalities were recognized as having different needs than large urban centers. Municipalities with fewer than 500 people were permitted to conduct their business through open meetings of the adult population. This measure applied to more than half of the country's municipal governments.

Often smaller population centers were overshadowed by a larger center within the confines of a single municipality. The Municipal Statute was the first legislation since the nineteenth century to offer remedies for the special problems of these "lesser local entities" *(entidades locales menores)*. Municipalities were also permitted to apply for charters granting extra powers, including taxation, to fit their particular circumstances. Special charters could also empower municipalities to govern themselves by elected commissions or professional managers instead of the previously mandatory mayor and council arrangement. The implementation of these changes, however, was deferred until the return of elected local governments.

The civil governor's power to intervene in local affairs was also limited. He could no longer summarily dismiss office holders, nor unilaterally alter local budgets. Challenges to local policies or officers were to be resolved through the courts, not administratively. Since many municipalities were too small or poor to provide needed services, the statute permitted, and indeed on occasion required, them to band together. Thus, several towns might share the expense of a doctor, veterinarian or pharmacist, or even build and maintain a road between themselves.

The statute provided for increased popular participation in local government. Women heads of household received the right to vote. Voting age was reduced from twenty-five to twenty-three. Mayors were to be chosen locally rather than by the central government. As noted, smaller communities were able to manage their affairs in open meetings. To counter *caciquismo,* the secret ballot and proportional representation were instituted.

The dictatorship did not equate local autonomy and popular participation in government with the maximum extension of democratic principles. Indeed, *caciquismo* under the constitutional regime was characterized by the manipulation of an untutored electorate within the framework of formally democratic institutions. In keeping with Maurist tradition, the Municipal Statute fell back on corporativism to reconcile increased popular interest in the hands of the propertied classes. Two-thirds of each municipal council were to be elected popularly, while one-third were to be chosen as the special representatives of the

Church and leading business and social organizations. The influence of the corporate representatives was magnified by the statute's provisions for fewer meetings of the full municipal council and the delegation of most responsibility to a smaller, permanent commission of the council. This conservative paternalism was implicit in Calvo Sotelo's reference to the Municipal Statute as "not won by the people, but for the people."[18]

The responsible and autonomous municipal government, which the dictatorship saw itself giving to Spain, had improved services as its corollary. Many municipalities embarked on development programs stimulated alike by the Municipal Statute's grant of new powers, the governmental delegates, and the general climate of expansion and regeneration engendered by the dictatorship.[19] The regime furthered this process by mandating new responsibilities in health, education, housing, and highways.[20]

Increased responsibilities made local finances important. Better administration resulted in improvements here. In Priego de Córdoba, an Andalusian town of 19,000, annual expenses in the year before the dictatorship were 329,000 pesetas against revenues of 185,830 pesetas. During the dictatorship's first complete fiscal year, expenses decreased to 322,850 pesetas, while income rose to 321,775.[21] One administrative measure contributing to such improvements was elimination of tax farmers. In one year that step boosted Alicante's revenues from 2,229,619 pesetas to 3,390,222 pesetas, an increase of 47.4%.[22] In the smaller town of Benisa in the same province expenses fell from 84,604 pesetas in 1922 to 82,538 pesetas in 1924 while income rose from 58,407 pesetas to 104,921 pesetas.[23] Increases of that magnitude indicate the degree of laxity, corruption, and favoritism that had traditionally plagued local finances. Another concern of many municipalities was retirement of past debts. During the first months of the dictatorship, 41,243,773 pesetas in back debts were retired, some of which had been pending more than five years.[24]

Most of these positive early results stemmed from the dictatorship's new town councils and the scrutiny they received from the government delegate. In subsequent years the regime supported efficiency in municipal finances with permanent legislation.[25] The Municipal Statute required the use of the same budget categories by local government throughout the country. The statute also distinguished between "obligatory" and "voluntary" services, requiring municipalities to meet the former before the latter. Local budgets had to be publicly announced, and the municipal secretary had to approve their soundness and legality.[26] Although the statute denied the civil governor the right to intervene in budget matters, citizen's groups could appeal inequitable or illegal provisions to local representatives of the finance ministry. These officials could then bring suit against the municipality in an administrative court. These measures helped sustain the progress made in the dictatorship's first months. In Priego de Córdoba, for example, revenues from a major income tax increased 66.7% during the first two years of the dictatorship, while the tax rate itself decreased 65.4%.[27]

Most municipalities, however, found themselves in a less enviable position. The rate at which the dictatorship whetted appetites for development and mandated new responsibilities far outpaced the increase in resources from improved administration. Early in the dictatorship, then, uncovering new sources of revenue became important. Before 1923 municipalities derived their income from several sources.[28] Primary support came from the *consumos,* or excise taxes, on basic consumer products. Other revenues were produced by fines, license, inspection and notarization fees, as well as such muncipal services as transportation, schools, and hospitals. The 1877 Municipal Act also allowed municipalities to require up to twenty days labor service per year, redeemable by cash payment. Levies similar to head or pool taxes elsewhere in Europe were also permitted. The municipalities' major remaining source of income came from a fixed share of various state taxes collected locally.

Taxes of this sort, and particularly the *consumos,* were heavily regressive. Social inequity was compounded by economic disadvantage. With the bulk of its revenue derived from the poorest sectors of society, local government was forced to operate within narrow fiscal limits. Most town councils dealt with this problem in a piecemeal manner. One small levy of the same basic type was piled on top of the other, until an incredible fiscal maze existed. The system had become exceedingly inelastic. Additional revenue could only be extracted in two ways: a substantial improvement in the honesty and efficiency with which the system was administered or its restructuring along less regressive lines.

Both alternatives, however, ran up against the privilege and personalism that stood at the center of local society and politics. Flores de Lemus had sought to alleviate this dilemma in the 1911 Municipal Revenue Act. That measure kept the basic tax structure intact. But it established new levies on luxury items and placed a measure of the burden for increasing expenses on the shoulders of those benefiting directly from such new services as sewers, refuse collection, and street lighting and paving. In the 1924 Municipal Statute Flores de Lemus expanded both these features. He also included a small, socially oriented tax on uncultivated land. More importantly, he extended the municipalities an increased share of national and provincial taxes assessed locally. But with both the state and provinces running increasing deficits of their own, there was never any possibility that revenue sharing would generate enough income to eliminate municipal deficits. Moreover, borrowing opportunities were limited by competition with other public and private borrowers, the chronic insolvency of most local governments, and the remoteness of many of them from the principal capital marketplaces of Madrid, Barcelona, and Bilbao.[29]

The Municipal Statute gave local credit the most systematic attention of any legislation to date. Ordinary budgets for routine operating expenses were required to be in balance. Borrowing was only to finance extraordinary budgets for long-term development programs. None of this is to say, however, that the dictatorship discouraged borrowing. What Calvo Sotelo argued for was not an end to deficit spending, but intelligent use of credit.[30] That his position was inconsistent with the assignment of many new responsibilities to the municipalities was another matter.[31]

Local governments needed a new source of credit to fund their deficits. To supply that need the dictatorship established the Local Credit Bank (Banco de Crédito Local) in May 1925. By the end of 1929 the bank had issued 215,411,574 pesetas in loans to various municipalities.[32] During the same period municipal indebtedness increased from 924,376,800 pesetas to 1,388,023,900 pesetas.

Municipal Debt

1923	792,078,300 ptas.
1924	–
1925	–
1926	924,376,800 "
1927	944,603,100 "
1928	1,078,998,200 "
1929	1,388,023,900 "

SOURCE: Successive editions of the *Anuario estadístico*.

In other words, possibly as much as 68% of the increase in municipal debt between the time that the Local Credit Bank began issuing loans at the end of 1925 and the end of the dictatorship was underwritten by that bank. The state's role in facilitating this growing debt was greater than that statistic suggests, since the National Insurance Institute also extended sizable loans to local governments for health and education purposes.

What those figures could mean on a local level can be seen in Priego de Córdoba.[33] In four and one-half years under the dictatorship, Priego's regular budget expenditures increased 81%. With improved administration and new taxing powers, incomes also increased. Indeed, the deficit that had plagued Priego during the last years of the constitutional regime was virtually eliminated. Dramatic as the increase in regular budget expenditures was, it did not encompass the ambitious development program originated after Primo's takeover. The Municipal Statute anticipated this need with its provisions for local extraordinary budgets, and the establishment of the Local Credit Bank in 1925 provided the necessary credit. However, for Priego, at least, the bureaucratic wheels turned exceedingly slowly in Madrid. Although Priego had virtually completed preparation of its development plan in 1924, it was not until February 1927 that the Local Credit Bank approved a 1,350,000-peseta loan for the community's 1,535,000-peseta program.

Priego did not fulfill its pledge to fund the remaining 185,000 pesetas of its plan, primarily through special taxes *(contribuciones especiales)* on those benefiting directly from the new expenditures. That problem, and a general underestimation of costs, brought the project to a premature conclusion in October 1929. During those years Priego paved a number of streets and improved its water and sewage treatment systems.[34] But it did not build the new town hall and school, which had been important parts of the original plan, even though it had spent 1,350,511 pesetas, an amount almost equal to the Local Credit Bank's original loan.

Certainly, building projects of the sort carried out in Priego were needed in many Spanish towns, and the dictatorship deserves credit for stimulating them. Still, the projects appear to have been hastily conceived and irresponsibly funded, not just exceeding the ability of local governments to fund them out of current revenue, but exceeding their ability even to meet the debt service charge. In Barcelona, Spain's largest city, for example, there were complaints in 1930 that local finances had been mishandled.[35] During the greater part of the dictatorship, the mayor of Barcelona was the baron of Viver. On leaving office after Primo's fall, Viver claimed that his administration had considerably increased municipal services while decreasing the city's debt service from 21% to 20% of its total budget. The mayor's critics argued that those figures concealed a significant financial deterioration. In 1923, Barcelona's municipal debt stood at 427,797,000 pesetas, by far the highest in Spain. By 1930 the municipality's contracted liability had more than doubled, to 882,029,500 pesetas. The debt service charge had grown even more rapidly, from 21,795,000 pesetas to 53,470,000. Those increases represented a jump in the mean liability per inhabitant from 588 pesetas to more than 1,000. That figure is particularly striking when compared against a burden of national debt per inhabitant of only 874 pesetas.

However, what was truly problematic was that Barcelona had nearly exhausted its resources for funding these obligations. By 1930 the state itself was too hard-pressed to offer much help.[36] With credit contracting nearly everywhere, and the regular budget's shortfall amounting to 27 million pesetas, or nearly one-sixth of expenditures, there was little likelihood that the city could raise the money it needed in the private capital marketplace. Faced with this situation only weeks after the dictatorship's fall, Manuel Argüelles, Calvo Sotelo's successor in the finance ministry, called for austerity in municipal finance and asserted new review powers for the central government over local budget making and borrowing.

The onset of the depression certainly complicated local finances. Nonetheless, to blame the problems of Barcelona and other cities on that event is, to an extent, to reverse cause and effect. Municipal deficits were part of a larger problem of rapidly increasing public indebtedness at every level. That increase was not sustainable indefinitely. It contributed to a widespread unease in the financial community that, in turn, compounded the contraction in credit that began nearly a year before the American stock market crash.

The dictatorship's curious device for municipal borrowing, the Local Credit Bank, aggravated this problem. Although a semiofficial institution, it drew on private banks for much of its management and funds, relying especially on Recasens's Bank of Catalonia (Banco de Cataluña). The irony in this situation was that resistance to taxation from Spanish elites had helped place the state in tight fiscal straits in the first place, precluding significant aid to municipal government. But after 1925 a portion of that same elite, the bankers, was able to use the Local Credit Bank as its middleman, guaranteeing security and a high rate of return on the funds private financial institutions processed through it to local governments. Worse, this device largely eliminated the scrutiny that either the state or private bankers acting on their own might have given to the value of local development projects and of the ability of local communities to support their long-term costs.

A final way in which the dictatorship sought a civic awakening at the municipal level was through new personnel policies.[37] Under the constitutional regime, municipalities exercised virtually unrestricted patronage power over nonelective government posts. Kenneth Medhurst has described the results of this system as "low levels of administrative efficiency and little continuity of administrative effort. Offiicials who regarded their appointments as pieces of personal booty rather than opportunities for public service were unlikely to pursue local politicians to create effective local services and were unqualified to administer them."[38]

The dictatorship sought to overcome this problem by establishing a national civil service system for local government employees, especially the secretary, the auditor, and the tax collector. The secretary was the most important. He was the chief clerk in most municipalities as well as corporation counsel and notary. His signature was required to certify municipal accounts and most other government acts. Equally important, he was in charge of much of the day-to-day administration. He was also responsible for reporting irregularities in municipal affairs to higher authorities, generally the civil governor. He occupied, in short, a highly anomalous position, at once the municipality's employee and the monitor of its performance.

The dictatorship eliminated some of the most obvious pressures on the secretary's independence by establishing minimum salaries for municipalities of different sizes. The regime made his dismissal from office more difficult by requiring a quorum of three-fourths of the town council's members and a two-thirds majority of those present for this purpose. All secretaries were also required to join a newly established National Secretarial Corps, with admission of future members to the corps contingent on a certain minimum of professional training and a formal examination. Municipalities were required to hire their secretaries from this group. Similar, though less stringent, measures were applied to the auditors and tax collectors. These measures were part of a larger effort at every level of government to replace political operatives with apolitical, and presumably more efficient, bureaucrats.

Nonetheless, if these personnel changes were consistent with the dictatorship's war on *caciquismo,* they were at variance with its pledge of increased municipal autonomy. As Medhurst has pointed out, the attempts of the dictatorship and subsequent regimes to improve the quality of municipal employees and to insulate them from improper influence largely failed for several reasons.[39] Local government service in a poor, but highly centralized, state could not avoid being unattractive to the best public servants. It was far removed from important decision making, and its salaries were consistently meager. Additionally, no legislation could undo the fact that isolated government employees in a small town are subject to a far wider variety of informal influences than bureaucrats in a large ministry in the capital.

Important defects in the dictatorship's legislation compounded these problems. Although the regime recognized the secretary as chief of local government employees, it gave him virtually no disciplinary power over those responsible to him. Another mistake was the creation of an adjutant secretary post in cities of more than 100,000 population. The division of authority between the secretaries and the adjutants was not clearly delineated. Friction between them snarled the affairs of several large cities before the adjutant post was abolished. Finally, although the dictatorship required higher professional standards for new administrators, it did little to encourage those already in such positions to upgrade their qualifications.

In general, the regime's municipal legislation gives the impression of a poorly coordinated series of false starts. Promises of important improvements were made in municipal self-government, services, and personnel. But in few of these areas were basic and lasting changes realized. Worse, the regime frequently widened the gap between governmental promise and performance that had been so conducive to civic apathy before 1923. In 1927, Primo received a letter from a town in Asturias bemoaning that, three years after enactment of the Municipal Statute, it had "neither light, nor good roads, nor police."[40] Priego de Córdoba may, in a fashion, have moved forward in this period. But in 1928 in the neighboring town of Carcabuey typical old complaints persisted of the mayor lining his pockets with money earmarked for water-treatment and of the butcher selling meat from diseased animals.[41]

The Provincial Statute

An unintended consequence of early preoccupation with municipal reform was denigration of the provinces. As Primo informed Basque civic leaders, provincial government reform would have to wait until more pressing matters, such as municipal government problems, were resolved.[42] Primo was, in fact, sufficiently unconcerned with provincial government that he did not replace provincial assembly members until early 1924, months after he had begun similar changes with town councils.[43] Moreover, much of the autonomy granted the municipalities by the Municipal Statute was purchased at the provincial civil governor's cost. In similar fashion, many of the increased responsibilities entrusted municipal government came at the expense of the provincial assemblies. By the end of the dictatorship's first year, the diminishment of the provinces in mind and substance raised questions about their future.

The need to examine the role of the provinces also resulted from long-term trends.[44] The provinces were dependent for most of their income on the financially pressed municipalities. Lack of a solid revenue base meant that they could not readily perform the services needed to give them vitality. Moreover, the responsibilities mandated them by the central government were frequently back-up and support functions. But the failure of most municipalities to perform their basic health and education tasks meant that there was little to gain from the provinces developing more advanced services in those areas. Equally serious was the evolution of the civil governor's role from professional administrator to linchpin of *Caciquismo*. With most of his energies devoted to politics, he was seldom able, even if inclined, to give much attention to provincial needs. For these reasons provincial government seemed an expensive irrelevance and more an encumbrance than aid to sound administration. Moreover, the division of Spain into fifty provinces had been a product of the early nineteenth century. By the twentieth century improvements in transportation and communication had made possible an end to this fragmentation of administrative energies through the establishment of larger, regional units of government.

Retarding this development, however, was the fact that many politicians looked to the province to dilute growing regional consciousness at this time. The driving force behind regionalism was Catalonia. From 1912 to the fall of the constitutional regime, public discussion of local government was largely preempted by attempts to accommodate Catalan regional sentiment within the nation state.[45]

As captain-general in Barcelona, Primo had cultivated cordial relations with prominent regionalists, and his coup enjoyed initial support there.[46] Primo, for his part, was quoted on 14 September in *El Día Gráfico* as saying, "Catalonia will have nothing to fear from our coming to power . . . I have come to care for Catalonia so much that my greatest desire is to serve her."[47] The next day *La Veu de Catalunya* editorialized,

> The General has been reaffirmed in his intention to dedicate himself to the resolution of the internal problem of Spain, giving the regions all the power and liberty compatible with the existence of the state's unity . . . believing that in those regions lies the firm basis for the rebirth of the country, and he has repeated his great love for Catalonia, whose problem he wishes to solve with dispatch.[48]

Only one awkward moment interrupted these effusions of goodwill.[49] Just before Primo's train left for Madrid, cheered by a large crowd, his friend, the count of Güell, presented him with a statement of the

Lliga's goals that had been drafted by the president of the *mancomunidad*, Puig i Cadalfalch. Primo said he would accept the statement, but first its reference to Catalan nationalism would have to be changed to regionalism. That done, the new dictator's train departed, the beginning of a journey that would presumably produce a new form of regional government.

Indeed, although Primo took a hard line against separatism, he did not quickly abandon his commitment to regionalism. In January 1924, at the same time that Primo was replacing elected members of the Catalan *mancomunidad* with his own appointees, he spoke of the need to establish more supraprovincial bodies similar to it.[50] Calvo Sotelo shared Primo's interest in regionalism, and the Municipal Statute contained references to future regional units. Within and outside government it was assumed that the weakened provinces would give way to regions. Newspapers were filled with speculation about which cities would become regional capitals. Primo lent credence to these rumors through public statements and support for an abortive Castilian *mancomunidad* along the same lines as the Catalan *mancomunidad*.[51]

By early 1925, however, Primo had become an opponent of regionalism. He justified the shift on the ground that, after a year in power, it was apparent that regionalism was often only a thin cover for antinational feelings.[52] He had help in forming this opinion. The directory's secretary, Nouvilas, expressed the views of *juntero* officers when he opposed any concession to regionalism.[53] Barrera, Primo's successor as captain-general in Barcelona, was equally emphatic on this point.[54] Four days after the coup Alfonso himself asked Primo to come up with measures suppressing Catalan separatism.[55] The next day the government forbade use of the Catalan language in official functions, and made statements against national unity subject to prosecution in military courts. Other affronts to Catalonia included prohibiting display of the Catalan flag, proscribing the regional dance, the *sardana*, and changing Barcelona's street signs from bilingual to Spanish only.

Primo spent the next several months courting both sides. A new dictator with only shaky support from the crown and the army could hardly afford to offend either. At the same time, however, he did not want to break valued ties with leaders of the Lliga and the Barcelona based League for the Development of National Production (Fomento de Trabajo Nacional). His early economic and social measures met most of the needs of his wealthy friends.[56] Catalan financial institutions associated with the marquis of Comillas and the baron of Güell played a prominent role, along with the Basque Urquijo interests, in the telephone monopoly granted ITT in 1924. Primo's high tariffs on manufactures and low duties on raw cotton and oil were well suited to Catalonia. No less agreeable to the propertied elite there was his crackdown on anarchosyndicalists and his appointment of two ruthless enforcers of law and order, Martínez-Anido and Arlegui, to head the interior ministry and national policy.

What Primo could not grant, and what Catalonia would not rest without, was increased regional autonomy. When the count of Güell came to Madrid to protest the directory's early anti-Catalan policies, Primo could only apologize, saying that the *junteros* had played an important role in his coup and he could not oppose their wishes on an issue of such importance. In January 1924, still not without hope of a *modus revendi* with the region. Primo traveled to Barcelona to meet with Catalan leaders. After his discussions, as part of a general personnel change in provincial government throughout the country, he packed the *mancomunidad* with conservative politicians he could work with. But conflicts repeatedly broke out between local military commanders and the Catalans, forcing Primo and his new appointees to choose sides, generally on opposite sides of the fence. In spring and summer 1924, for example, a major dispute flared between army officials and the Barcelona bar association over the use of the Catalan language.[57] Again, finding he had no middle ground to stand on, Primo aligned with the army.

Increasingly resented by Catalonia, Primo turned his frustrations against many of his former associates there. Employment seekers, among others, soon learned that association with the Lliga had become a black mark on one's record.

This divorce never became total. Primo retained until the end close links with some of the region's most wealthy and powerful figures, as evident as late as 1928 in the award, against strong opposition from Basque and Madrid financiers, of the lucrative concession for the Exterior Bank of Spain (Banco Exterior de España) to a consortium headed by Recasens's Bank of Catalonia, the same institution that already played a leading role in the semiofficial Local Credit Bank.[58] He also sought to channel Catalanism into cultural channels by allowing considerable literary and artistic freedom. A Catalan language chair was even established in the royal academy. Primo held two meetings of his Council of State in Galicia in Summer 1928, rather than in Madrid, to show his interest in areas outside the capital. But the dictatorship's basic political thrust, and increasingly aspects of its economic program, alienated the bulk of the propertied classes there just as its repression of the CNT made it unpopular with the working class.

None of this boded well for regional government. After promulgating the Municipal Statute, Calvo Sotelo was entrusted with drawing up similar legislation for the provinces. Calvo Sotelo was aware of Primo's hardening line on regionalism, and attempted at least once to dissuade him.[59] But Primo was uncompromising, and Calvo Sotelo had little choice but to delimit carefully the powers of future regional confederations and to lay down stringent preconditions for their establishment. In public statements as well, Calvo Sotelo followed Primo's line on the profligate waste and inefficient duplication of services of the Catalan *mancomunidad*.[60]

Nonetheless, when Calvo Sotelo presented his draft of the Provincial Statute to the directory in early 1925, he was still taken aback to see how far Primo had reversed himself on his earlier regional sentiments. In particular, Calvo Sotelo could not understand how the dictator could insist on deleting all references to regional administration when it had been presupposed in the municipal legislation announced with much fanfare the year before. In the end, Calvo Sotelo assured Primo that requirements for regional formation set by the statute were sufficiently tough to prevent separatists from dismantling the national state. Persuaded that future interprovincial cooperation could be limited to ad hoc agreements in areas such as health and transportation, Primo accepted the statute. Almost simultaneously, he abolished the Catalan *mancomunidad*, the only effective regional administration up until that time.[61] His new position was that regionalism was inherently dysfunctional within a unitary state, and that legitimate local aspirations could be adequately expressed within the municipal and provincial formulas provided by the dictatorship.[62]

With regionalism proscribed, the Provincial Statute's purpose became articulation of a positive role for provincial government. The statute reversed tradition in dealing with this problem. It held that the provinces should be agents of the local administrations under them, with authority flowing up rather than down. Municipal governments were given a role in choosing the provincial government, and the provincial government's functions, in turn, were essentially to support the operations of those local administrations. The provincial assemblies also received genuine legislative powers, transforming them from the largely advisory bodies they had been. Their new status came largely at the expense of the civil governor who lost his position as their ex officio president.[63]

Expanded provincial government activity paralleled municipal experience. Efforts were made to fulfill long neglected responsibilities in education and health. In May 1928 thirty-eight provinces compacted to finance a large road-building program.[64] The Local Credit Bank issued

255 million pesetas in state-guaranteed interprovincial bonds to support the project. Overall, local roads, funded in considerable measure by the provinces, expanded considerably.⁶⁵ This activism reflected not so much a new role for the provinces as fulfillment of an old one. During these years the provinces began to function as the back-up for municipal government that they had long been declared to be.⁶⁶

Attempts were made to improve administrative personnel parallel to the reforms in this area for municipal government.⁶⁷ But the most important requisite for effective government at this level, as elsewhere, was money. With most of their revenue coming from the overburdened municipalities, and with new sources of revenue limited by Spain's general poverty, the provinces lived a meager life. Calvo Sotelo only partially alleviated their situation through a five-percent share in a state tax on agricultural income, a provincial head tax, a surcharge on certain state taxes, and a variety of minor taxes.⁶⁸ The state also agreed to underwrite a share of certain major provincial expenses such as highway construction.⁶⁹ Additionally, the provinces received a small share of state revenues in return for their collecting certain national taxes. Part of the funding for increased government activity also came from borrowing. Between 1922 and 1930 provincial indebtedness ballooned 133% from 104,329,800 to 242,907,102 pesetas.⁷⁰

The dictatorship deserved credit for attempting to make the provinces more responsive to local needs. But overall its program for provincial government foundered on the Catalan issue that Primo could not solve. With the Municipal Statute Primo turned a corner, but he could not go down the road that lay ahead. That edict had anticipated creation of regional government units between the municipalities and the state. But even for dictators, politics remain the art of the possible, and the ill will that had accumulated between the army and the Catalans since the turn of the century left Primo with scant opportunity to proceed in that direction. Indeed, as a soldier needing the military's support, he had even less freedom of action than civilian politicians before and after him. With many provincial powers already transferred to the municipalities, but with regional government itself precluded, the provincial statute was doomed to be an exercise in futility. Primo's fears of elections eliminated what opportunity remained for responsive, representative government at that level. With an appointed civil governor and an appointed council, provincial administration could not easily gain popular identification with its efforts.

Antipathy between the dictator and Catalonia was mutually reinforcing and escalating. The regionalism for which he had expressed sympathy in the first months of his regime increasingly infuriated him, and he attributed its persistence not to any failure on his part, but to the workings of a small group of antinational plotters.[71] In 1926 he ordered the count of Gimeno to investigate the University of Barcelona, which had been a separatist center.[72] In particular, Primo wanted the names of the professors fomenting antinational feeling. Unbelieving, Primo refused to accept Gimeno's conclusion that there was no such "radiating center" of militant Catalanism, but that the university was merely mirroring opinion around it.

With Primo operating on this basis, the Catalans could only become more estranged.[73] Even the region's small textile manufacturers turned against him, alienated by economic policies that relied on state spending as the motor for development rather than the mass purchasing power that their industry required. Catalonia's growing regional sentiment was also evident in a remarkable cultural flowering, as a variety of foreign authors were translated into Catalan and as the people of that region patronized local writers and theater as never before.[74] During a difficult time for journalism in other parts of the country, Catalans supported a number of new periodicals in their own language. As the Catalan movement deepened in intensity, it moved to the Left, led by *Acció Catalana,* the *Partit Republica Català,* and *Estat Català.* As leader of *Estate Català,* Francesc Macià was Catalanism's dominant figure.[75] He was involved in abortive attempts to assassinate the king in 1925 and to invade Spain from France with Catalan guerrillas in 1926. Seeking support for his cause, Macià met in Moscow with Bukharin and Zinoviev, traveled throughout Latin America, and presided over an assembly of Catalan groups in Havana. The most extreme of Catalonia's leaders, Macià embodied the unremitting militancy bred by the dictatorship's intransigence.

The tragedy in this was that, even though integral nationalists in other parts of Spain may have resented Catalonia's aspirations at times, Primo's attitude did not reflect the country. In December 1927 the National Library in Madrid sponsored a Catalan exposition. *La Época, El Sol,* and *El Debate* all took that occasion to pay tribute to Catalonia's contribution to the nation.[76] But for most Catalans the public face of Spain was the government in Madrid, and during the dictatorship Madrid generated little but hostility. The seeds sown by the dictatorship were reaped by the second republic when Catalonia's alienation produced one of the deepest cleavages leading to the civil war.[77]

The failure of the dictatorship's revolution in local government was nearly total.[78] Primo never found his "new men." He also backed away from the free elections that might have given meaning to his pledge of local self-determination. He postponed those elections originally on the grounds that the dictatorship was a temporary government soon to leave power. But as he clung to office, the gap between his promises and his actions deepened the apathy and cynicism he had set out to destroy. That same gap between word and deed was present in his mandating more responsibilities to local government than he provided revenues to meet them.

Nowhere, however, were the regime's policies more lacking than in Catalonia. Apart from the Basque provinces and a few other northern areas, Catalonia was the only part of Spain where there had been a widespread civic awakening before the dictatorship. Much of Catalan sentiment, of course, defined itself in opposition to the central government, seeing it as corrupt and negligent in meeting the region's special needs. But the popular interest and participation in local government there could have been held out as a model for the rest of the country. By doing so Primo might have reduced the distance between that area and the rest of Spain and simultaneously given additional life to local government. Instead, he yielded, perhaps unavoidably, to centralist elements that saw not just the separatist movement, but the vitality of Catalan life in general, as a threat to the Spanish state. Soon there was no other alternative to the deepening estrangement between the dictator and Catalonia than the collapse of the regime itself. Primo's search for the elusive key to national regeneration had begun, but could not end, with local government. Thus, the latter years of the dictatorship were marked by a growing number of economic and social initiatives and a declining sense of political direction.

NOTES

1. The phrase "Pocket Iron Surgeons" is taken from Tusell, "The Functioning," p. 21. On the delegates generally, see his *La crisis,* pp. 85–116.
2. See, for example, Rubio, *Crónica,* pp. 58, 61 and 84.
3. The dictatorship's legislation on the delegates is listed in Enrique las Heras Marin, *Auxiliar indicador de la legislación española* (Madrid: Editorial Reus, 1929), pp. 179–80, 34, and 176.
4. On the Explorers *(Exploradores)* themselves, see *Unión Patriótica,* 15 October 1926, pp. 9–11.
5. Maura Gamazo, *Bosquejo,* 1:95.
6. E. T. L., *Por pueblos,* pp. 37–38, illustrates the primacy of this political purpose.
7. Ibid., p. 75.
8. Ibid., pp. 41–43.
9. Payne, *Politics and the Military,* pp. 229–30.
10. Ortega, *España encadenada,* p. 225.
11. E. T. L., *Por pueblos,* pp. 213, 225, and 237–38.
12. Ibid., pp. 101–8, 117–19, 121–26, and 139–79.

13. This negative assessment of the delegate's performance is supported by the unpublished research of Enrique Moral Sandoval. In a 1 June 1973 conversation he indicated that few delegates ever achieved much success apart from reforming local finances. In Catalonia they also played an important role in repressing expressions of regional sentiment.

14. Tusell, "The Functioning," p. 22.

15. Calvo Sotelo, *Mis servicios,* pp. 29–64, discusses the drafting of the Municipal Statute.

16. Luis Jordana de Pozas, "Significación del Estatuto en la historia del municipalismo español," in *Cincuentenario del Estatuto Municípal,* ed. Instituto de Estudios de Administración Local (Madrid: Instituto de Estudios de Administración Local, 1975), p. 18.

17. General accounts of the changes brought by the Municipal Statute are contained in Calvo Sotelo, *Mis servicios,* pp. 29–64; Pemartín, *Los valores,* pp. 427–72; and Ceballos Teresi, *Historia económica* 5:205-7.

18. Calvo Sotelo, *Mis servicios,* p. 60. The dictatorship's ambivalent commitment to democratic government was also evident in a November 1925 statement of Calvo Sotelo, declaring "the current [municipal] corporations have not converted municipal government into an electoral instrument; precisely because their members have not had to be preoccupied with political intrigues, their honest and brilliant administration has excelled;" "A Guisa," *Anuario de la vida local 1925* 2:vii.

19. See, for example, the building program of Priego de Córdoba, the planning of which began in mid-1924, well before the establishment of the Local Credit Bank in 1925; Valverde, *Memorias de un alcalde,* pp. 31–59. See also José de Ucelay, "Servicios municipales," *Revista de Obras Públicas* 74, no. 2444 (1 January 1926): 28–32.

20. For a partial listing and commentary on these new mandated responsibilities, see las Heras, *Auxiliar,* pp. 453 and 661–62; José de Ucelay, "Las obras municipales y el servicio hidraulico," *Revista de Obras Públicas* 74, no. 2450 (1 April 1926): 183–85; and J. Oller Piñol, *Martínez Anido* (Madrid: Librería General de Victoriano Suárez, 1943), pp. 185–86. The extent of these responsibilities should not be exaggerated. They were certainly very heavy in terms of the limited resources available to meet them in many Spanish municipalities. But many needs considered basic in western Europe were still unmet by local government years after the dictatorship. See, for example, Instituto de Estudios de Administración Local, *La hacienda en el municipio rural español* (Madrid, 1949), pp. 55–73.

21. Valverde, *Memorias de un alcalde,* pp. 29–30.

22. Calvo Sotelo, "A Guisa," *Anuario de la vida local* 1:ix.

23. *Unión Patriótica,* 1 December 1926, p. 24.

24. Calvo Sotelo, "A Guisa," *Anuario de la vida local* 2:ix.

25. This legislation is discussed by Antonio Saura Pacheco, *Presupuestos de las entidades locales,* (Madrid: Instituto Estudios de Administración Local, 1948), pp. 63–81 passim.

26. The position of the municipal secretary is discussed in greater detail below.

27. Valverde, *Memorias de un alcalde,* pp. 29–30.

28. José García Hernández, "Hacienda estátal y hacienda local" *Revista de Estudios de la Vida Local* 13, no. 73 (1954): 3–50 and Antonio Saura Pacheco, *Principios y sistemas de haciendas locales* (Madrid: Instituto de Estudios de Administración Local, 1949), pp. 123–29.

29. In the *Añuario de la vida local 1925,* pp. 12–16, Calvo Sotelo identified the principal factors determining access to credit, in order of their relative importance, as proximity to credit centers, the size of the town seeking credit, the fiscal soundness of that town together with its overall level of economic development, and whether or not it was a provincial capital. Thus, a number of small towns in the Basque provinces were able to engage in considerable borrowing, while larger communities in other parts of the country, further removed from major economic centers, were starved for credit. Generally, however, it was the larger cities that were able to borrow most freely. In *Mis servicios,* pp. 42–43 n. 1, Calvo Sotelo reported that during the fiscal year 1924–25, municipal debt

in the country amounted to 797.3 million ptas. Of that total, 461 million was owed by Barcelona alone, 127 million by Madrid, 48.5 million by Bilbao, 30 million by Corunna, and more than 4 million each by Oviedo, Santander, Málaga, Gijón, and Zaragoza.

30. Calvo Sotelo, *Mis servicios,* pp. 46–47.

31. Town councils in the period complained persistently that they were in an impossible position, and that either their responsibilities had to be reduced by the state or their revenues increased. This sentiment is echoed by E. Nicanor Puga, José María Pí y Suñer, and Fernando Cuesta, *Informe sobre las haciendas locales* (Madrid: Unión de los Municipios Españoles, 1927).

32. Calvo Sotelo, *Mis servicios,* p. 49.

33. Priego's finances were detailed by the city's mayor under the dictatorship; Valverde, *Memorias de un alcalde,* pp. 29–50, passim.

34. Municipal improvement programs elsewhere are discussed in *Unión Patriótica,* 1 October 1926, pp. 27–28, and 1 December 1926, pp. 24 and 31.

35. Criticism of this sort includes Pedro Corominas et al., "La revisión de la obra económica de nuestras corporaciones locales durante la dictadura," *Revista Nacional de Economía* 30, no. 89 (January–February 1930): 113–16; "Nuevos aspectos de la actuación financiera de nuestras corporaciones locales durante la dictadura," *Revista Nacional de Econòmia* 30, no. 90 (March–April 1930): 303–5; and Dalmacio Iglesias, *Política de la dictadura* (Barcelona: Espasa Calpe, 1930), pp. 110–27 and 211–24.

36. Iglesias, *Política de la dictadura,* pp. 110–27 and 211–24, passim.

37. The following account of the dictatorship's legislation for local administrators is drawn largely from Antonio Bullón Ramírez, *Historia del secretariado de la administración locale* (Madrid: El Consultor de los Ayuntamientos y de los Juzgados, 1968), pp. 203–39; and J. I. Morillo-Velarde Pérez, *El alcalde en la administración española* (Seville: Universidad de Sevilla, 1977), pp. 75–92.

38. Kenneth Medhurst, *Government in Spain* (Oxford: Pergamon Press, 1973), p. 198.

39. Ibid., pp. 199–200.

40. AHN Leg. 524 (14 May 1927).

41. *Hojas Libres,* February 1928, pp. 84–85. Still more striking is Primo's difficulty in finding a capable mayor for Madrid; ibid., July 1927, pp. 50–56, and December 1927, pp. 49–56.

42. Rubio, *Crónica,* p. 97.

43. Acedo Colunga, *Calvo Sotelo,* pp. 67–69.

44. The historical evolution of the provinces is discussed briefly by García de Enterría, *La administración española,* pp. 51–66, and José María Mandoli Giro, "El derecho provincial," *San Jorge* 8 (1952): 61–63.

45. Tusell and Chacón, *La reforma de la administración local,* pp. 133–69.

46. Primo's close ties with the Catalans antedated his appointment as captain general. In November 1921, Cambó introduced a bill against the wishes of Maura, the president of the government, to allow Primo to inherit his grandeeship free of all taxes; *Hojas Libres,* June 1927, pp. 60–66. On the Barcelona economic elite, see also AHN Leg. 318 (Bancos, April 1924).

47. Maximiano García Venero, *Historia del nacionalismo catalán* (Madrid: Editora Nacional, 1967), 2:310.

48. Ibid.

49. Ibid.

50. Calvo Sotelo, *Mis servicios,* pp. 17–19.

51. Maura Gamazo, *Bosquejo* 1:118–28, and Ceballos Teresi, *Historia económica* 5:135–36.

52. Pemartín, *Los valores,* pp. 92–102.

53. Maximiano García Venero, *Santiago Alba* (Madrid: Aguilar, 1963), p. 239.

54. Pabón, *Cambó,* 2:471.

55. Fernando Díaz-Plaja, *De la dictadura a la guerra civil,* vol. 2 of *La España política del siglo XX* (Barcelona: Plaza & Janes, 1972), pp. 17–18. See also José Manuel and Luís

de Armiñan, *Epistolario del dictador* (Madrid: Javier Morata, 1930), pp. 71–74; Melchor Fernández Almagro, *Historia del reinado de Alfonso XIII* (Barcelona: Montaner y Simón, 1934), pp. 451–52; and Maura Gamazo, *Bosquejo* 2:58. Primo's adoption of a harsh, repressive line against Catalonia is criticized in *Hojas Libres,* October 1927, pp. 39–42, and February 1928, pp. 43–51.

56. Ben-Ami, *The Origins,* p. 163; and Colectivo de Historia, "La dictadura de Primo de Rivera y el bloque de poder en España," *Cuadernos Económicos de I.C.E.* 6 (1978), and "La via nacionalista del capitalismo español," vol. 2, p. 205. A key figure in Primo's relationship with the Catalan elite was Joaquín Milans del Bosch y Carrío. Formerly a member of the king's military household, Milans served as provincial governor in Barcelona for much of the dictatorship. He also championed local interests as head of an association of exporters and as head of the government's regulating committee for the cotton industry; see, for example, AHN Leg. 138, Exte. 300.

57. Javier Tusell, "Abogados catalanes contra la dictadura (1924)," *Historia 16* 4 (October 1979): 46–54.

58. Colectivo, "La dictadura," p. 210. Reflecting the continuing loyalty of some conservative propertied groups was the founding of a Patriotic Union newspaper in Vilafranca del Panedés by "mature men with the liberty that comes from not needing to depend on anyone"; *Heraldo del Panadés,* 2 March 1929, p. 1.

59. Calvo Sotelo, *Mis servicios,* pp. 67–70.

60. See, for example, his comments in the *Anuario de la vida local 1925,* pp. 15–18.

61. Revesz, *Frente al dictador,* pp. 22–27.

62. Díaz-Plaja, *De la dictadura,* pp. 70–73.

63. Kenneth M. Medhurst, "The Central-Local Axis in Spain," *Iberian Studies* 2, no. 2 (Autumn 1973): 82.

64. Velarde, *La política económica,* p. 56.

65. Ceballos Teresi, *Historia económica* 7:383, records a 26% increase, from 15,968 km. in 1927 to 20,118 km. in 1929. However, the large jump he cites in every category of road building from 1927 to 1928 makes it difficult to have complete confidence in this statistic.

66. A sketch of provincial services as they were expanded by the second republic and early Franco regime is contained in Instituto de Estudios de Administración Local, *Estudios y estadísticos sobre la vida local en España* (Madrid, 1943), 1:458–61, 478–82, and 484–505. On the dictatorship, see *Anuario de la vida local 1925,* 1: viii–xi; *Avance de la provincia en el quinquenio 1923–1928;* and *Unión Patriótica,* 1 October 1926, pp. 26–27.

67. Bullón, *Historia del secretariado,* pp. 231–39.

68. Information on provincial taxes can be gleaned from Saura Pacheco, *Presupuestos,* pp. 49–63; las Heras, *Auxiliar,* pp. 149–50, 177–79, 261–62, 734–36, and 744–53; Higinio Paris Eguilaz, *El movimiento de precios en España* (Madrid: Consejo Superior de Investigaciones Cientificas, 1943), pp. 130–31.

69. Acedo Colunga, *Calvo Sotelo,* pp. 73–74.

70. *Anuario estadístico 1934,* p. 536.

71. Primo, *La obra,* p. 10, is his retrospective statement on the matter.

72. Maura Gamazo, *Bosquejo* 1:165–67.

73. Borja de Riquer, "El nacionalismo catalán: La hegemonía de la Lliga Regionalista," *Historia 16,* Extra 5 (April 1978): 53.

74. García Venero, *Historia del nacionalismo catalán* 2:330–31, and Albert Balcells, *Cataluña contemporanea, 1900–1939* (Madrid: Siglo Veintiuno, 1976), p. 21.

75. On the growth of radical left Catalanism, see Enrique Ucelay da Cal, "Estat Catala: The Strategies of Separation and Revolution of Catalan Radical Nationalism (1919–1933)" (Ph.D. diss., Columbia University, 1979).

76. Rubio, *Crónica,* pp. 304–10, passim.

77. For the dictatorship and Catalonia during the later years of the regime, see Maura Gamazo *Bosquejo* 2:124, 128, and 222–25. For a moderate Catalan perspective on the

dictatorship in this period, see Voltes Bou, "Enfoque Barcelonés," pp. 114–20 and 136–43. Even during the final months of the dictatorship, there was a foreshadowing of future developments when Streseman, the German foreign minister, declared on a visit to Madrid that Catalonia was Spain's "minority" problem; Rubio, *Crónica,* p. 413.

78. Different aspects of the dictatorship's failure are discussed for Asturias by Ruiz González, *El movimiento,* p. 185, and for Catalonia by Pabón, *Cambó* 2:471.

4

Attempts at a New Compact

The Patriotic Union

Primo intended the Patriotic Union to give national structure to the civic awakening initiated by his local government reforms.[1] The union's origins were several. In November 1923, anticipating the directory's promised early end, Catholic conservatives met in Valladolid to form the UPC (Unión Patriótica Castellana) to continue its work. Many of those present had been opponents of Santiago Alba, the former Liberal minister from that province. They were linked to the province's small landowners, where Alba had had stronger ties with local industrialists. Also helping found the UPC was Ángel Herrera, editor of the Catholic Madrid daily *El Debate* and a backer of previous attempts to win over men of small property and the working classes to the church and conservatism. The UPC held rallies in central Spain in November and December. At approximately the same time, former supporters of what had been the Conservative party organization in Primo's native province of Cadiz claimed similar purposes in founding Civic Action (Acción Ciudadana).

Primo himself, after a state visit to Italy in late November, became interested in using these efforts to unite his supporters into a single movement. Working with him, and linked to both the Cadiz and Valladolid groups, was his brother José. In April 1924, Primo launched the Patriotic Union as his chosen vehicle for national regeneration. Its original platform was "Religion, Monarchy, and the Constitution of 1876."[2] In proclaiming these three principles Primo committed himself to the country's basic political and social institutions as he had found them at the time of his coup. His goal was not so much to transform existing structures as to infuse them with a new spirit.

Most immediately, the union was a connecting link between the dictatorship and the nation, rallying support to the regime and attempting to keep it in touch with popular needs and aspirations. The politicians of the constitutional regime were allowed to participate, but only if they renounced their past political affiliations. This test was understandably difficult and degrading for most of those who had been nationally prominent only a short time before. But the main goal of the union was not to win the support of the old elite, but to mobilize the energies of the previously politically inactive. As Primo put it,

> We are going to prepare Spain for government by those who have not governed. Those that have already governed have done nothing for the country.[3]

The union was not born with a well-defined program. It was to draw its identity from the action of the regime, and that action was said to be a broadly apolitical and technical work of national reconstruction. For the present the directory was concerned with the Moroccan War, local government, tariff revision, agricultural credit, and the railroads.[4] Beyond those immediate objectives,

> Nothing requires nor even advises the formulation of advance programs, which can in any event already be deduced from the action of the directory: a policy of order and economy, of justice, of the development of labor, of military and social discipline, of protection for the wealth of the nation, of the normalization and efficient conduct of public services. On these and many other points patriots may unite, regardless of their political orientation.[5]

After the dictatorship, the Patriotic Union was to become the spawning ground for new political parties. By virtue of their immaculate conception within the union, such parties would not represent narrow interests. Instead they would offer genuine, if competing, versions of the national good.[6] According to the union's official organ,

> the current organization of the Patriotic Union will disappear when it has finished its generative mission as mother of new parties and of new values which will be grouped together along programatic lines. Within these parties will be able to belong some of the old politicians once they have been reformed. The current leaders, once their mission has been completed with themselves covered with glory, will need their well earned rest and perhaps will remain as a reserve without intervening directly . . . in the future political contests that should begin then.[7]

The day the dictatorship would hand over power to the union seemed close at hand to many in 1924. Primo himself had encouraged such speculation by initiating electoral reform and new voter registration lists. In speaking on behalf of the organization, Primo spoke of leaving government soon to return to the army.[8] He qualified those remarks on other occasions, but the impression was nonetheless created that he did not intend to prolong the dictatorship, and that it was the Patriotic Union that would inherit the work of reform.

Primo promoted the movement with fanfare. From April until June 1924 he spoke on its behalf in southern Spain.[9] In July and August he turned to Galicia, Asturias, and other areas in the north. Although Primo had declared that no favoritism would be shown members of the union, actual practice proved the reverse. When Calvo Sotelo, as director general of local administration, ordered members of town councils and provincial assemblies chosen without regard to political affiliation, Primo countermanded him by requiring membership in the union.[10] The state's patronage was apparent at every level. The delegates held town meetings to recruit members.[11] Civil governors oversaw the growth of the organization at a provincial level, and the interior ministry supervised it nationally. To no one's great surprise Primo named himself to head the union.[12]

The Patriotic Union was the most confused initiative of a regime conspicuous for its contradictions. Few of its members came from pre-1923 political and economic elites, and few of its leaders would attain prominence again after the dictatorship, failing generally even to be resurrected by Franco. In many instances their obscurity was well merited. It was also a product of a rigid society with few opportunities for mobility, apart from brief and partial periods of exception such as the dictatorship.[13] The *clases medias* were the backbone of the Patriotic Union and the hoped for source of Primo's "new men." They exhibited the same fear of the working classes below and resentment of privileged groups above that fueled radical right movements elsewhere in interwar Europe. The union's bulletin declared that

> the dictatorship was necessary to sweep away the swarming parasites that were sucking the nation's blood. Before the dictatorship Spain was the fief of four privileged families. Today, thanks to the dictatorship, Spain belongs to the Spaniards. And Spain has been saved.[14]

The union's 1925 platform called for an end to the system of personalism, or *recomendaciones,* by which the old order had perpetuated itself and excluded outsiders from participation. It stated,

> It is necessary to abolish the basic causes of faith in the omnipotence of the recommendation, a pernicious and enervating system, which disregards merit in order to be captivated by the name of a "god-

father," which aims for a reverse selection process, rejecting the best talents, conscious of their worth, and instead turns to an improper, unconfessable source of guidance, resting content with mediocrity and remaining totally rooted in favoritism and intrigue. In this way, there will be a rebirth of faith in the worth of one's own labor, and the best minds will no longer despair.[15]

With similar thrust the sixth of the Patriotic Union's ten commandments in 1929 called for a single chamber parliament, abolishing the constitutional regime's Senate, which had given extra weight to the nobility.[16] That same commandment, on the other hand, committed the union to at least partial corporate representation in parliament, diluting the working classes' strength and increasing the propertied classes' influence. A Patriotic Union newspaper in Catalonia declared,

It is the moment of the Patriotic Unions born in every country to check the excessive, sporadic advance of democracy, which has been transformed from a peaceful and generative river into a devastating flood. Political and social progress cannot be held back if it stays within its banks. . . , but it is indispensable to contain and return flood waters to the river channel.[17]

In short, members of the Patriotic Union did not want to destroy the structure of society. They wanted to strengthen and affirm it, simultaneous with promoting their own position within it.[18]

The *clases medias* were Primo's *neutra masa,* but they were as sharply divided against themselves as against the rest of society. Those divisions carried over into the Patriotic Union.[19] Many of the union's members were Maurists, Traditionalists, and Social Catholics and saw the union, and the dictatorship generally, as an opportunity to make dominant ideals that had been peripheral before 1923. In the countryside, where the union drew much of its strength, peasant and medium-sized landholders, bypassed by the processes of change sweeping the country, could see the organization as championing a return to traditional values. Particularly striking is how closely the new motto adopted by the union, "Religion, Fatherland, and Monarchy," paralleled the old Carlist cry of "God, Fatherland, and King." But the union also attracted republicans and even a few Socialists. Indeed, Primo courted those groups, praising their sincerity, if not their principles.[20] The union also sponsored charitable undertakings for the urban poor, such as soup kitchens and clothing distribution.[21] Not all union members, however, were primarily motivated by ideals, nor from the *clases medias.* Large numbers of one-time rural *caciques* joined the movement much as they had previously supported the old dynastic parties.[22]

They curried the favor and patronage from the central government needed to maintain their local influence. The union also attracted a variety of job seekers in city and countryside alike.

This motley band did not lend itself to a single unifying purpose. Moreover, because Primo did not think in systemic terms himself, he had little sense for the importance of political principle to others. Regarding the union as a group of sincere patriots, he thought their common dedication to national regeneration was sufficient in itself to produce a clear direction and purpose for the organization. He did not understand that national regeneration was only a platitude and that any attempt to give it specific content risked irreconcilable differences of opinion. This difficulty was evident in his 5 July 1926 welcoming speech to the union meeting in Madrid responsible for drafting a program.

> Within the Patriotic Union should be admitted all manner of thought, and we should organize our work, most probably, through division into subgroups so that even the smallest details will be attended to. I hope that within a few brief days a definite orientation will arise from this gathering that will serve as the program to be followed in all 50 provinces.[23]

Similar appeals over the next three years followed the failure of this meeting. At a local level, beyond expressing loyalty to the dictatorship, individual union chapters did little other than proclaim moralistic pieties and advocate pork-barrel public works and special-interest legislation benefiting their area. The program of the chapter in the small town of Padruenda in Galicia was sufficiently exemplary to be reported in detail in the union's national bulletin. It called for the repression of blasphemy and elimination of work on Sunday, together with local highway construction, better postal service, increased agricultural services, and reduced taxes on alcoholic products manufactured by members as well as free laboratory analysis for members of those products.[24]

Latent in the *clases medias'* social position was a national socialist predisposition that Primo could have played upon. But his inclinations were never so radical. Moreover, he had not taken office as head of a mass movement from below, but through a coup from above, and needed the support of established groups to govern—groups that accepted the dictatorship but did not see it as having more than a limited instrumental value. The power centers with which he coexisted, particularly the church, had strong constituencies, substantially overlapping with his own. Primo himself acknowledged, "the support of the army means . . . [that the union] is apolitical."[25] He and Alfonso disagreed publicly about the need for the Patriotic Union in the Basque provinces and Catalonia, where active monarchist groups already existed.[26] In both areas, in fact, the union remained weak. Nor were large industrialists, financiers, or aristocrats likely to be enthusiastic backers of a radical Patriotic Union.[27]

In 1924, Primo's call for patriots to band together in the moment of their country's extremity did not call for any elaborate rationale. As that challenge faded, Primo sought to hold the union together with nationalist rhetoric. He also assigned it special projects, such as carrying out the 1926 plebiscite. He entrusted its women's section with a literacy campaign. Large rallies were another device to buoy the union's morale as well as his own prestige. It was difficult, however, to sustain a movement whose main purpose was to support a dictator whose own purpose was in continual flux. In the latter half of 1924, Primo said the union was ready to take power. The union proclaimed itself the directory's heir in its 1925 platform. But Primo then perpetuated the dictatorship, moving from directory to civil government. He also abandoned his pledge to uphold the 1876 Constitution, part of the original Patriotic Union program, and began saying that the union and the regime's corporate economic and labor organizations provided more representative government than the constitutional regime's parliament. Primo spoke, as well, of his reform mission as longer term than originally anticipated, but one that he now planned on seeing through to completion.

In mid-1926 he said he would convene a National Assembly, a largely government-appointed grouping of notables, to help him with his work and to improve communication between him and the country. Rather than imbue the dictatorship with an aura of legitimacy, that announcement provoked fears about its indefinite continuance—especially among the old politicians and intellectuals. The king's reluctance to sign the necessary enabling legislation delayed the project for more than a year. Primo also confronted the first serious attempt to overthrow the dictatorship in June 1926, and in the fall he became embroiled in an ongoing dispute with the artillery corps. Throughout 1926 as well, he engaged in a running and acrimonious debate with landlords and merchants over tax legislation. These difficulties, and Primo's worsening diabetes, contributed to the tone of doubt and uncertainty that crept into his public statements in 1927. His emphasis was not on new promises, but old pledges. After all the words about a new era, "we . . . have to persevere in our action so that the people will not see themselves defrauded," he declared,

> If . . . providence has marked out a man to be the leader of a people, that same providence cannot grant such men an eternal existence . . . it will be enough then if we can mark out the general outlines that will lead to the enrichment of our mother country.²⁸

Less confident than during the first days of the civil government, he had begun to look for a way to exit from power. With recurring frequency his governing team described itself as "temporary," "transient," and "exceptional."²⁹

Anticipation of the dictatorship's end gave importance to the Patriotic Union as Primo's heir. Primo fueled this speculation in Spring 1928 by talking openly of stepping down in order to remarry and enjoy a quiet retirement. Madrid buzzed with rumors of a new cabinet dominated by Primo's ministers, but also including a few prominent private citizens and old politicians.³⁰ But just when the regime most needed the organization, it discovered what a weak reed it was. Even Primo's earlier statements about the readiness of the union to take power had usually been followed by injunctions to strengthen itself, which betrayed at least a doubt about the organization's vigor. Attempts to breathe new life into the union through one reorganization plan after another only made it more suspect with public opinion.³¹ Martínez Anido showed the dictatorship's concern during a Summer 1928 speech in La Coruña:

> We have governed for five years, and the country will become tired as the son is restless from the extended guardianship of his father. It is necessary, then, that the Patriotic Union be strengthened in order that it might receive power with strong hands, for if that does not happen, we will be worse off than we were and communism will come.³²

However, it was unrealistic to expect that the regime could attract many supporters to the union by proclaiming its own impermanence. In the meantime the union had lost many of its more idealistic original members. Its few Liberals and republicans grew disillusioned with the dictatorship's illegality and arbitrary rule. Conservative elements were of different minds. A minority, remaining active in the union, such as José María Pemán Pemartín, sought to move the organization in a fascist direction, making it the basis of a permanent dictatorship.³³ Others, less avowedly ideological, became disenchanted after rubbing shoulders with ambitious ne'er do wells and place seekers of the sort that Calvo Sotelo labeled "soup and spoon men." Primo repeatedly called on the union to pull itself together quickly, but such an amorphous melange did not naturally cohere about any organizing principles.³⁴

In the monarchist daily *ABC,* the Traditionalist leader, Victor Pradera, questioned in October 1928 the viability of such an artificial organization.[35] Even *El Debate,* which had originally supported the union, joined its critics that year. By having kept the union so long without principles, Primo left it dominated by the unprincipled. The remaining members were, according to his governor in Santander, General Chacón,

> the most ramshackle collection of dolts that could ever be gathered. A selection has been made of all the fools in the country—a group of pretentious and intriguing backbiters.[36]

Primo's relationship with the union revealed an enormous capacity for self-delusion. He seemed convinced that the union represented a positive new force in national life and valued its expressions of *adhesión.* Calvo Sotelo denounced this faith.[37] He saw both Primo and the union's leaders as political neophytes, living in a fool's paradise and offering each other false encouragement. Above all, he was critical of the union's discouraging Primo from restoring constitutional rule.

The Somatén civil militia was another false prop for Primo.[38] The Somatén was indigenous to Catalonia and traced its origins to the middle ages. Its modern history began in the mid-nineteenth century when it became a Catalan equivalent to the French National Guard. As a volunteer, bourgeois militia defending law, order, and property, it spread to several cities outside Catalonia during the years of labor unrest following World War I. In September 1923, Primo ordered the organization extended throughout Spain, looking to it for social peace and to reduce the expensive military establishment. Firmly integrated into the army command, the Somatén appeared a stronger defense of the social order than the Patriotic Union and was dominated at its higher levels by wealthy landlords, industrialists, and financiers. Its lower ranks, however, were filled by many of the same fortune seekers and misfits that discredited the union. The Somatén had a special appeal for thugs, little men eager to exercise the little authority it conferred. To judge from its bulletin, there was not much that united it besides a rabid fear of bolshevism. The artificiality of that purpose in a troubled but not yet polarized country meant in the end that the Somatén had no more cement holding it together than the union.

Primo did not become fully aware of the shortcomings of these groups until the abortive revolt of former Conservative leader José Sánchez Guerra and certain artillery units in January 1929. That rising was easily suppressed. But not a single group of the Patriotic Union of Somatén rose to defend the regime. According to Calvo Sotelo, Primo was completely disillusioned with both organizations.[39] The union's lack of vitality was further evident after the dictatorship's collapse. With official patronage removed, it quickly shrank from a mass movement of more than one million members to a handful of rightist agitators seeking to prop up Alfonso's tottering throne.[40]

The Patriotic Union's failure was indicative of the regime's ambivalent political position, appealing for mass support from the *clases medias* but needing to maintain the backing of elite groups. Suspended between the two, the dictatorship lacked the firm support of either. For the Patriotic Union this meant an absence of purpose and spirit—problems compounded by the dictator's own frequent changes of direction. The ultimate tragedy here, however, does not lie in the fate of the union, but in the energies and resources squandered on it. As the regime proceeded down this deceptive path, it moved steadily further away from an understanding of the country's real needs and aspirations. At the same time, the attention lavished on the union, together with the favors showered on its members, drove a wedge between the regime and public opinion. By the time the dictatorship began to write a new constitution, it found itself out of touch with much of the country.

The National Assembly and Constitutional Reform

Primo had not taken power as a constitution maker. For more than a year after his coup, he upheld the 1876 constitution, stating that he had only suspended, not repealed, it.[41] By late 1925, however, this commitment had become more intermittent and soon began to fade altogether as Primo's growing self-confidence in power combined somewhat paradoxically with increasing uncertainty over a free electorate. There was also the example of Italy. Little was known in Spain about either Mussolini or fascism.[42] But viewed from a distance it did appear to many that somewhere in the forcefulness and energy of the Italian dictator's new order, a greater future was being prepared for Italy than was obtainable through the continuation of decadent parliamentarianism.

Primo shared his thoughts in 1926 with the journalist Andrés Revesz. During the course of their interviews he declared,

No human institution is eternal. The parliamentary system, which perhaps was useful in a particular age, has passed into history. Today it is no longer indispensable, nor of much other value, for the welfare of the country. One could even say that it is frequently deleterious for the orderly conduct of public business.[43]

At another point he acknowledged the value of Mussolini's work.[44] He added, however, that Spain required conservative solutions, not the revolutionary surgery performed in Rome. Primo declined to be specific on future political institutions, other than to renew his faith in his local government reforms and the Patriotic Union. When Revesz asked him how he was going to replace the Cortes, he answered,

> with a completely new and original system of which I can still not give details. We will find ourselves with a system as democratic as parliamentarianism, but much more effective.[45]

Somewhat inconsistently he added that no constitutional changes would be implemented without the approval of the king and the Cortes.

There was, them, reason for uncertainty concerning Primo's purposes when, several months after the formation of the civil government, he spoke about convening a National Assembly.[46] According to Primo, the dictatorship had successfully steered Spain through the immediate crisis he had found on taking power. He was now ready to complete the work of national reconstruction and looked to the National Assembly to provide him with the best minds in the country for that task. Here was an echo of his initial plan for government in 1923, which reappeared again in 1929. As dictator Primo presumed he could attract the finest technical expertise to give the programmatic shape to his regenerationist impulses. He and his immediate governing circle could then serve as overseers guaranteeing legislative implementation, as well as order. The plebiscite approving the assembly and voting confidence in the government was a public collection of signatures, not a secret-ballot referendum. Free drinks, food, and other hoopla accompanied the four-day effort, and no opposition campaigning was permitted. Not surprisingly, Primo received an overwhelming endorsement. Still impressive is the fact that the 7,506,468 men's and women's signatures collected represents nearly twice the political mobilization achieved under any election during the constitutional regime.[47]

The plebiscite stirred controversy. Sánchez Guerra spoke for the outraged politicians when he told Alfonso that illegal action overthrew the Constitution of 1876.[48] He warned the king that if he did not want to be dragged down by the dictatorship, he would have to dismiss Primo immediately. The former Liberal leader, the count of Romanones, was quoted in the underground *Hojas Libres* as saying that Alfonso's cooperation with the dictatorship's plans for the assembly had enmeshed him thoroughly in the regime's illegality.[49] A tense half-year followed between Alfonso and Primo when the king refused to sanction Primo's project.⁵⁰ The old politicians took heart. Once regular cabinet meetings at the royal palace nearly ceased.⁵¹ Speculation recurred about the forced abdication of the king in favor of one of his heirs. Alfonso's position was none the easier for Primo's seeming ability to mobilize support in the plebiscite and in large public rallies of the Patriotic Union. In spring 1927, moreover, Alfonso suffered an illness that briefly threatened his life. At about the same time, Primo had a bad fall that nearly killed him. Those incidents, so close together, underlined the desirability of restoring regular government.

Expediency as well as principle, however, argued against a return to the old parliament. Primo was not certain enough of the identification between the country and the Patriotic Union to be confident that free elections would leave power in the hands of its new men. Similar doubts about the popular will were evident in his backing away from the local government elections promised in the Municipal and Provincial Statutes and in his handling of the plebiscite. Resorting to a plebiscite did show a certain confidence in his public support that was confirmed by the results. But the manner in which he conducted it suggests his sensitivity to criticism and unwillingness to accept even a limited opposition. Two months later *El Debate* opined that Spain was not responding to Primo's call.⁵²

Primo had to worry as well about the politicians. His continuing disparagement of them, which they could not answer in the press, had taken its toll. But the only alternatives to their return were the untested Patriotic Union and the growing republican movement. These circumstances cheered the politicians early in 1927 when they thought Alfonso might call for parliamentary elections. But Primo could hardly be expected to play their game, nor could Alfonso impose such a course on him. In the end dictator and king compromised. Alfonso agreed to sign the decree convening the National Assembly. In return Primo removed from the assembly's name the work "constituent" *(constituyente)* with its connotation of autonomy in constitutional matters, subject to plebiscite approval. Nonetheless, along with advising the government on its programs, preparation of a constitutional draft remained the Assembly's principal purpose.

Primo's concession was significant, for it meant that he still had not freed himself from having an elected parliament pass judgment on that proposal and, presumably, his dictatorship as a whole. Alfonso had hoped that that step would mollify the old politicians. But Sánchez Guerra left Spain, even though the king sent his own private secretary, the marquis of Torres Mendoza, along with the duke of Alba and Gen.

Rodríguez Mourelo to dissuade him.[53] From exile the former Conservative leader was a rallying point for antidictatorship sentiment and, increasingly, for opposition to Alfonso himself.

Self-interest as well as principle made the Assembly a crucial issue with the politicians. The personalism on which their power had rested could only be kept alive by continual favor giving. They knew perhaps better than Primo how much the lines of dependency through which they had governed had deteriorated during the dictatorship's first four years. Indeed, Primo's men appear to have recognized, too, that the Assembly's three-year extension of the dictatorship might be as significant in its impact on the politicians as any constitutional proposal produced by that body.[54]

Primo's statements about instituting rather than restoring normality and his public reservations about universal suffrage heightened these anxieties.[55] The Patriotic Union specifically denounced the politicians for wanting

> a Parliament elected by universal suffrage. They have to be thickhead fools and pharisees! Have we not learned that honest elections are a fiction without a well developed civic spirit, and that a Parliament without honest elections is another fiction? And do we believe that the civic spirt, which those politicians undermined, can now be brought to life by magic?[56]

But just as the dictatorship feared that a restoration of parliamentary government would bring the return of its enemies, many politicians feared that any departure from liberal principles meant their permanent exclusion from power. Accumulated ill will and the threat that the dictatorship and politicians perceived in each other precluded dialogue. Their estrangement made it harder for Primo to retreat from power, but by prolonging the dictatorship it would also eventually destroy the old politicians' chance of returning to office.

Against this troubled background the National Assembly met for the first time on 10 October 1927. There were three types of members in the assembly: the representatives of national, provincial, and local government; the representatives of "activities, classes, and values;" and the representatives of the Patriotic Union.[57] The national-government representatives were senior bureaucrats, jurists, and military officers. The provincial-government members were elected by the provincial assemblies, while the municipal representatives were chosen by province-wide votes of the municipal councils. Since the dictatorship had appointed both the municipal and provincial governments, this selection process produced few unwelcome surprises. The Patriotic Union members tended generally to be local functionaries of the organization. The interest-group members accounted for nearly a third of the entire body. Here Primo hoped to attract the independent talent needed to legitimize the assembly and assure its effectiveness. His success was notably incomplete. Professional groups, and particularly bar associations and university faculties, frequently rejected Primo's invitation or elected as their representatives exiled or imprisoned enemies of the regime such as Miguel Unamuno and Ángel Ossorio y Gallardo. Ramiro de Maeztu was the only prominent intellectual to serve. Altogether sixteen academicians participated, "but none were among the intellectual figures that inspired Spanish youth in the first half of the century."[58] Among the Socialist leadership, Largo Caballero, Saborit, and Llaneza were inclined to participate, and Llaneza even met privately with Martínez Anido to discuss the matter. But rank-and-file resistance from the UGT resulted in the Socialists' standing aside.[59] Few of the embittered old politicians collaborated apart from opportunistic or rightist members of the Conservative party such as Juan de la Cierva, César Silió, Antonio Goicoechea, and Gabriel Maura.

The assembly was, then, narrower and more conservative than Primo had wished. More members came from traditional rural areas than in other legislatures in this century.[60] Old Castile and Western Andalusia had greater representation than their population alone allowed, while Catalonia had less.[61] For a regime dedicated to bringing "new men" into government, most participants were older than in past parliaments.[62] Only 11.6% of the assembly was under thirty-seven years of age, compared with 29.2% for the 1907 Cortes. More significantly, leadership positions within the assembly were concentrated in the hands of the ex officio and national-government members.[63] Those groups occupied 28.2% of the seats, but controlled 54.9% of the leadership posts. No less striking was the scant representation of the Liberal party and the left-of-center reformists from before 1923.[64] The Assembly's general mediocrity and lack of political balance made a mockery of Primo's pledge that it would be more select and representative than the sham parliaments of the constitutional regime.[65]

Primo could not quite trust even this tame body. He did not allow it legislative initiative. The assembly could only discuss measures presented to it by the government. Even then, each deputy could only address the full body briefly. Primo had charged the assembly with helping him draw up new legislation, but was afraid of its criticism. Although he sought the assembly's help on the constitutional project, he entrusted little else of significance to it. Typically, he asked the assembly to review a minor aspect of inheritance law when he had already charged a nonassembly committee with a complete revision of the civil code, including all inheritance matters. The government decreed a change in the tax on earned income without any prior review by the assembly. In those instances when Primo did turn to that body for advice, he frequently rejected its findings.

Primo had little understanding of a loyal opposition. Even when the prestige and programs of the government were not involved, he cut off debate once sparks flew. The basic pattern was set in the first month. Primo upbraided García Guijarro, a Traditionalist member, for saying, with regard to the provisional rules for the assembly, that "the sad experience in Spain has been that everything transitory becomes permanent."[66] Another Traditionalist, Pérez Bueno, asked, "Is this the freedom of an assembly member?" Primo shouted back that it was necessary to maintain order, and that he was determined to do so. The dictator's sense of order was exhibited when Victor Pradera criticized the government for undermining the independence of the judiciary.[67] Pradera was not allowed to finish his speech and was abused so badly that he walked out of the assembly.

With more than 300 members the assembly was too large to function in an advisory capacity. But when broken into separate committees, it lost what little representative aspect it had. It also suffered from the inexperience of many of its members. Without party ties and whips, the ill-assorted and poorly organized assembly lacked cohesion. When entrusted with a project, such as recommendations for the 1929 and 1930 budgets, it frequently debated the matter at great length without being able to reach consensus. The assembly had, in the words of one critic, "all of the defects and none of the advantages" of an elected parliament.[68]

These same problems marred the work of the section responsible for the constitutional draft. Presiding over the section was Yanguas Messia, who had served as the civil government's foreign minister until January 1927.[69] Among the leading figures were Gabriel Maura, son of the late Conservative leader, and the former Maurist ministers, César Silió and Antonio Goicoechea. Juan de la Cierva was another former Conservative minister. In varying degrees these one-time parliamentarians were sympathetic to devices such as corporatism and weighted voting to keep representative government from becoming too representative of the working classes. The rightist intellectuals Maeztu and Pemán were even more critical of parliamentary government. The Traditionalists, led by Pradera, regarded parliament as a sham and sought to replace it with a quasi-medieval Estates-General of classes. With a similar but less extreme critique of the social atomization and volatility produced by liberal government were the Social Catholics. Speaking for the sector's more moderate, liberal minority were the less well-known Carlos María Crehuet and the academic García Oviedo. No ready consensus could come from such diverse opinions, with some members arguing for simple modifications in the 1876 Constitution and others repudiating parliamentary government altogether.

The final draft resulting from their compromises was a pastiche of the political philosophies of the fragmented Right that predominated in the section.[70] The most significant innovation was transformation of the Senate into a Council of the Realm with important changes in membership and powers. Half of the council was to consist of permanent members, serving either ex officio or by royal appointment. The ex officio seats were held by members of the royal family, military captains general, the archbishop primate of Toledo, and the presidents of the council of ministers, supreme court, supreme financial court, and supreme military court. Only a third of the elected members were to be chosen by universal suffrage. The remaining two-thirds were to be selected by various corporate interest groups. The term of office for these latter members was ten years. Effective power within the council was to be held by a Permanent Commission selected by the membership from its own ranks.

The authority granted the council was considerable. It was to arbitrate disputes between executive and judicial branches of government. It also reviewed the constitutionality of all legislation. The council had authority to either recommend or review appointments to the Supreme Court and the various ministries. All questions of regency, and royal education and matrimony, were to be submitted to it as well as all diplomatic treaties, including any secret clauses. The council of ministers was also required to consult with the council before taking action on matters of public order or interlocal government cooperation and autonomy. The council could also veto any act of the lower house that was not approved by ninety percent of the deputies there. When the lower house was not in session, which could be as much as eight months of every year, the council could legislate in its place, although such acts would later have to be referred back to that chamber for approval. The king's powers under the constitutional proposal were almost as impressive, including a veto over new legislation. Once appointed, all ministers were only responsible to the monarch.

The significant changes attempted here become more evident when it is seen how little authority was left to the lower house. That house took the name Cortes alone. It was depicted as a unicameral legislature in its own right, though as seen, this was hardly the case, given the council's broad legislative functions. Half this Cortes was to be chosen by universal suffrage on the basis of a modified proportional representation scheme involving provincial electoral lists and a very small number of representatives elected nationally. Of the remaining half, a limited number would be royal appointees, while the majority would be corporate representatives. The Cortes could not vote confidence on any government or minister. Nor could it initiate constitutional, diplomatic or treaty changes, or any tax or budget legislation. The constitutional draft guaranteed many of the same civil and religious liberties as the 1876 constitution, but here too wide discretionary powers over interpretation and even temporary suspension of those rights were held by the council. The proposal reflected the increased appetites of radical conservatives, while it mirrored the growing social anxieties of more traditional conservatives. For radicals it was a forward, if somewhat reactionary, step; for more moderate conservatives it was a final attempt to establish defensive frontiers for Spain's structure of privilege before the anticipated collapse of the dictatorship unleashed a wave of leftist reaction. Provisions for corporate representation and royal appointment exhibited the fear of many assembly members of popular electoral majorities. Corporatism also served as a device for transforming the *clases medias'* interest in preserving order into a prop for elitist government.[71]

The constitution makers, however, had overreached. As they had moved to the Right, large sectors of opinion had moved to the Left. Primo himself was upset over the authority granted the king and over the even more considerable powers given the council at the expense of the more democratically elected Cortes.[72] He was certainly not a total champion of parliamentary democracy, but the draft put him in a difficult position. To use it to leave power, he had to legitimize it. Fear of his nemesis, the old politicians, had led him to break his promise at the assembly's opening that an elected Cortes would review any basic constitutional changes. In July 1928 he publicly claimed the right to submit whatever draft the assembly might produce to a plebiscite.[73] He maintained this position consistently in the year remaining before the assembly completed its work. But for the politicians of the old regime a constitutional plebiscite was anathema, and Alfonso felt that he had little chance to retain his throne after the dictatorship without their support. Still, Primo had outmaneuvered his monarch on other occasions and could hope to do so again if necessary. By Spring 1929, however, Alfonso had begun to disassociate himself from his no-longer-popular dictator. Not a single cabinet meeting was held at the palace between February and July.[74] As the king became uncooperative, Primo grew petulant, even ordering the various ministries in May to cancel their subscriptions to the monarchist periodical *La Monarquía*.[75]

More than even Alfonso, however, what left Primo stymied was the constitutional draft itself. How was any document so patently undemocratic to win popular support at the polls? Without much enthusiasm, about all he could do was test public opinion. For several weeks in July he lifted the censorship to allow public discussion of the proposal. Notwithstanding his own misgivings, he was stunned by the strength of the opposition to it and to his regime.

Primo set out to salvage what he could. On 26 July he announced a plan to open the National Assembly to various professional groups, intellectual figures, working-class organizations, and, most importantly, former political leaders under the constitutional regime. He hoped the new members might provide the modifications and legitimacy needed to make the proposal acceptable.[76] But this was a classic case of reaching out too late with too little. Those for whom Primo had shown little regard, now showed little concern for his call. There was a touch of sadness in his words in mid-September when he said,

> The news that we have received concerning the attendance of the ex-presidents (of the Council of Ministers, the Congress of Deputies, and the Senate) has not been favorable. They must know why they have done what they have. They would have been received in the assembly with courtesy and a correct attitude by the governmental majority. But they did not come.[77]

The final agony of the regime began. Its fiscal and economic programs were in disarray. The exit from power on which it had planned for two years was now blocked. Its critics were steadily mounting and, worse, had begun to talk as if the dictatorship had already passed into history. Even in smaller cities far from the capital, the sense existed by fall 1929 that the regime's days were numbered.[78] Primo sought to check the ebbing of his authority, declaring that national reconstruction had only just begun and required additional years of dictatorial rule. Privately he cast about for a way out. When he was hunting in mid-November with Alfonso and the duke of Alba at Navalperal, the rumor was that the quarry would be the dictator himself.[79] But Primo refused to leave office in disgrace, fearing that an elected successor government would repudiate him and his dictatorship. Alfonso was equally unrelenting. The king could not afford to use his decree powers to ease the exit of his unpopular government. He refused to sign the assembly's constitutional draft into law or to authorize a plebiscite on it.

Checked at every turn, the regime was riven by internal dissension. The focal point was Primo's fear of elections. Rather than face the electorate himself, or even head the government when elections were held, Primo wished to hand the premiership over to his minister of development, Guadalhorce, while he quietly retired. Not all of those to be left behind acquiesced. Calvo Sotelo claimed to convince him to consider a gradual transition to democratic government beginning with municipal, then provincial, and finally national elections, at the end of which he could hand power over to a duly elected successor under the terms of the 1876 Constitution. The improbability of this plan would be confirmed in Alfonso's fate in April 1931. Primo, for his part, soon reverted to saying, "I could never stoop to an electoral conflict with all its corruption and low tricks."[80] Aunós was sympathetic to Primo, while Yanguas believed that the assembly's constitutional draft might somehow be salvaged.

The drifting government's unpopularity and internal divisions led Guadalhorce, Calvo Sotelo, and Callejo to consider resigning.[81] By early December, however, Primo had managed to secure the cabinet's backing for a plan that, in his own words, would permit the regime "to die well."[82] Together with his ministers he presented the project to the king at the end of the month. It called for the continuation of the dictatorship largely as it was until 13 September 1930. During this transition period local governments would be reconstituted with half their members appointed by the interior ministry and the other half chosen locally on a corporate basis. Only in the smallest *pueblos* would direct elections for half of the members be permitted.

Meanwhile the National Assembly would be reorganized, and its life extended another three years. Primo hoped that the various groups that had so far refused to participate could somehow be persuaded to enter the assembly and give it legitimacy. From the ranks of the assembly Alfonso would be free to choose a new cabinet. That cabinet would constitute the effective government, for Primo anticipated the assembly's never meeting together, apart from its separate committees, for more than fifteen days each year.[83] During the three years of the new assembly's life the cabinet would use its decree powers to lay down gradually the foundations of a new constitutional order. Remarkably, after all that had transpired, Primo could still say "constitutions can have no other origin nor structure than that which is imposed by he who governs."[84]

As striking as the unreality of the plan is the fear that motivated it. Primo referred throughout the proposal to "those . . . so-called political parties and their organs of action which consist in at least half of the ambitious, the sectarian and the meddlesome."[84] Above all, he worried about the king's giving the old politicians a forum, whether in a parliament or through elections, to hurl their "attacks and defamations" against him.[86] Primo did his best to equate the "public interest" with "the prestige of the dictatorship."[87] He warned Alfonso that if he "wants . . . to save his country and save his dynasty," he should not make any radical break from the dictatorship.[88] Alfonso's fears, however, were not the same as his premier's. The king felt that he could only be hurt by continuing to support a discredited government. The king's rejection of the plan left Primo isolated and frustrated. His bitterness was evident in a year-end statement to the nation written directly after his audience with the king. Primo said very little about his long-standing enemies among the intellectuals, old politicians, and working class radicals. Instead he reserved his harshest complaints for conservative elements whose withdrawal of support was slowly sealing the fate of his regime.[89] On 5 January Guadalhorce, Calvo Sotelo, and los Andes formally proposed to the dictator elections to the old Cortes of the constitutional regime. They recommended as well that he preside over a caretaker cabinet while the elections were conducted. As might have been expected, Primo preemptorily rejected their suggestion, saying, "I do not need, want, nor expect balloting."[90] That dispute led to the jettisoning of Calvo Sotelo from the cabinet. Departure of the unpopular minister, however, could not alter the fact that the regime had little firm support. The student demonstrations of the past two years against the government reached a new peak. Artillery officers who had rebelled a year earlier in Ciudad Real against the regime were cheered after their trial at every train station on their way to prison in Pamplona. With the king also removing his backing, Primo turned to the army leadership on 26 January, asking for an expression of confidence from the captains general of the various military districts. Several weeks earlier, however, a senior officer banquet had given scant applause to two addresses by Primo.[91] Response to this latest appeal was tepid, and rumors circulated about an imminent coup planned by Gen. Manuel Goded in Cadiz. With the military turning against him, Primo had no alternative but to resign. On 28 January his dictatorship came to an end.

Primo's regime attracted interest in other countries.[92] With only eleven months separating his coup and Mussolini's March on Rome, many comparisons were made of Spain and Italy. In a visit to Italy two months after his takeover, Primo said, as part of a formal address, to Mussolini, "your figure is not only Italian, but global. You are the apostle of the campaign that Europe has embarked upon against disintegration and anarchy."[93] Drawing the comparison still more strongly, Primo said that Mussolini's coming to power "prepared the ambience, electrified the atmosphere, and today guides Spain on the road to the restoration of progress and order."[94]

More than rhetoric united the two dictators. They strengthened the diplomatic ties between their countries.[95] Mussolini proffered Primo occasional advice and followed his regime with interest.[96] For his part, Primo adopted many fascist policies and trappings—large rallies, a plebiscite, repression of dissent, promotion of large families, and extreme nationalist hyperbole deflecting attention from internal divisions. Cults of personality enveloped both dictators. As in Italy, Primo's political organization was an avenue of mobility for "new men." While appealing rhetorically to the little man, both dictators were also quick to strike deals with the economically powerful. Both sought to substitute economic growth for social change but defeated their purpose with programs favoring large producers at the expense of foreign trade and domestic purchasing power. To many of his contemporaries this record sufficed to make Primo a fascist in all but name. Particularly striking is the sense of common purpose shared by Italian and Spanish political exiles in France.[97]

Primo, however, never applied the label *fascist* to his government and consistently claimed that his purpose was less extreme than Mussolini's. Indeed, when he compared himself to Mussolini, it was almost always as a fellow restorer of order, not as a political innovator. Primo's choice of heroes in instructive. In 1923 he acclaimed Mussolini as his model along with the regenerationist prophet of 1898, Joaquín Costa, and the nineteenth-century liberal republican Francisco Pi y Margall.[98] In accepting an honorary doctorate from the University of Salamanca in 1926, he again identified with Mussolini, but also with the German president Hindenberg.[99] The Patriotic Union showed similar confusion, linking Primo with Mussolini as well as with Richelieu, Bolívar, Washington, Cisneros, Bismarck, Cavour, and, most improbably of all, Lenin.[100]

The ideological fog suggested by these self-proclaimed antecedents derived only partly from Primo's intellectual imprecision. It was also connected with the way he became dictator. Unlike Mussolini, Primo had not been the leader of a mass party from below, capable of strengthening his hand in dealings with the powerful established interests he faced after taking office. The Patriotic Union was an organization decreed from above, lacking the identity and purpose that came through a struggle to take power from below. As a movement of the *clases medias,* it foundered in part on the contradictions of that group. But, even more, it failed because its new idealists never had the chance to serve as an assimilative core before they were washed away by an overnight wave of self-seekers.

What this meant was that Primo lacked the social and political reference points needed to clarify his sense of purpose. He and the country had grown up under parliamentary government. One of his more radical ministers went so far as to attribute Primo's fall to the fact that "the general was a man educated in the practice of liberal politics, and it did not seem to him that interruption of that system ought to last any longer than was necessary to revitalize it."[101] At the same time, though, a lifetime as a soldier had imbued him with values of hierarchy and authority, principles that fearful conservative backers reinforced him in. Without a firm base of support Primo fluctuated between parliamentary government and authoritarianism. Without solid backing from the *clases medias* or established elites, he wavered between fascist and traditional conservative poles. Oscillating rhetoric and policies alienated one sector of society and then another. Torn back and forth by events and conflicting pressures he neither returned to the 1876 Constitution, institutionalized his own regime, nor found an alternative political formula.

While Primo's political thought became more muddled, a new *caciquismo* grew up beneath him.[102] This development was not immediate or altogether intended. Even General Jordana, a member of the directory, did not succeed in placing a friend of his in the state lottery system.[103] Primo may have looked to conservative groups to staff his regime but nonetheless claimed that careers in government belonged to the talented and dedicated, regardless of their personal connections or, even, their political opinions.[104] He never quite saw, however, nor could he altogether afford to see, the difference between ambitious careerists and sincere reformers. Nor, as someone personally involved in the network of favoritism and deals that characterized government under the constitutional regime, was he above securing special advantage for himself, family, and friends.[105] A lax administrator, tolerant of the vices of those who governed under him, Primo found it difficult to prevent his "new men" from finding employment for friends and relatives or from influencing the awarding of government contracts in return for private advantage.[106] He periodically attacked these abuses but seldom went so far as to dismiss offending officials.[107] As his energy and sense of purpose declined, opportunities for misuse of office expanded.

The lines of patronage and obligation that had constituted the political and administrative infrastructure of the constitutional regime were adapted to the dictatorship.[108] The struggles for influence of the old politicians became the infightings of Primo's governing team. Calvo Sotelo and Martínez Anido each had family roots in the Galician province of Lugo and competed to advance their respective retainers there.[109] The king had his favorites to advance, too.[110] Even low-level government workers relied on favoritism rather than on merit or seniority for promotion. Political influence was particularly rife in the postal service.[111] Local administrators, such as Cruz Conde in Seville, used access to the central government's patronage to establish themselves as new *caciques,* organizing rallies and conducting a plebiscite for the dictatorship rather than manufacturing election results for the constitutional regime.[112] The material rewards from proximity to power could be great. The count of Mieres went from the verge of bankruptcy to considerable wealth after his friend, Guadolhorce, became development minister.[113] Primo rewarded his childrens' tutor by naming him director of the Canal of Isabel II, a post paying 30,000 pesetas yearly. Service to the Patriotic Union also brought substantive benefit, with high-ranking officials in that organization also holding important posts in various public enterprises.[114]

The military held privileged positions, with former directory generals assuming particularly lucrative posts under the civil government. General Mayandia was president of the Superior Railroad Council, while General Hermosa was president of the Fuel Council.[115] General Gómez Jordana collected separate administrative salaries in excess of 100,000 pesetas annually. Among others to benefit from Primo's patronage were General Acha as president of the National Economic Council; General Milans del Bosch as provincial governor of Barcelona and president of the Cotton Junta; and General Gómez Nuñez as a member of the National Economic Council, Fuel Council, and Official Motor Transport and Automobile Commission.[116] Primo rewarded General Correa for turning his back on his fellow artillery officers during their crucial showdown with the regime by naming him to a highly paid position with the Fuel Council. As captain general in Barcelona, Barrera was able to engage in a number of profitable business dealings, including arranging for his son to be in charge of the advertising for the Barcelona exposition.[117] Soldiers in important civilian positions could also supplement their usually generous salaries by resorting to graft. General Burguete, for example, was said to have made nearly 300,000 pesetas by collecting a commission of 10 pesetas on each new uniform for the Civil Guard.[118]

Such lucrative posts were sinecures, rewards to the faithful. Less fortunate and less content were many junior officers appointed to minor positions in government ministries.[119] The swollen ranks of the officer corps furnished many recruits for civilian bureaucratic positions. By filling civilian vacancies with officers, Primo hoped to reduce an expensive military establishment. But the officers generally lacked preparation for their new posts and were frequently treated with disdain and relegated to paper shuffling, which offended their sense of importance. They also complained that as soldiers in civilian positions they received the retirement benefits of neither branch of government service.

The army's ranking generals worried about this slighting of the military. They were also concerned when some officers petitioned to return to the military with a higher rank than they had left in order to keep abreast of others in their group *(plantilla)*. These problems reinforced the anxiety of some generals over the army's apparent complicity in the public's eyes for supporting an increasingly unpopular dictatorship presided over by a military man. The army's misgivings were evident in a military court's acquittal of former Conservative leader Sánchez Guerra for his attempt to overthrow the regime in January 1929.

Primo's primary difficulty, however, was less the military than his failure to find an alternative to the 1876 Constitution. His abuse of the old politicians, rather than bullying them into acquiescence of his regime, had driven most of them into irreconcilable opposition. But if he could not return to the system dominated by them, neither could he secure the support of significant sectors of opinion for the institutionalization of his regime or for the establishment of some new authoritarian government. At a political impasse and without a sure base of support, he could only drift and equivocate, with decreasing control over the events buffeting his regime.

His legacy was not creation of a new political system, but destruction of the old. He neither restored parliamentary government nor found an alternative to it. For all his rhetoric and legislation, *caciquismo's* structure and functioning continued under his dictatorship much as they had under the constitutional regime. That much the regime itself confessed in denouncing the large number of "wheel greasing" middlemen *(intermediarios)* who continued from the old order to do business under the dictatorship.[120] Venality persisted despite the declaration the government felt driven to make that there was a clear distinction between the old *caciques* and its new local authorities.[121] What, in fact, was undone was not the personalistic nature of government, but the specific web of personal relations that had sustained the old politicians. Primo's ill-assorted appointments of conservative idealists, ambitious careerists, and army officers to different administrative levels did not make the bureaucracy an efficient tool of government.[122] But his dictatorship did interrupt for six years the patterns of favor giving and vote collecting by which the constitutional regime's politicians had sustained themselves. Once the old network disintegrated, there was no easy way to restore it. The sustained public discrediting of politicians also made their return unlikely. More basic than personalities, however, the old politics' requisite of a low level of civic consciousness was eroded by communication and educational advances under the dictatorship. Indeed, by continuing the old jobbery while fostering opinion antithetical to such practice, Primo added to criticism of the dictatorship.

The political failure of the dictatorship, then, had several origins. Clumsiness and inexperience explain many of its problems. But the basic difficulty was one of conceptualization. Primo had a disconcerting faith in the ease with which fundamental political change could be effected. As a pundit, he would have been naive. In power he was arrogant. Primo believed in the regenerationist myth that Spanish society was held in check by a corrupt system of bossism that extended from Madrid down to the smallest *pueblos*. He felt that that system had created an artificial gulf between the government and the nation, and he was determined to destroy it. Neither he nor his ministers anticipated the contradictions that soon arose.

When Primo shied away from local government elections, it was clear that popular sovereignty could not be readily reconciled with dictatorial rule. The regime's wide-ranging interventionism in local affairs made a mockery of its promises of administrative decentralization. Rapidly increasing municipal and provincial indebtedness suggested an inconsistency in the dictatorship's simultaneous pursuit in a poor country of expensive development programs and fiscal responsibility. And the Patriotic Union's failure testified to the inadequacy of Primo's belief in the *neutra masa* as a store of talented and selfless "new men."

The last problem was the greatest. Primo defined his government inclusively. He thought it possible to fashion a broad political center, ranging from the republicans and Socialists on the left to Traditionalists on the right. All but working-class radicals and regionalists were welcome. However, the social divisions that did so much to facilitate his dictatorship in the first place undermined that consensus and prevented him from finding a constitutional formula by which he could leave office. A dictator who sought to represent all Spaniards ended by representing none.

NOTES

1. The Patriotic Union's most important self-definition is José María Pemán, *El hecho y la idea de la Unión Patriótica*. The union's origins are discussed by Shlomo Ben-Ami, "The Forerunners of Spanish Fascism: Unión Patriótica and Unión Monárquica," *European Studies Review* 9, no. 1 (January 1979): 52–54; Tusell, *La crisis,* pp. 116–17 and 134–35; and José Luis Gómez Navarro, María Teresa González Calbet, and Ernesto Portuondo, "Aproximación al estudio de las élites políticas en la dictadura de Primo," *Cuadernos Económicos de I.C.E.* 10 (1979): 186–88.

2. Primo accompanied the founding of the Patriotic Union with repeated public assertions of fidelity to the 1876 Constitution, most notably on 15 April, 25 April, and 1 July 1924. These statements were reprinted in December 1926 in one of the early issues of the *Unión Patriótica*, showing the formal commitment of that organization a full year after establishment of the civil government to the old parliamentary institutions.

3. Maura Gamazo, *Bosquejo* 2:145.
4. E. T. L., *Por pueblos,* p. 215.
5. Ibid., pp. 216–17.
6. This principle was enunciated as part of the union's program in 1925; Rubio, *Crónica,* p. 186. There is some evidence that the dictatorship made preliminary inquiries well before then, seeking to enlist the support of prominent Spaniards in the formation of new parties from within the union; Ortega, *España encadenada,* pp. 232–33.
7. *Unión Patriótica,* 1 November 1926, p. 27.
8. Maura Gamazo, *Bosquejo* 1:81, and Ceballos Teresi, *Historia económica* 5:214–15.
9. Maura Gamazo, *Bosquejo* 1:75 and 81–89.
10. Calvo Sotelo, *Mis servicios,* pp. 332–33.
11. See E. T. L., *Por pueblos,* pp. 213–45, for the general failure of this effort.
12. The union's organization is outlined in *Unión Patriótica,* 15 October 1926, pp. 28–29; 15 November 1926, p. 20; and 15 January 1927, p. 2.
13. This point is raised with regard to the dictatorship generally by Linz, "Spanish Cabinet," pp. 176–77.
14. *Unión Patriótica,* 15 December 1926, p. 8.
15. Rubio, *Crónica,* p. 186.
16. *Heraldo de Panadés,* 7 September 1929, p. 1.
17. Ibid., 13 April 1929, p. 1.
18. Similar conflict between traditional "in" groups and insurgent "out" groups was endemic to Southern and Eastern Europe in the interwar period. See, for example, Andrew C. Janos, "The One-Party State and Social Mobilization: East Europe between the Wars," in *Authoritarian Politics in Modern Society,* ed. Samuel P. Huntington and Clement H. Moore (New York: Basic Books, 1970), pp. 204–36.
19. The dictatorship's opponents perceived the union's widely divergent membership as a weakness; *Hojas Libres,* June 1928, pp. 4–5.
20. See, for example, *Unión Patriótica,* 1 December 1926, and Maura Gamazo, *Bosquejo* 1:145.
21. Ben-Ami, "The Forerunners," p. 55.
22. Maura Gamazo, *Bosquejo* 1:134–35.
23. *Unión Patriótica,* 1 October 1926, pp. 9–16.
24. Ibid., 15 November 1927, p. 29.
25. Ibid., 1 December 1926.

26. On the troubled relations between the regime and the union with monarchist groups in the Basque provinces, see AHN Leg. 354 (17 December 1924) and Leg. 492 (3 February 1925); *Unión Patriótica*, 1 December 1926, pp. 25–29; and Calvo Sotelo, *Mis servicios*, p. 333.
27. Expressing their coolness was Ceballos Teresi, *Historia economica* 5:204–14.
28. Rubio, *Crónica*, p. 263.
29. See, for example, *Unión Patriótica*, 1 July 1927, p. 1.
30. *Hojas Libres*, May 1928, pp. 79 and 86.
31. The government's sensitivity on this point is evident in *Unión Patriótica*, 15 July 1927, pp. 5–6.
32. Fernández Almagro, *Historia del reinado*, p. 514.
33. On interest within the union in fascism, particularly in Madrid, see *Unión Patriótica*, 15 October 1926, pp. 20–31 and 15 December 1926, p. 30.
34. One such appeal is contained in *Unión Patriótica*, 1 July 1927, pp. 1–2.
35. Rubio, *Crónica*, p. 355. Liberals also questioned the inherent contradiction in Primo's denunciation of the "artificiality" of the dynastic parties under the constitutional regime and his attempt to impose a single party by administrative fiat; Ortega, *España encadenada*, pp. 231–34.
36. *Hojas Libres*, April 1927, p. 62.
37. Calvo Sotelo, *Mis servicios*, pp. 333–34. No more positive was Martínez Anido; Pabón, *Cambó* 2:523.
38. A recent analysis of the Somatén leadership is Rosa Martínez Segarra, "Grupos económicos en el Somatén," *Cuadernos Económicos de I.C.E.* 10 (1979): 209–24. A more critical contemporary view of the members attracted to that organization's lower ranks is Quintiliano Saldaña y García Rubio, *Al servicio de la justicia*, pp. 34–39.
39. Calvo Sotelo, *Mis servicios*, p. 333.
40. The union claimed a membership of 1,319,428 according to *Unión Patriótica*, 15 July 1927, p. 6.
41. Maura Gamazo, *Bosquejo* 1:140.
42. Payne, "Spanish Fascism," p. 6.
43. Revesz, *Frente al dictador*, pp. 16–17.
44. Ibid., p. 18–19.
45. Ibid., p. 17.
46. For Primo's own explanation of the purposes of the assembly, see Díaz-Plaja, *De la dictadura*, pp. 118–23.
47. *Unión Patriótica*, 1 October 1926, p. 5. Especially striking is the fact that the highest percentages of eligible voters to endorse the regime were in the traditional *cacique*-controlled provinces, especially Almeria with 85%, Ciudad Real with 83%, Jaén with 88%, and Murcia with 86%.
48. Maura Gamazo, *Bosquejo* 2:19–25.
49. Díaz-Plaja, *De la dictadura*, pp. 122–23 and 126–27.
50. The strength of opposition to the Assembly owed perhaps as much to Primo's timing as to the idea itself. Antonio Maura had suggested in November 1923 that Primo consider something along those lines; Pabón, *Cambó* 2:536. Had he acted immediately on Maura's idea while the old politicians were still off balance and the country still looked at the directory as a brief transitional government, he might have succeeded.
51. PG, *Diario de la Presidencia del Gobierno, 1924–1930*.
52. Rubio, *Crónica*, p. 241.
53. *Hojas Libres*, July 1927, pp. 28–41.
54. See, for example, *Unión Patriótica*, 1 October 1926, pp. 16–17.
55. On the distinction between a "new" and the "old" normality, see ibid., 15 December 1926, p. 8, and 1 July 1927, pp. 1–2.
56. Ibid. 15 December 1926, p. 8.
57. This description of the composition of the National Assembly is largely drawn from Linz, "Spanish Cabinet," pp. 76–103.

58. Ibid., p. 91.
59. *Hojas Libres,* April 1927, pp. 39–42.
60. Linz, "Spanish Cabinet," p. 82.
61. Ibid., p. 89.
62. Ibid., pp. 99–100.
63. Ibid., pp. 83–84.
64. *Hojas Libres,* November 1927, pp. 62–68 discusses Primo's failure to attract support from these groups.
65. On that claim, see *Unión Patriótica,* 1 July 1927, p. 2.
66. Rubio, *Crónica,* p. 295.
67. Maura Gamazo, *Bosquejo* 2:278. Pradera's conflict with Primo in the assembly is also discussed in *Hojas Libres,* January 1929, pp. 45–46.
68. Fernández Almagro, *Historia del reinado,* p. 518.
69. The membership of the constitutional section is described by Mariano García Canales, *La teoría de la representación en la España del siglo XX* (Murcia: Universidad de Murcia, Publicaciones del Departamento de Derecho Político, 1977), pp. 115–16.
70. Asamblea Nacional Consultiva, *Anteproyecto de constitución de la Monarquía española y otras leyes complementarias* (Madrid: Nueva Imprenta Radio, 1929).
71. On the varied uses to which corporatism was put in other parts of interwar Europe, see Charles S. Maier, *Recasting Bourgeois Europe* (Princeton: Princeton University Press, 1975), pp. 9–10, 13–14, 353–54, 515–16, 580–82, and 590–94.
72. Fernández Almagro, *Historia del reinado,* p. 532, and Calvo Sotelo, *Mis servicios,* p. 337.
73. Maura Gamazo, *Bosquejo* 2:158.
74. PG, *Diario de la Presidencia.*
75. AHN Leg. 1, Exte. 259.
76. Pabón, *Cambó* 2:567–68.
77. Maura Gamazo, *Bosquejo* 2:289.
78. A 23 November letter from the head of the Catholic Agricultural Federation of Corunna (Federación Católica Agraria de la Coruña) warned Primo's aide, Maximo Cuervo, of the dangerous extent to which the regime had become an object of ridicule in Northwest Spain; AHN Leg. 139, Exte. 379.
79. Ciges Aparicio, *España bajo la dinastía,* p. 449.
80. Calvo Sotelo, *Mis servicios,* p. 338.
81. Ciges Aparicio, *España bajo la dinastía,* p. 449.
82. Calvo Sotelo, *Mis servicios,* p. 338.
83. Ibid., p. 347.
84. Ibid., p. 345.
85. Ibid.
86. Ibid., p. 346.
87. Ibid., p. 343.
88. Ibid., p. 348.
89. Díaz-Plaja, *De la dictadura,* pp. 160–61.
90. Calvo Sotelo, *Mis servicios,* p. 354.
91. Ciges Aparicio, *España bajo la dinastía,* p. 450.
92. See, for example, Douglas L. Wheeler, *Republican Portugal* (Madison: University of Wisconsin Press, 1978), pp. 188, 209, 212, and 246; and H. S. Ferns, *Argentina* (New York: Frederick A. Praeger, 1969), p. 172.
93. The full text of the speech is quoted by Duarte, *España: Miguel Primo de Rivera,* pp. 195–98.
94. Ibid., p. 198.
95. John F. Coverdale, *Italian Intervention in the Spanish Civil War* (Princeton: Princeton University Press, 1975), pp. 31–37. In fact, however, relations between Italy and Spain were not as close as opponents of the two dictators frequently thought. The outsized anxieties of Spanish dissidents is evident in *Hojas Libres,* April 1924, pp. 82–85.

96. On this interest and especially the impact that the collapse of the Spanish dictatorship had on Mussolini, see Renzo de Felice, *Mussolini il duce* (Turin: Giulio Einaudi editore, 1974), pp. 129, 131, 229 n. 1, 305 n. 2, 555, and 782.

97. This shared identity is evident in *Hojas Libres,* August 1927, pp. 92–95. A more recent attempt to place the dictatorship in a fascist context is contained in pp. 75–76 of an untitled paper by Joaquín Romera Maura in *The Identification of Pre-Fascist Elements in Certain Modern Societies,* ed. American Universities Field Staff (Rome: Center for Mediterranean Studies, 1971).

98. Duarte, *España: Miguel Primo de Rivera,* p. 69.

99. *Unión Patriótica,* 15 October 1926, p. 16.

100. *Unión Patriótica,* 1 March 1927, pp. 1–2.

101. Aunós, *Soldado,* pp. 51–52.

102. Typical of the personnel changes brought by the dictatorship was the turnover involved in the transformation in 1924 of the Supreme Court of the Finance Ministry (Tribunal Supremo de la Hacienda) into the Supreme Court of Accounts of the Kingdom (Tribunal Supremo de Cuentas del Reino); AHN Leg. 1, Exte. 210.

103. AHN Leg. 34, Exte. 2588.

104. An 11 April 1924 memo, for example, emphasized the importance of following correct administrative procedures in new appointments; AHN Leg. 1, Exte. 76. This same theme was an article of faith with the Patriotic Union; *Unión Patriótica,* 15 February 1927, pp. 1–2, and 1 March 1927, pp. 1–2.

105. See, for example, AHN Leg. 139, Exte. 391.

106. Particularly active on Primo's staff in finding positions for friends and associates was Maximo Cuervo; AHN Leg. 138, Extes. 96, 144, and 253.

107. In 1928, for example, he ordered an end to abuses in government building contracts, stating that such construction was to be undertaken without favoritism and at the lowest cost; AHN Leg. 2, Exte. 1518P. No evidence seems to exist, however, of punishment of violators of these guidelines or of any other type of administrative follow through.

108. For Primo's office's review of patronage appointments to different ministries, see AHN Leg. 46, Extes. 8221 and 8365, and Leg. 33, Exte. 2086.

109. *Hojas Libres,* July 1927, pp. 91–93.

110. See, for example, AHN Leg. 33, Exte. 1651.

111. *Hojas Libres,* January 1929, pp. 55–59.

112. Cruz Conde's rapid rise in Seville under the dictatorship is discussed in *Hojas Libres,* July 1927, pp. 83–88. The efforts of the mayor and the Patriotic Union in Cadiz to support the plebiscite are described in AHN Leg. 524 (16 September 1926).

113. *Hojas Libres,* October 1927, p. 71.

114. *Unión Patriótica,* March 1927, pp. 1–2.

115. *Hojas Libres,* October 1927, pp. 76–78.

116. Ibid.

117. Cánovas Cervantes, *Apuntes históricos,* p. 60.

118. *Hojas Libres,* April 1927, p. 49.

119. The guidelines by which officers were appointed to civilian posts, as well as the problems that soon ensued, are detailed in AHN Leg. 1, Exte. 99, and Leg. 47, Exte. 8944. Primo's own justification for this policy is contained in *Curso de Ciudadanía,* p. ix.

120. *Unión Patriótica,* 15 February 1927, p. 26, and 15 March 1927, p. 23.

121. Ibid., 15 January 1927, p. 23.

122. Primo's failure to live up to his promise of bureaucratic reform was evident in the complaint of *El Noticiero Universal* on 24 December 1925 that the cost of living in Barcelona could be significantly reduced if the state bureaucracy and its red tape were reduced; AHN Leg. 524 (13 January 1926). The persistence of personalism in politics and administration after the dictatorship is lamented by Joaquín del Moral *Oligarquía y "enchufismo"* (Madrid: Galo Sáez, 1933), pp. 103–7.

Part Three

ECONOMIC REFORM

5
Finances

Taxation

The dictatorship's development program was expensive. Its financing says much about the regime and the limits of its power.[1] Changes in fiscal policy could conceivably have produced revenue.[2] But Primo did not have a coherent view of the measures required. In his first months he promised to cut the size of the bureaucracy by not filling one of every four attrition vacancies and by firing negligent civil servants, while setting higher standards for those remaining.[3] He even reduced the number of government chauffeurs and explored the possibility of cutting expenses by replacing rented government office space with new construction.[4] At the same time, however, he supported most of the constitutional regime's social and economic initiatives and began new programs of his own. Later, his initial plans for the civil government included simultaneously balancing the budget, reducing the national debt, and financing extensive public works.

Fiscal chicanery was one way to resolve these contradictions temporarily. But for the dictatorship to have full financial freedom meant that any independent monitoring agencies had to be eliminated. In June 1924 the absorption of the General Intervention Agency of the State by the Accounts Tribunal of the Kingdom realized this condition.[5] The latter body was administered by the marquis of Cabriñana, a close associate of Primo. The Accounts Tribunal also acquired a new name. As the Supreme Court of the finance ministry, it was ultimate arbiter on financial matters. In other words, the ministry of finance was supervised by a dependent agency of that ministry.[6]

Dramatic cost-cutting displays and statistical manipulation might succeed with public opinion, but they could not produce the revenue necessary for either existing expenditures or new programs. Fiscal year 1923–24 ended with a deficit of 431,339,000 pesetas.[7] The deficit

Short Term Treasury Obligations

1923	3,724,000,000 ptas.
1924	4,325,000,000 "
1925	4,825,600,000 "
1926	5,225,000,000 "

SOURCE: *Diario de las Sesiones* (8 and 30 May 1934), pp. 3,028 and 3,082.

for the second trimester of 1924 alone was 115,362,000 pesetas. Even though the government reduced costs and increased revenues for fiscal year 1924–25, it still ended that period with a deficit of 116,884 pesetas.[8]

The dictatorship needed additional funds, and here some of the constraints on its authority quickly became apparent. Revenue could come from only a limited number of sources: increased tax rates, improved tax collection, a restructured revenue system, or increased borrowing. A government promising economy was reluctant to opt for the first. Except for a few limited increases, tax rates remained much the same under the civil government as the directory. Not surprisingly, the dictatorship became interested in tax reform and enforcement, impelled in part by the outpouring of denunciations of the tax system and tax fraud elicited by Primo's early regenerationist promises.[9] But protests from large property owners forced him to abandon his attempt in 1925 to improve collection of land taxes by accelerating the cadastral survey begun under the constitutional regime.[10] Merchants also protested tighter enforcement of tax laws affecting them.[11] In January 1925, Primo declared:

> I have to say that we plan to embark positively on the modification of the tax law in order that each one pays what he owes, and that the mediation of pettifoggers is done away with. Taxes will be enacted in accord with the law, and the law itself will provide the sanction; but the taxpayer will not be ruined and exploited. . . . All the world will pay, but with equity and much enthusiasm.[12]

But the opposition aroused by his first efforts in this direction appears to have at least briefly tempered his zeal, and he took little action on this pledge during the directory's remaining months.[13] The budget for fiscal year 1925–26 showed a deficit of 337,250,000 pesetas.[14] The directory funded its deficits through short-term treasury obligations, the most convenient but most unstable and costly method.

Much of current economic thought is characterized by the belief that moderate budgetary imbalances and governmental deficits are not inherently bad. It is argued that the financing of such shortfalls soaks up private savings and puts them to work for the general good. Whatever the merits of this thinking, it had few adherents in Spain or elsewhere in western Europe during the 1920s. Deficits were generally regarded as indications of fiscal mismanagement, if not of instability.

The new civil government was at first no exception to this thinking. As finance minister, Calvo Sotelo sought to raise new revenue through improved tax collection and an overhauled tax structure. The key to both goals was information. How much untaxed wealth was there, and where was it located? To answer these questions, Calvo Sotelo issued three decrees in early January 1926.[15] The first required landlords to reveal the current market and rental value of their properties. The penalty for small undervaluation was a fine, with expropriation reserved for gross fraud. The second edit strengthened earlier legislation, requiring the registration of all lease, sublease, and sharecropping arrangements in a municipal register. Failure to comply was punishable by fines up to 25,000 pesetas, as well as the invalidation of each unregistered lease. The latter sanction was significant, as it would make it difficult to enforce a contract or secure an eviction. The final decree required merchants to maintain a standard register of their transactions. This accounts book would be open for government inspection of all times and would be the basis for taxation. Compliance was to be enforced primarily through fines. The accounts book was also necessary as evidence in legal proceedings. No businessman could sue for breach of contract or failure to make payment unless his book recorded the transaction accurately.

This approach to tax fraud was naive. Spain in the 1920s was an archetype of amoral familism.[16] Fraud has been a way of life for so long that almost everyone had a stake in it. In this situation it was easy to mobilize sentiment behind tax reform in principle but difficult to carry through any specific measure. Calvo Sotelo also suffered from an exaggerated sense of dictatorial power. Spain simply did not have the administrative resources to manage a sophisticated system of direct taxation. But Primo's finance minister thought he could overcome that deficiency through intimidation alone, with that intimidation made especially problematic by being directed mainly against merchants and property holders to whom the regime looked for political support.

Calvo Sotelo had sought to sweeten disclosure by promising that a general tax reform and rate reduction would soon follow. But who could risk disclosing his wealth without first knowing what others would do and, more significantly, what the government would do with this information? Certainly, it would have been difficult to reverse that sequence. There was no way that Calvo Sotelo could have pledged himself to any future tax system without prior knowledge of the available sources of revenue. But what he should have realized was that this was the same dilemma that had bedeviled earlier finance ministers and that, if there had been any quick, easy method of cutting through it, it would have been attempted decades earlier.

Landlords, merchants, and bankers responded to this legislation with a storm of criticism, far greater than that of 1924.[17] Interestingly, Calvo Sotelo received little support from other sectors of the public, who presumably had something to gain from merchants and landlords paying an increased share of the nation's taxes. At first Primo stood behind his finance minister. When the Madrid Mercantile Union criticized the disclosure measures as inflationary, the dictator declared that the true cause of high prices in Spain was the "lack of organization" among shopkeepers and their stocking an excessive number of luxury goods.[18] As before, Primo found it more difficult to take a hard line against the socially and economically influential large property owners. In the end the government retreated on the disclosure of landed wealth, retaining only the rent register and the sales book for merchants.

Calvo Sotelo had other plans for raising government income. After the fall of the dictatorship he declared that improved administration in the finance ministry increased revenue substantially without any parallel jump in tax rates.[19] However, the improvement in most tax categories is not significantly ahead of general economic indicators, suggesting that the increased revenue resulted from little more than an upturn in the business cycle.[20]

In any event, tax administration was less important than reforming the tax structure itself. There were three dimensions to this problem: the fiscal, or the government's need for funds; the economic, or the need to encourage resource development; and the social, or the need to promote a better distribution of wealth. The government did not agree on how to proceed in these different areas.[21] Primo himself was captivated by the single tax.[22] He saw a progressive tax on capital as a way of simplifying the tax structure, providing the government with operating capital, and promoting economic growth. He declared early in 1926 that the government should also begin reducing the national debt by 1928.

Calvo Sotelo shared Primo's desire for a simplified fiscal structure based on direct, progressive taxes.[23] He was also committed to reducing the national debt. But he felt that taxes should be based on income rather than capital. Moreover, he was willing to go further than Primo in challenging the traditional prerogatives of private property. He wanted the tax system to discourage rural landlord absenteeism and to encourage full utilization of agricultural resources. Expediently, if somewhat inconsistently, he also wanted to extract additional revenue from government monopolies, despite the regressive nature of that income.

Primo's enthusiasm for the single tax notwithstanding, Calvo Sotelo had the same independence as other ministers. As seen, he used that freedom to enact his ill-fated disclosure decrees. He also modified the law on inheritance taxes in April 1926.[24] The change he instituted was to tax an estate before its distribution rather than after. He also strengthened the penalties for fraud. In May he established a five percent luxury tax. Slightly higher land and stamp taxes were also imposed that year, as well as new taxes on industrial sales and transportation.

None of these measures was particularly important. They only amounted to small increases in revenue, and each of them was enacted within the general tax framework inherited from the constitutional regime. Even Calvo Sotelo's disclosure decrees were only attempts to improve the efficiency of the existing system. Basic reform, including adoption of a tax on aggregate personal income and an extension of direct taxation, remained long-term goals.

In the spring and summer of 1926, however, Calvo Sotelo was embroiled in controversy. After supporting his finance minister through the initial waves of criticism triggered by the disclosure decrees, Primo began to express some doubts publicly. Privately, he urged Calvo Sotelo to base future reforms on a capital tax and administrative decentralization. Calvo Sotelo did not argue. He worked into the fall on a proposal reconciling his thinking with Primo's. The result was a mixture of lofty principle and problematic application similar to many of the regime's other initiatives.[25] To increase direct taxation, Calvo Sotelo recommended a new tax based on overall financial standing. In addition to income and profits, the tax would take into account a taxpayer's other assets and liabilities. This measure would have established the modern, comprehensive income tax in Spain. Other parts of the package included taxing earnings from invested capital more heavily than those from personal labor and penalizing single individuals while granting a moderate incentive to large families. What rendered the package unrealistic was its transferring primary responsibility for revenue collection to municipal councils, formed of equal numbers of taxpayers and government employees. The proposal was unveiled in December 1926. By promoting the plan as the heart of any future change in the tax system, the regime preempted public discussion and

Budget Deficits

1923–24	575,334,000 ptas.
April/June 1924	166,073,000 "
1924–25	417,145,000 "
1925–26	608,381,000 "
July–December 1926	147,283,000 "
1927	612,478,000 "
1928	703,237,000 "
1929	924,459,000 "

SOURCE: *Diario de las Sesiones* (22 May 1934), p. 3027.

prevented the emergence of more practical ideas. With derisive reference to Calvo Sotelo's hometown in Galicia, the underground opposition journal *Hojas Libres* awarded him the sobriquet "the Necker of Lugo."

Little reform was achieved thereafter. In 1927 charges were made for drivers' licenses. Also in that year minor changes were made in the tax on income from personal labor, requiring workers earning more than 3,250 pesetas per year to pay that tax. Since few actually earned that much, the tax did not open up any major source of revenue. It did, however, strain relations with the Socialists.[26]

Banking and Budgets

Opposition from established interest groups clearly worked against the efforts of directory and civil government alike to fund their programs through increased tax revenue. The resulting fiscal straits of the dictatorship should not be exaggerated, but neither should they be understated. Primo was even forced to seek occasional financial backing for his government from Juan March, a notorious robber baron noted for corrupting politicians and for large-scale tobacco smuggling.[27] Financial shortfalls of the magnitude faced by the dictatorship, however, went far beyond even March's legendary wealth and could not be funded easily without the help of the banks.

From the first days, however, there was tension between the regime and the large Madrid and Bilbao bankers.[28] Bankers' support of a public debt subscription in October and November 1923 helped to legitimize the regime and provided it with one of its early milestones. At the same time, however, bankers worried that the government would turn to foreign lenders, declaring that Spain should be developed with national capital. Financial circles buzzed in 1923 as well with rumors of an impending attack by the directory on the privileged, semiautonomous

Bank of Spain, and bankers were upset by Primo's incompatibility legislation, which challenged the close ties between themselves and the former leaders of the Liberal and Conservative parties. Indeed, the rhetorical thrust of the regime toward a rising of the *neutra masa*—however vague that call might have been—implied a challenge to them as elites as well as to radical leftists. Always present, at least under the surface, this tension occasionally flared into the open. In September 1927, for example, banking leaders were in consternation after the Supreme Court's prosecutor characterized them as a tight-knit, selfish oligarchy whose "grasping and tenacle-like power was being extended throughout the nation."[29]

Nonetheless, the mutual self-interest of the bankers and the regime in working together generally proved stronger than the divisions between them. Cooperation with the dictatorship brought tangible rewards to the bankers, and as long as they provided that cooperation the regime tended to support their interests. Before the dictatorship Primo had owned a heavily mortgaged farm in Chamartin. Chronically short of money, he had fallen behind on both interest and principal payments on that estate. A widely current rumor held, however, that he was able to pay off that debt in full after his coup as the result of receiving a 300,000-peseta loan from the Arnus Bank in Barcelona.[30] About the same time, the government awarded that financial house the concession for the salt mine at Torrevieja without requiring competitive bids and for only half the amount previously charged.

Primo responded handsomely as well to one of the bankers' earliest requests—subsidies for the financially troubled railroads in which they had a substantial stake. Among the petitioning bankers had been the marquis of Urquijo, who after becoming head of ITT's newly established telephone monopoly in Spain, appointed Primo's son to a lucrative legal position with the company. The two families found jobs for each other's dependents, and their correspondence ranged from the desirability of daylight savings time to increased funding for the Industrial Credit Bank that the marquis headed.[31]

Primo shielded the Urquijos and other large bankers from the demands of merchant and bar associations for closer government regulation and sounder accounting and investment practices. The rapid expansion of banking capacity during World War I and the immediate postwar period had proved insupportable. To maintain their highly extended positions many banks had been forced into speculative ventures during a period of contraction and slow recovery. Not everyone could gamble and win. The penalty for the losers was insolvency.[32]

To protect bankers from themselves the constitutional regime had established the Superior Banking Council (Consejo Superior Bancario) in 1921. Initially opposed by the banking community, this measure was eventually so watered down as to become almost meaningless, with effective control of the council slipping into the hands of the bankers themselves. Primo showed little interest in this situation until a series of bank failures in 1925 led him to increase the council's investigative, licensing, and punitive powers in May 1926. His commitment to reform, however, may be questioned, since the council continued to be dominated by the large banks.

His reluctance to deal firmly with the large banks was also evident in his reaction to the failure of Bilbao's United Mining Credit Bank (Banco Crédito de la Unión Minera), the biggest to collapse in 1925.[33] Responding to irate depositors' demands for punishment of the bank's officers, a local judge had imprisoned Juan Nuñez, the bank's director general. The king, however, interceded with Primo on Nuñez's behalf. Nuñez was soon out of jail, the judge out of a job, and the entire scandal hushed up and out of public view.

Banking influence was also evident in the creation of CAMPSA, the national oil monopoly.[34] Funding for the dictatorship became especially important after announcement in 1926 of its long-term public-works program. The lucrative oil distribution system domintted by Shell and Standard interests was an obvious nationalization target. Banker complaints against foreign investment helped create the climate for that takeover. Bankers, and especially the Urquijos, were also its principal beneficiaries because of the large stake they received in quasi-public CAMPSA. Indeed, how little the government actually cleared for itself is striking—somewhat less than four times the amount of the match monopoly and only half that of the tobacco monopoly. Primo and his entourage, though, could hardly complain. Their use of CAMPSA as a rich source of patronage did little for its profitability.[35] Shortly, after establishment of CAMPSA, the pattern of favor reciprocated by favor continued with the Patriotic Union soliciting financiers to contribute to a bejeweled military baton and a new house to be given the dictator as part of a national show of appreciation.[36]

Large private banks also profited from the expanding public banking system.[37] Rather than require private banks to fund low yield, high-risk development projects directly, the regime relied on government banks. The first was the Local Credit Bank established in 1925 to provide municipal and provincial governments with long-term investment funding. The Savings Bank for the Development of Small Properties was founded to finance internal agricultural colonization and low-income

Monopoly Revenue
(in Ptas.)

Year	CAMPSA	Tobacco	Matches	Lottery	Totals
1922–23		227,100,000	34,200,000	277,400,000	538,700,000
1923–24		245,200,000	34,200,000	295,800,000	575,200,000
April–June 1924		64,300,000	13,100,000	57,200,000	134,600,000
1924–25		266,200,000	40,100,000	324,900,000	621,200,000
1925–26		261,900,000	43,800,000	351,100,000	656,800,000
July–December 1926		135,400,000	23,600,000	184,100,000	343,100,000
1927		277,100,000	39,800,000	370,000,000	686,900,000
1928	112,500,000	285,400,000	41,400,000	387,900,000	827,200,000
1929	148,900,000	293,100,000	38,800,000	413,300,000	394,100,000

SOURCE: The figures on CAMPSA are from Calvo Sotelo, "CAMPSA," in *Lecturas*, ed. Velarde, pp. 392–93. The statistics on tobacco are from *Anuario estadístico 1930*, p. 290. The figures on the match and lottery monopolies are from I.N.E., *Principales actividades*, p. 135.

housing. The Industrial Credit Bank, established during the constitutional regime, was given extended lending authority in December 1926 and April 1927. Finally, the Exterior Bank of Spain was instituted to finance foreign commerce and win back business that Spaniards in other countries were giving to foreign banks.

One historian unsympathetic to the large private banks has viewed these measures as an attack on the banking establishment and as indicative of a strong reformist thrust in the dictatorship.[38] More research is needed on the state banks, but it is unlikely that it will sustain that interpretation. Primo relied heavily on the directors of large private financial institutions to run the state banks and, more importantly, counted on government-guaranteed bond issues subscribed by the private banks to provide much of the state banks' operating capital. The state banks were intermediaries providing the surety of profit needed for private bankers to mobilize and invest capital in useful, but not necessarily highly profitable, areas. The money spent in this way was considerable. By 1928 the outstanding loans of the Industrial Credit Bank amounted to 460 million pesetas,[39] and those of the Local Credit Bank to 315 million pesetas.[40]

Widespread corruption existed. Particularly serious was the allegation that the newly created Technical Construction Company (Técnica de la Construcción, S.A.) was a privileged recipient of many contracts funded by the Local Credit Bank.[41] Martínez Anido and other government and bank officials were said to have high positions in the company. More generally, the state banks' bond issues paid a high rate of interest—so high that oversubscription was a problem and would-be purchasers complained that "insiders" preempted the market.[42] The state banks passed these high interest charges on to their borrowers, despite the fact that the purpose behind those banks had been to provide low-cost capital for investments in the national interest. As shown earlier, many borrowers were left with an uncomfortably large debt burden by the end of the dictatorship for which the state itself was finally responsible.[43]

If financing the dictatorship brought bankers tangible benefits, the centerpiece of that cooperation was their backing of public debt issues. With this funding the regime established itself as the principal motor of the economy, virtually preempting the capital market place. Various categories of government debt issues constituted 75.5% of more than 29 billion pesetas in estimated public and private borrowing at the end of 1929.[44]

After 1926 an extraordinary budget was used to fund expanding deficits while retaining a formal commitment to a balanced budget.[45] O'Donnell had employed this device in 1859. During the First World War, González Besada and Santiago Alba had proposed such budgets. The 1924 Municipal Statute also included provisions of this sort. Ideally, the extraordinary budget was an amalgam of special social and economic development programs.[46] In practice, the lines separating the extraordinary and the ordinary budgets were not so clear. A number of routine expenses were covered by the extraordinary budget, while the ordinary budget continued to finance important builing projects. This budget has since been labeled Keynesian. In a strict sense of that broad word, this was not the case. Calvo Sotelo argued that the correct time to implement an extraordinary budget was not in a time of declining state revenues—that is, in a recession—but during a period when state finances were in an upswing.[47]

The extraordinary budget was originally intended to finance a ten-yer development program costing 3,535,000,000 pesetas. By the end of the dictatorship less than 37% of that amount had been spent. The yearly totals were:

July–December 1926	81,074,538 ptas.[48]
1927	312,914,648 "
1928	445,931,225 "
1929	459,793,090 "
Total	1,299,713,501 ptas.

The regime claimed its floating the debt issues funding the budget constituted a "full vote, a most strong vote of confidence in the government" as much from "banking circles which have stood out in the financial and economic activities of the country as from small capitalists."[49] The end of the extraordinary budget came in 1929. The government's difficulties in maintaining the peseta's exchange rate led to an invitation to the peripatetic French central banker Charles Rist to visit Spain that year.[50] Rist told Calvo Sotelo that if he wished to preserve Spain's international credit rating, as well as curtail the decline in the peseta, he had to place a ceiling on state expenses, avoid further debts, and abolish the extraordinary budget. Spain's finances were in such precarious shape by this time that the government had little choice but to follow his advice.

Before its termination the extraordinary budget contributed to a significant expansion of the national debt. The yearly totals were:

1923	15,644,798,000 ptas.[51]
1924	16,221,123,000 "
1925	16,957,528,000 "
1926	17,369,474,000 "
1927	18,419,134,000 "
1928	18,936,786,000 "
1929	20,301,431,000 "

Most striking is that the increase for the later years took place despite the leveling off of military expenses connected with Morocco. Total Moroccan related expenses in 1929 were 332 million pesetas less than they had been in fiscal year 1924–25.[52] Military expenses apart from Morocco actually rose during this period, reflecting Primo's interest in the army's good will.

The dictatorship's deficits were inconsistent with its commitment to reduce the national debt. Not all Spaniards were aware of how contradictory its policies were. Free from a critical parliament, the regime deluded itself and much of the country into believing it was taking positive action to reduce the debt. The first step was consolidation, beginning in January 1927.[53] At a conversion cost of approximately 393 million pesetas, Calvo Sotelo consolidated 5,317 million pesetas in floating treasury debt. He took pride that this operation resulted in a lower overall maintenance charge for the treasury. However, what was gained in this way was largely lost through the tax discounts used to facilitate the changeover.[54] As principal sellers of the old issues and buyers of the new, the banks were well placed to profit from the transaction.[55]

Consolidation was preliminary to the main goal of amortization.[56] An amortization department *(caja de amortización)* was established in May 1926 to manage a sinking fund, using surpluses from the ordinary budget to retire outstanding debt issues. The only significant amortization took place in early 1928 when 3,407 million pesetas were converted from floating to amortizable debt. This operation reduced the internal floating debt from 8,668 million pesetas to 5,261 million pesetas.

The question of indebtedness extends beyond the central government's formal obligations. Many loan issues floated by private and quasi-public concerns were guaranteed by the dictatorship.[57] Their rapidly rising yearly totals were:

1923	161,381,500 ptas.
1924	168,488,500 "

1925	305,088,100	"
1926	351,017,500	"
1927	367,614,500	"
1928	518,664,500	"
1929	637,079,900	"

Among the important state-backed securities were those of the Transatlantic Corporation, the Ebro Hydrographic Confederation, and the National Touring Foundation. As many of the issuing authorities were not on solid financial footing, the government's guarantee represented a very real increase in its liabilities.

Local-government indebtedness also increased under the dictatorship, in large measure as a result of the borrowing authority granted by the municipal and provincial statutes. The central government was ultimately responsible for much of this debt, especially the loans granted by the Local Credit Bank. Overall local-government indebtedness increased by 693,421,200 pesetas during the period.[58] As if the problem was not sufficiently complicated, some of the dictatorship's corporate economic organizations also had borrowing and taxing powers. In most instances their loans were of minor significance. However, 1,100 million pesetas in railroad debt alone were issued during the period.[59] Notes amounting to 163,600,000 pesetas were also issued in 1925 and 1927 to support the regime's housing program. Additionally, the State Mortgage Bank (Banco Hipotecario de España) floated its own bonds during the period. These latter, however, were solid securities and represented only a formal liability for the state. Such a plethora of bond-issuing authorities makes it difficult to determine governmental indebtedness during the period.[60] However, one does not need a precise number to understand the basic point that the dictatorship funded much of its program through credit underwritten by the large financial institutions.

From the large banks' point of view, this approach to development had much to recommend it. Under Primo their assets and profits ran dramatically ahead of most other economic indicators. From 1922 to 1929 the total capital invested, on reserve, and on deposit at the six largest banks increased from 2.4 to 4.3 billion pesetas.[61] The competitive position of the large banks compared with smaller financial institutions also improved. For the five largest, the total number of branches increased from 156 to 791 between 1922 and 1929.[62] Since the government notes they purchased provided them with capital at low rates from the Bank of Spain, they were also able to extend their control over industry.[63] These investments were generally in heavy industry and transport. Railroads, shipping, coal, steel, and cement, incidentally, received disproportionately large subsidy and tariff protection and benefited more directly from the regime's building programs than consumer-oriented light industries such as textiles.[64] Overall, then, the dictatorship's method of funding its programs helped to carry forward the momentum from World War I toward a strong bank role in Spain's structure of economic and political privilege.

The Peseta

During Primo's last years in power this arrangement came under increasing criticism, especially from the textile-producing Catalonia.[65] Fear grew that the dictatorship's rapid increase in indebtedness threatened economic instability and could not be sustained indefinitely. The fate of Franco's similar economic program in the 1950s supports this view. Under Primo, however, it was international currency speculators who pricked the bubble. In the mid-1920s a large quantity of short-term capital had entered Spain as a result of peseta purchases abroad. Several factors occasioned this speculative movement. The Moroccan War was concluding favorably, prompting expectations of a balanced budget. Spain also had strong gold reserves. Approximately 61% of its currency was gold backed.[66] The economy was also sharing in the general European business recovery. The dictatorship itself inspired the confidence of the international financial community with its debt consolidation and promise of fiscal responsibility. Carlos Vergara y Cailleaux, the governor of the Bank of Spain, even offered some indirect encouragement to speculators. Although declaring that Spain had no need nor immediate interest in returning to the gold standard, he attested in a foreign journal to the general strength of the economy and stability of the country's finances. Primo himself encouraged merchants to strengthen the peseta by reducing their stock of foreign goods.[67]

These factors led many to believe that the peseta was likely to be revalued upward by as much as 25% to its parity value of 5.18 pesetas to the American dollar.[68] There is no reliable indicator of international payment transactions for Spain in this period.[69] Nonetheless, Juan Sarda has estimated that as much as 700 million pesetas in short-term capital entered the country by 1927.[70] The exchange rate of the peseta moved significantly upward in international currency markets. The dictatorship attributed the peseta's strength to the soundness of its own policies, not to speculation. Calvo Sotelo and Primo talked publicly about restoring the gold standard.[71]

The collapse began in 1928. The least noticed yet most basic pressure on the peseta that year was the increased interest rates of the European central banks.[72] Tight money constricted the speculative capital used to purchase pesetas. Another cause of the peseta's decline was the nationalization of British, Dutch, and American oil interests. This act sent shock waves through international financial circles. Primo felt called to asure the British-owned Rio Tinto Company personally that it would not be next. Nonetheless, Shell's Henri Deterding declared economic war on Spain.[73] Led by Shell and Standard, western oil companies refused to supply Spain. The country no longer seemed attractive for foreign investment of any sort. A more tangible blow to Spain's payment position was the forty-million-peseta indemnization awarded Shell.[74] The year 1928 was also one of the worst for agriculture in the twentieth century. Imports of wheat and other cereals required large foreign exchange outlays. At the same time that imports were up, wine and olive oil exports fell.[75] Those commodities had been important export earners. These developments reminded speculators of Spain's underlying poverty and the fact that it was inherently more of an importer than exporter.

The dictatorship had little comprehension of the long- and short-term factors working against the peseta and exhibited "naive ideas . . . [about] the prestige of the currency" similar to Mussolini's "Battle of the Lira."[76] All the regime seemed to understand was that there was a sustained, external attack on the currency. Since it had proclaimed the strength of the peseta as a sign of the economic improvement it had brought, it felt compelled to defend it.[77] In no sense does it appear to have recognized that the "norm" it intended to preserve was the result of temporary, highly aberrational circumstances. Certainly a country can find it desirable to intervene briefly against speculative fluctuations in the true value of its currency. But all that can be accomplished by a sustained defense of an overvalued currency is the exhausting of foreign exchange and gold reserves. This happened in Spain in 1928 and 1929. In the midst of its effort to check the peseta's decline, the regime was still seriously considering the gold standard. That measure could be entertained only on the basis of blind faith or ignorance, given Spain's continuing trade and budget imbalances. The report of Flores de Lemus's commission on the gold standard, demonstrated the inadvisability of that course.[78]

Tactics to defend the peseta were also poorly thought out.[79] The first mistake stemmed from the Bank of Spain's reluctance to permit use of its gold reserves. That decision required the government to resort to credits, which signaled to speculators how far the regime was willing and able to go in the peseta's support. This error was compounded by the use the regime made of those credits. Loans were contracted with London, Paris, and New York banks for use by the Exchange Intervention Committee established in June 1928.[80] Thus the foreign banks intended as instruments of the peseta's defense knew in advance precisely how much Spain had in reserve at any particular moment. They were as well situated to speculate against the currency as to bolster it.

Calvo Sotelo chaired the intervention committee ex officio as finance minister.[81] The committee also included the director of the treasury, the president of the Superior Banking Council, the president of the stock exchange, and the governor, subgovernor, and a director of the Bank of Spain. It had an operating capital of 500 million pesetas, one-half of which was borrowed from the Bank of Spain and one-half from the treasury. The committee intervened in international exchange markets on an on-again, off-again basis through October 1929.

It encountered many difficulties. Not the least was the marquis of Cabia, the subgovernor of the Bank of Spain.[82] He saw the folly of trying to maintain an artificial exchange rate, and his opposition complicated the committee's work. In arguing against the regime's policy, he spoke for private bankers who feared that a peseta defense might lead to a capital exodus out of the country and were afraid of the tightening of credit that would ensue. The close ties of the bankers with the Bank of Spain and the Superior Banking Council put them in a strategic position to hamper the defense both inside and outside the committee.[83]

Throughout the summer of 1928 the committee strove to maintain an exchange rate of 29.5 ptas./£1. By September, pressure on the peseta had become so intense that it dropped its support level to 30.2 ptas./£1. By February 1929 the peseta was at 31.25 ptas./£1, and by June it had fallen to 34.27 ptas./£1. That low point prompted a final paroxysm of activity from the committee, raising the peseta to 32.08 ptas./£1 in September. By that date, however, the whole effort had become so costly as to be insupportable.[84] A run on the peseta that month broke the committee's ability to continue the struggle. In October the regime formally abandoned the effort. Two months later Primo publicly labeled the defense a mistake in *Hoja del Lunes*.[85] In doing so he repudiated his finance minister. A short time later Calvo Sotelo resigned, and within two weeks the dictatorship itself collapsed.

In his last days in power Primo attacked conservative interests for not rallying to the regime they had benefited from. The banking community was among his primary targets. Some of his anger was misdirected. Bankers could hardly be faulted for failing to underwrite what Primo himself eventually conceded was a misguided defense of the peseta. Nor could he fairly blame them after 1928 for disassociating themselves from a government growing too weak to defend their interests. The selection of Calvo Sotelo as president of the Central Bank in February 1930 suggests that even in the dictatorship's inglorious aftermath, they did not altogether turn their back on the fallen regime.[86]

At a deeper level, however, much of Primo's sense of abandonment and hurt was justified. He may have been conservative at heart, and vague and inconsistent in thought. He may also have lacked the instinct for social and economic engineering of his ministers. But, like them, he was animated by a sense of crisis, a belief that Spain stood at the crossroads in the 1920s. Within the intuitive, individualist framework of his thought, economic development was important in itself, but also because it promised to reduce social divisions.

Primo's amorphous vision and his lack of a strong independent power base, however, meant that he had little to set against the clearer and narrower purposes of wealthy, well-entrenched elites. Resistance from landowners to increased taxation and reliance on financiers for funding and favors helped incline fiscal policy in the 1920s toward dangerous, short-term expedients. Financiers had encouraged Primo in those policies but were quick to criticize when they proved economically counterproductive and politically ruinous.

NOTES

1. A critical examination of Primo's search for revenue is Felix Benítez de Lugo, *Obra económica, financiero, y moneteria de la dictadura* (Madrid: n.p., 1930), pp. 54–84.

2. Partial lists of the dictatorship's fiscal legislation are contained in Calvo Sotelo, *Mis servicios*, pp. 493–505, and las Heras, *Auxiliar*, pp. 126–39.

3. On Primo's attempt to reduce the state bureaucracy by attrition, see AHN Leg. 35, Exte. 2704 (2 April 1924); on his effort to improve performance, see AHN Leg. 1, Exte. 364 (26 January 1926), and AHN Leg. 32, Exte. 1179 (30 April 1924).

4. AHN Leg. 35, Exte. 2654 (31 March 1924) and AHN Leg. 1, Exte. 89 (26 April 1924).

5. José G. Ceballos Teresi, *Política y economía* (Madrid: El Financiero, 1934), pp. 331–33, describes this change. See also Castrillo Santos, *¿Se ha redimido España?*, pp. 93–101.

6. Ceballos Teresi characterized this situation as "the absurdity of the administrative centers themselves being the inspectors of their own actions"; *Historia económica* 5:332. Primo himself acknowledged the problematical nature of the state's official budget figures in a 2 April letter to the duke of Tetuán, in which he wrote: ". . . the budget . . . as you put it very well, ought to be sincere. But I believe that even faulting that, it can still be efficient"; Armiñan and Armiñan, *Espistolario del dictador*, p. 80.

7. These are finance minister Marraco's statistics cited in a 22 May 1934 Cortes debate; *Diario de las Sesiones*, p. 3026. See also Ceballos Teresi, *Política y economía*,

pp. 228–30, and pp. 364–69; as well as *Anuario estadístico 1925:26*, p. 367, for financial statistics during this period.

8. Fiscal year 1923–24 ran from 1 April 1923 through 31 March 1924. In 1924, Spain changed to a fiscal year running from July to 30 June. A special trimesterly budget was drawn up to cover the interim period from 1 April through 30 June 1924. According to Marraco's statistics, which are identical to those used by Indalecio Prieto in the debate over the dictatorship's financial record, expenses for 1923–24 were 3,048,386,000 ptas. compared with 2,941,724,000 ptas. for 1924–25. Income during that same period increased from 2,617,047,000 ptas. to 2,777,840,000 ptas.; Ceballos Teresi, *Historia económica*, 7:426–27.

9. On early petitions for tax reform, see AHN Legs. 29, 30, and 31 and Ceballos Teresi, *Historia económica* 5:189–93. Denunciations of fraud implicated the great as well as the small. The Rio Tinto Company was the subject of repeated and particularly serious allegations; see AHN Leg. 29, Exte. 96, and AHN Leg. 30, Exte. 393.

10. For the protest of the property owners, see AHN Legs. 35, 36, and 37. During this same period small shopowners also actively protested a new tax on bottled products and tighter customs regulations; AHN Leg. 36, Extes. 3863, 3866, and 3867 and Leg. 38, Extes. 3252–53. Manufacturers appear to have been pursued for less vigorously.

11. AHN Legs. 36, 37, and 38.

12. Díaz-Plaja, *De la dictadura*, p. 265. For antecedents of this concern with tax reform and better tax collection, see Calvo Sotelo, *Mis servicios*, pp. 124–25.

13. An effort was made, however, to extend the work of the cadastral survey of landed property in April 1925; Pemartín, *Los valores*, pp. 189–91.

14. *Diario de las Sesiones*, 22 May 1934, p. 3026.

15. Ceballos Teresi, *Historia económica* 6:18–30. A few months later in Torrelodones in the province of Madrid itself, a glaring example of the abuses he was trying to correct was discovered and attracted considerable interest from Primo; AHN Leg. 42, Exte. 6935.

16. On the concept of amoral familism, see Edward C. Banfield, *The Moral Basis of a Backward Society* (The Free Press of Glencoe, 1958).

17. Far more letters and telegrams resulted from these actions than from anything else done by the finance ministry during the dictatorship; AHN Leg. 41. See also Miguel Avilés Fernández, Santos Madrazo Madrazo, Emilio Mitre Fernández, Bonifacio Palacios Martín, and Isabel Redondo Castro, *El siglo XX/ Los primeros treinta años* (Madrid: EDAF, 1974), pp. 217–19.

18. Maura Gamazo, *Bosquejo* 1:152–55.

19. José Calvo Sotelo, *En defensa propia* (Madrid: Librería de San Martín, 1932), pp. 64–65; and Benavides, *La política económica*, p. 22. For evidence of the corruption and inefficiency chronically plaguing the finance ministry see AHN Leg. 1, Exte. 205, and AHN Leg. 31, Exte. 831.

20. INE, *Principales actividades*, pp. 85, 101, 121–22, and 126–37.

21. Calvo Sotelo, *Mis servicios*, pp. 256–60.

22. This idea had a modest measure of popular support; see, for example, AHN Leg. 37, Exte. 4379, and AHN Leg. 42, Exte. 7273.

23. The fullest statement of Calvo Sotelo's views on tax reform is contained in his "Orientaciones económicas y tributarias," pp. 310–24 in *Curso de Ciudadana* (Madrid: Junta de Propaganda Patiótica y Ciudadana, 1929).

24. Even this modest act stirred controversy; see AHN Leg. 43, especially Exte. 7650.

25. Calvo Sotelo's proposal is summarized in Pio Ballesteros, "Medio siglo de hacienda española," *Anales de economía* 8, no. 32 (October–December 1948): 403–4 and Pemartín, *Los valores*, pp. 179–89. The text is contained in Ceballos Teresi, *Historia económica* 6:85–148.

26. This act provoked more protests to the finance ministry than even Calvo Sotelo's 1926 disclosure legislation. The protests are recorded in AHN Leg. 47, Exte. 8650.

27. John Brooks, "Annals of Finance:Privateer—1," *New Yorker*, 21 May 1979, pp. 66–72 passim, and *Hojas Libres*, August 1927, pp. 62–69.

28. Catalan banks were not as large. At the end of 1920 the deposits in millions of ptas. of the largest Madrid and Bilbao banks were 423.5 for the Hispano Americano Bank, 84.7 for the year old Central Bank, 335.4 for the Spanish Credit Bank, 255.3 for the Urquijo Bank, 188.9 for the Bank of Bilbao, 133.0 for the Bank of Vizcaya, and 142.1 for the United Mining Credit Bank. After the collapse of the Bank of Barcelona the next largest Catalan bank, the Hispanic Colonial, had only 51.1 million in total deposits. The underdeveloped state of Catalan banks, primarily commercial deposit institutions making short-term rather than long-term industrial loans, mirrored the small size of most manufacturing plants in that region. For bank deposit figures, see Roldan et al., *La formación* 2:256–59. Catalan bankers also complained before and during the dictatorship about discriminatory tax legislation; see AHN Leg. 36, Exte. 4131 (August 1924). Additional statistics on Catalan banking interests in the 1920s are contained in AHN Leg. 319, Bancos 1927. Recent contributions to understanding the relationship between the regime's finances and the banking community are Nicholas Belford, "El sistema bancario durante la dictadura de Primo," *Economía política de la dictadura de Primo de Rivera, Cuadernos económicos de I.C.E.,* ed. Carlos Velasco Murviedro, 10 (1979): 227–66; Ángel Melguizo Sánchez, "El presupuesto de Calvo Sotelo," ibid., pp. 401–42; and Juan Muñoz, "La expansión bancaria entre 1919 y 1926. La formación de una banca nacional," *La via nacionalista del capitalismo español,* vol. 2, *Cuadernos económicos de I.C.E.,* ed. Carlos Velasco Murviedro, 6 (1978): 98–162.

29. On the debt subscription, see AHN Leg. 318, "Bancos noviembre 1923 and mayo 1923." For the type of foreign loan offer feared by the bankers, see, AHN Leg. 39, Exte. 535 (5 March 1925). On rumors of an attack on the Bank of Spain, see *Las Finanzas* 3, no. 95 (23 October 1923): 1447. On banker response to incompatibility legislation, see ibid. and ibid. 2 (13 November 1923): 1503–4. The quotation is from AHN Leg. 319, "Bancos septiembre 1927."

30. *Hojas Libres,* April 1927, pp. 44–45.

31. See, in particular, AHN Legs. 39 (9 November 1923, 1 March 1924, 14 March 1924, 23 September 1924), 35 (April 1924), and 524 (28 July 1926 and 21 March 1927). On relations between Primo and the Marquis of Quintanar of the Plus Ultra Insurance Company, see AHN Leg. 42, Exte. 7201 (3 July 1926).

32. On the demand for greater bank regulation, see AHN Leg. 39, Exte. 5549–50 and 5552 (9 March 1925), and *Las Finanzas* 7, no. 266 and 268 (22 February and 8 March 1927) and 269 (15 March 1927), p. 5465. On the banking's problems generally, see Canosa, *Un siglo,* pp. 91–94 passim. On Cambó's legislation in 1921, see Muñoz, *El poder,* pp. 53–55. The privileged position of the banks extended to favored treatment against the competing savings banks. The complaints of the latter are contained in AHN Leg. 41, Exte. 6630 (1 December 1925), and Leg. 44, Exte. 7892 (16 February 1927) and Exte. 7944 (15 March 1927). For more on the savings banks, their relationship to the dictatorship, and competition with the private banks, see José Francisco Forniés, "El ahorro popular durante la dictadura: Las cajas de ahorro y montes de piedad," *Economía política de Primo de Rivera, Cuadernos económicos de I.C.E.,* ed. Carlos Velasco Murviedro, 10 (1979): 267–98.

33. AHN Leg. 41, Exte. 6662; Leg. 40, Exte. 6304; Leg. 318, "Bancos febrero through mayo and diciembre 1925," and Leg. 319, "Bancos enero 1926." See also Tuñón de Lara, *Poder,* p. 121, and *Hojas Libres,* September 1927, pp. 82–89. For related criticism of Primo's response to the collapse of the Bank of Barcelona, see Ortega, *España encadenada,* pp. 240–43.

34. CAMPSA was perhaps the single most controversial and enduring act of the dictatorship and has yet to receive the study that it deserves. On the bankers' opposition to foreign investment generally, see *Las Finanzas* 7, no. 165 (15 February 1927): 5391, and 7, no. 267 (1 March 1927): 5427. Many sectors of the business community, however, were opposed, especially those with ties to foreign capital; see, for example, AHN Leg. 45, Exte. 8214. There is further indication here too of the king's willingness to use his influence with the government to advance his own financial interests; see, in particular, AHN Leg. 50, Exte. 9813. Calling for most attention is an explanation of the private

interests involved in CAMPSA. The potential importance of this question is underscored by the fact that in the comparisons between tobacco and oil monopolies, tobacco revenues are artificially low due to the large profits siphoned off by Juan March; see Brooks, "Annals of Finance: Privateer—1," pp. 68–72 passim.

35. On the division of CAMPSA into separate patronage fiefs, see *Hojas Libres,* December 1927, pp. 45–48. On the substantial employment turnover and patronage opportunities brought by CAMPSA, see also AHN Leg. 47, Extes. 8731 and 8747. Primo was also accused of receiving shares in the monopoly; *Hojas Libres,* July 1927, pp. 74–77.

36. *Hojas Libres,* February 1928, p. 76 and June 1928, pp. 70–71. In the end neither was the house built nor the baton purchased. Primo did, however, keep the 4 million ptas. to buy them that the union had collected from banks and companies with government business. He also accepted the gift from his native city Jerez of the house he had been born in; Ciges Aparicio, *España bajo la dinastía,* p. 447.

37. For a brief introduction to this question, see *The Banker* 29, no. 26 (June 1928): 461; Ceballos Teresi, *Historia económica* 6:426–31; and AHN Leg. 319. On the origins of the Exterior Bank, see in particular, AHN Leg. 318, "Bancos 1924." Calvo Sotelo typifies the official stance of the regime in his account of the Local Credit Bank, *Mis servicios,* pp. 47–52.

38. Juan Velarde Fuertes, *Sobre la decadencia económica de España* (Madrid: Editorial Tecnos, 1969), pp. 336–37.

39. Velarde, *La política económica,* p. 130.

40. Calvo Sotelo, *Mis servicios,* p. 49.

41. *Hojas Libres,* July 1927, pp. 78–80.

42. The first annual report of the Local Credit Bank discusses the problem of interest rates; AHN Leg. 319, "Bancos agosto 1926." For the preempting of public bank issues, see AHN Leg. 319, "Bancos junio 1928."

43. See above, pp. 104–6 and 118.

44. If the more than 3 billion ptas. of heavily government-backed railroad borrowing are included among the state's liabilities, the public debt share increases to 87%. Underscoring the importance of these figures is the underdeveloped state of the stock market with the total shares of all private, as well as quasi-public enterprises such as CAMPSA, amounting to less than 12 billion ptas., only slightly more than 28% of the total of public and private bonds and shares; *Anuario estadístico: 1929,* p. 263. For evidence of banking investment patterns before the dictatorship, see the report of the Banco de Vizcaya, AHN Leg. 318, "Bancos noviembre 1923." For more on the regime's impact on private capital market places, see Manuel Aguilar. "La actividad en la construcción de obras públicas y la valoración de la peseta," *Revista de Obras Públicas* 77, no. 2520 (1 March 1929): 92–96 and Federico Reparaz, "Las obras públicas y la cotización de la peseta," *Revista de Obras Públicas* 79, no. 2567 (15 February 1930): 66–71. Relevant statistical information is contained in Ceballos Teresi, *Historia económica* 5:153, 233, and 470; 6:198 and 353; and 7:143.

45. Among the sources of the extraordinary budget are Calvo Sotelo, *Mis servicios,* pp. 478–89; *Diario de las Sesiones,* 3 March 1932, pp. 4237–45; Castrillo Santos, *¿Se ha redimido?* pp. 36–37; Santiago Alba, *Para la historia,* pp. 111–13; Gabriel Sole Villalonga, *La deuda pública española y el mercado de capitales* (Madrid: Instituto de Estudios Fiscales, 1964), pp. 54–57; and *Las Finanzas* 10, no. 377 (25 February 1930): 154–55 and 158. For an interesting defense, see Ceballos Teresi, *Política y económia,* pp. 343–64.

46. A partial listing of these programs is contained in Pemartín *Los valores,* pp. 291–92.

47. *Diario de las Sesiones* 18 May 1934, p. 2952. See also Calvo Sotelo, "Orientaciones," pp. 324–25.

48. The statistics are Indalecio Prieto's and were given by him in a Cortes debate with Calvo Sotelo; *Diario de las Sesiones,* 18 May 1934, p. 2973.

49. *Unión Patriótica,* 1 December 1926, p. 22.

50. Rist made similar visits to other southern and eastern European countries in the 1920s. The influence of British, French, and American bankers in such instances during this period generally is discussed by Richard Hemming Meyer, *Banker's Diplomacy* (New York and London: Columbia University Press, 1970).
51. *Diario de las Sesiones*, 23 May 1934, p. 3053.
52. Ceballos Teresi, *Historia económica* 7:428–29.
53. Velarde, *Politica económica*, pp. 128–29.
54. A detailed analysis of the conversion and its cost to the government is Benítez de Lugo, *Obra económica*, pp. 85–106.
55. Not surprisingly, consolidation was strongly praised by leading financiers, including Julián Cifuentes, director of the Hispanic American Bank; the marquis of Urquijo, the president of the Urquijo Bank; and Julio Collado, the director of the Central Bank; *Las Finanzas*, 7, no. 163 (1 February 1927): 5333.
56. *The Banker*, June 1928, pp. 474–75; and Sole Villalonga, *Le deuda pública*, pp. 54–57.
57. *Anuario estadístico 1934*, p. 536.
58. *Anuario estadístico 1928*, p. 385, and *Anuario estadístico 1931*, p. 419.
59. Calvo Sotelo, *Mis servicios*, pp. 465–71, describes various government-related credit operations in the period.
60. There are many peculiarities and irregularities in government budget and debt statistics for the period. Some of these are raised or discussed in Sole Villalonga, *La deuda española*, pp. 13–15; F. Edmond Tyng, Jr., "The Gold Standard for Spain?" *The Foreign Securities Investor* 11, no. 13 (9 June 1926): 4; and Benítez de Lugo, *Obra económica*, pp. 9–53.
61. Ildefonso Cuesta Garrigós, "Los grandes bancos españoles: Su evolución (1922–1943)," *Moneda y Crédito* 11 (December 1944): 49. The six were the Central Bank, the Hispanic and American Bank, the Spanish Credit Bank, the Bank of Bilbao, the Bank of Vizcaya, and the Urquijo Bank. See also Banco Urquijo Servicio de Estudios en Barcelona, *Las fuentes de financiación de la empresa en España* (Madrid: Editorial Moneda y Crédito, 1968), p. 22.
62. Velarde, *Sobre la decadencia*, p. 148.
63. Cuesta Garrigós, "Los grandes bancos," pp. 50–51; and Muñoz, *El poder*, pp. 210–11 and 215–17.
64. Nadal, "Spain," p. 472.
65. Velarde, *Sobre la decadencia*, pp. 191–93.
66. *The Banker*, June 1928, p. 462.
67. Rubio, *Crónica*, p. 134.
68. Typifying this optimism is Tyng, "The Gold Standard."
69. Antonio Bermúdez Canete, "Los presupuestos de la estabilización," *Revista Nacional de Economía* 31, nos. 93–94 (September–December 1930): 146.
70. Sarda, *La intervención*, p. 9. Much of this was thought to be French, Dutch, and Swiss.
71. Calvo Sotelo, *Mis servicios*, pp. 271–328, describes the government's interest in restoring the gold standard as well as its response to the fluctuations in the peseta during the period. The financial community was less sanguine and more realistic in its appraisal of the peseta's rise. See, for example, *Las Finanzas*, 25 January 1927, p. 5330 and 8 March 1927, p. 2. For a retrospective view see *Las Finanzas*, 25 February 1930, pp. 179–83. Exporters, especially of wine and minerals, were not pleased by the stronger peseta; see, for example, AHN Leg. 44, Exte. 7985, and AHN Leg 45, Exte. 8025.
72. The declining availability of capital for currency speculation in Europe is placed in a wider international context by Charles P. Kindleberger, *The World in Depression 1929–1939* (Berkeley and Los Angeles: University of California Press, 1973), pp. 65–76. On the peseta's fall itself, see Fernando Eguidazu, "La crisis de la peseta y la caída de la dictadura," *Economía politíca de la dictadura de Primo de Rivera, Cuadernos económicos de I.C.E.*, ed. Carlos Velasco Murviedro, 10 (1979): 299–352.
73. Prior to launching his boycott, Deterding traveled to Spain to meet with the dic-

tator. Accustomed to respect, even from the heads of government, the oil magnate had to wait three hours in Primo's outer office before the dictator received him; Jellinek, *The Civil War,* p. 80.

74. Bermúdez Canete, "Los presupuestos," p. 492.
75. Ibid., p. 491.
76. Nadal, "Spain," p. 477.
77. The peseta crisis provoked perhaps as much controversy as any other issue during the dictatorship; see AHN Leg. 48, Exte. 9173, and AHN Leg. 47, Exte. 8703.
78. Antonio Flores de Lemus, "Dictamen de la Comisión Nombrada pro Real Orden de 9 enero de 1929, para el estudio de la implantación del patrón oro," in *Lecturas,* ed. Velarde, pp. 497–516. The economic ignorance of Primo is also evinced in Maura Gamazo, *Bosquejo* 2:188–90 and 186–97. Calvo Sotelo gave an interview a few days before resigning, during which he admitted that he had little idea why the peseta had been under such downward pressure. In response to the question "How do you explain the change in the exchange rate?" he answered, "We are undoubtedly dealing with a case of financial madness. The phenomenon is so anomalous, so absurd, that it will not be much longer until it dissipates." The quotation is from Ceballos Teresi, *Historia económica* 7:148–49.
79. Bermúdez Canete, "Los presupuestos," pp. 496–97, and Benítez de Lugo, *Obra económica,* pp. 107–49.
80. Although relying on foreign capital for this particular purpose, Calvo Sotelo continued to assure Spanish bankers of his commitment to domestic capital for supporting the work of the government; Calvo Sotelo, "Orientaciones," p. 326.
81. Bermúdez Canete, "Los presupuestos," p. 490, and Sarda, *La intervención,* pp. 8–11, describe the organization and operation of the committee.
82. Bermúdez Canete, "Los presupuestos," p. 490.
83. Leftist critics of the regime charged that, after profiting from the dictatorship's financial profligacy, the large banks also sought to detach themselves from its ensuing downfall by large purchases of foreign currency; *Hojas Libres,* July 1928, p. 62.
84. It is difficult to arrive at a cost figure for an undertaking with such complicated financing and so many separate operations. With the conclusion of the intervention, the government floated a 300-million ptas. interior loan to redeem its short-term overseas obligations. How much of this can be regarded as outright loss is not clear. In 1934, Prieto calculated the total cost as 72,469,438 ptas. but offered little indication how he arrived at that sum; *Diario de las Sesiones,* 24 May 1934, p. 3061. Other aspects of this question are developed by Tamames, *Estructura,* pp. 543–44, and Sarda, *La intervención,* pp. 9–10. The regime's resulting fiscal straits are evident in Primo's appeal for funds to the president of the Guipuzcoa provincial deputation in December 1929; AHN Leg. 51, Exte. 10429.
85. Díaz-Plaja, *De la dictadura,* pp. 158–59, and Maura Gamazo, *Bosquejo* 2:274–75.
86. For an indication of the extent to which the banking community turned against Primo, see *Las Finanzas* 10, no. 373 (28 January 1930): 80–81. On Calvo Sotelo's selection as Central Bank president, see *Las Finanzas,* 10, no. 377 (25 February 1930): 188.

6
Transportation and Energy

Transportation and energy were increasingly important parts of the dictatorship's modernization program. The regime saw improved efficiency in transportation and energy subsectors, achieved through government sponsored oligopoly, as removing a major economic bottleneck. It also looked to infrastructure investment in these areas as a motor for growth. Support for public-works spending had been present since the first days of the regime and was particularly pronounced among banking and industrial elites.[1] As seen, however, funding these programs was difficult. Worse, basic flaws in conception and execution undermined both transportation and energy programs.

Transportation

Railroads were one of the most controversial economic issues inherited from the constitutional regime.[2] Spain's poor, thinly spread population did not generate the concentrated demand needed to maintain rail profits. The First World War's demands on the system forced most companies to choose between maintenance of equipment and of dividend schedules. Vitally dependent on keeping their credit lines open, they opted for the latter. With many companies on the verge of collapse, the government stepped in with a series of politically unpopular rate increases and cash advances. Stopgap measures, however, were not enough to put the railroads on a stable footing.

Primo handled this problem by asking General Mayandia, an army engineer and member of the directory, to put the development ministry to work on comprehensive legislation. The ministry proposed a far-reaching consolidation, reducing Spain's nearly eighty rail companies to three or four large operations, each emanating in a different direction from Madrid. This reorganization presumed a substantial, permanent increase in government regulation. It also flew in the face of the banking community's public and private recommendations.³ The large banks had a considerable stake in the rail companies, and they joined with them in urging a counter program of still higher rates and more state support for new equipment purchases.⁴

Primo retreated in the face of this opposition. Rather than decree policy, he included the rail companies in decision making. He organized the Superior Railroad Council (Consejo Superior de Ferrocarriles) as the government's main advisory body. It was composed primarily of rail-company representatives and also included spokesmen for rail customers and employees. Primo envisioned advisory and administrative functions for the council. Its first project was to draw up a program to replace the regime's aborted plan.

The 1924 Railroad Statute that resulted was composed eclectically from several reforms proposed during the last years of the constitutional regime.⁵ It declared that the railroads themselves were responsible for their day-to-day operating expenses, and conceded that they should be permitted to raise their fares to achieve that objective. Capital improvements, on the other hand, were generally the state's responsibility. In order to finance the latter a special Railway Funding Agency (Caja Ferroviaria del Estado) was established with authority to issue bonds.

The council united the rail companies and the government in a close working relationship, cemented together by the financial resources of the agency. Within this framework the regime showed a predilection toward the larger companies at the expense of the smaller. After the fall of the dictatorship, Guadalhorce declared that the regime never relinquished its original goal of consolidating the country's many small railroads into several large concerns. In any event, it is clear that the large lines received disproportionate aid. Of the 746,647,087 pesetas granted by 31 December 1929 for improvements in fixed and moving stock, nearly 98% of that amount went to the four largest companies:

North	297,263,691 ptas.⁶
Madrid, Zaragoza, Alicante	294,453,597 "
Andalusia and South of Spain	79,253,896 "
Western National	50,632,291 "

The larger companies also had disproportionately greater representation on the council and were especially dominant on its executive committee.⁷ They used their positions to take over many smaller railroads and to eliminate competitive lines.

The state's role in rail matters increased. The country's poverty precluded fulfillment of the statute's pledge of significantly higher fares. As the rail lines were unable to meet their operating expenses through passenger fare and freight revenues, they had little choice except increased dependence on the agency. Indeed, the agency represented an important step toward pooling the finances of the companies. In theory, a share of the more profitable companies' income funded the losses and investment needs of less profitable lines. In fact, little revenue was shared, and the agency drew most of its capital from its government-guaranteed bonds. While total agency revenue for 1926–29 was 1,516,898,000 pesetas, 99.4% of that amount was derived from either the agency's bonds, loans, the Exchange Intervention Committee, or outright government grants.[8]

Ties between the government and the companies grew tighter with establishment of the General Office of Railroads and Tramways in December 1925 as the coordinating link between the Superior Railway Council and the development ministry. On paper this step usurped much of the council's autonomy, making it a corporative adjunct of the national administration. In practice, however, the companies continued in many ways as the tail wagging the dog. In 1922 they had been in serious financial straits. But with the dictatorship's generous assistance many reversed their situation dramatically.

Improved cash flow provided for better service and the extension of rail transport to new areas.[9] In 1925 the council announced a long-term project for 9,000 kilometers of "urgent" construction, providing connections between existing lines. Progress was slow, with wide gauge track increasing from 11,319 kilometers in 1923 to 11,770 kilometers in 1929.[10] During the same period, narrow gauge track went from 4,916 kilometers to 5,246 kilometers. New construction, though limited, nonetheless provided opportunities for corruption. In at least one instance large sums were expended to obtain high profit guarantees from the government, with Primo and Alfonso themselves implicated as payoff recipients.[11] New track replaced much worn track during the dictatorship. Other improvements included electrification of key lines in the Cantabric Mountains and the Canfranc tunnel, which allowed more direct service with Paris.[12] As the government anticipated, construction and investment in equipment stimulated the economy, particularly steel production.

These benefits did not come cheaply. Their cost by major categories from 1926 through 1929 was:

Service Improvements	747,000,000 ptas.[13]
New Construction	512,000,000 "

Operating Grants	23,300,000	"
Subsidies and Advances	79,000,000	"
Takeovers	22,100,000	"
Superior Railroad Council Administration	5,100,000	"
Debt Service Charge	123,700,000	"
Total	1,512,200,000	ptas.

This sum was approximately equal to 11% of the state's regular budget during the period. Even an investment of this magnitude was not enough to put the railroads on a sound basis. If the original problem had been that the country was too poor to generate the traffic needed to support them, the dictatorship may even have exacerbated matters. Its development program contributed to economic expansion and increased rail traffic. But if the boom was ephemeral, the increase in the railroad's physical plant was not. Consequently, if the country was unable to support the system in 1923, the regime scarcely helped by increasing its size and cost by 1929. The rosy profits and dividends of the period were, in effect, regressive transfer payments benefiting a small group of stockholders and financial institutions. Especially well placed to profit were large banks as simultaneously holders of agency bonds and creditors and stockholders of the rail companies themselves. So costly a program was not sustainable indefinitely. The credit squeeze that began with the peseta's international decline precipitated a fall in railroad share prices and produced a renewed awareness by 1929 of the railroads' structural weaknesses.[14]

Shipping reveals a similar situation. Spain's limited production and purchasing capacities restricted shipping volume. But by the early

Steel-Production Indices

Year	Commercial steel, beams, and metal plate	Steel Rail
1913	100	100
1922	67	45
1923	92	71
1924	115	110
1925	125	150
1926	119	110
1927	136	159
1928	167	210
1929	199	177

SOURCE: José Luis Escario, "Política de obras públicas," *Economía Española*, 1, no. 5 (1933): 20.

Rail Company Dividend Totals

Year	North	Madrid, Zaragoza, Alicante	Central of Aragon
1922	12,384,000 ptas.	10,932,636 ptas.	2,802,833 ptas.
1923	12,384,000 "	10,934,132 "	2,907,744 "
1924	14,706,000 "	10,934,132 "	3,188,833 "
1925	14,706,000 "	13,916,168 "	3,756,085 "
1926	14,770,000 "	14,064,611 "	3,634,688 "
1927	14,706,000 "	14,164,500 "	4,011,409 "
1928	14,706,000 "	10,932,636 "	4,582,841 "
1929	14,706,000 "	14,164,500 "	4,651,704 "

SOURCE: *Anuario estadístico 1930*, pp. 287–88.

Rail Service Indicators

Year	Stations	Locomotives	Box Cars	Flatbed Cars	Employees	Tonnage (000)
1922	2,287	3,184	28,327	36,964	97,519	39,910
1923	2,300	3,220	29,980	37,786	101,327	35,848
1924	2,310	3,238	29,762	37,466	101,611	43,303
1925	2,315	3,325	31,639	38,121	103,737	41,489
1926	2,329	3,333	31,691	37,992	117,222	41,870
1927	2,328	3,519	33,772	39,020	114,509	45,659
1928	2,386	3,645	36,019	41,654	116,357	49,441
1929	2,345	3,585	34,815	40,972	115,829	49,136

SOURCE: Tonnage figures are from INE, *Principales actividades,* p. 101. The remaining statistics are from Ceballos Teresi, *Historia económica* 7: 374–75.

twentieth century, foreign exchange and international prestige considerations had led the state to support national carriers. That support enhanced interest in shipping among large financial institutions. Those institutions, in turn, served as catalysts for vertical and horizontal concentration of that sector.[15]

When Primo took power, shipping still had not recovered from the postwar slump, and the major companies lost little time in ingratiating themselves with the new regime. The Transatlantic Company—closely associated with Barcelona banks, shipbuilders, and Asturian and Rif mineowners—contributed 25,000 pesetas to a national tribute to Primo, 57,000 pesetas for patriotic centers in Madrid and Barcelona, more than 40,000 pesetas to the Somatén of Barcelona and Cadiz, over 53,000 pesetas for improvements in various royal palaces, in excess of 4,000 pesetas for its employees to travel to Madrid for a tribute to the royal family, and 1,000 pesetas for a tribute to General Barrera.[16] The company's largesse was not in vain. From 1924 through 1929 it received nearly 188 million pesetas in passenger-traffic subsidies alone.[17] Among other large carriers to benefit from the dictatorship's lavish and controversial subsidies were Sota y Aznar and Juan March's Transmediterranean.[18] However, what the country gained from these expenditures is questionable. From 1923 to 1930 the percentage of imports carried in Spanish ships increased slowly from 25% to 33%, still below pre–World War I levels and well below the wartime peak of 83%.[19] The percentage of exports carried in Spanish ships actually decreased from 26% to 24% from 1923 to 1930.

The dictatorship's highway program had similarly mixed results. Cars and trucks demonstrated during the First World War that they were no longer toys. After the war it was evident that highways could tie the country together economically and open it up to foreign tourism. But the constitutional regime had done little in this area. The only significant strides were made by the Catalan *mancomunidad,* the Basque provinces, and Navarra.[20] A modern highway system was one of the dictatorship's earliest goals.[21] Primo declared early in 1924 that the time had long since passed for Spanish highways to become something more than sheep and cow paths.[22]

Nonetheless, the directory limited itself to fulfilling the promises of the constitutional regime. In April 1924 it announced a three-year program of matching subsidies for repairs undertaken by local authorities.[23] The dictatorship provided 29 million out of 147 million pesetas spent in this way. In 1924, 898 kilometers of local roads were built. Although this total was almost as much as in 1922 and 1923 combined and nearly 60% of the total for 1920 through 1923, it was only a modest beginning.[24] Railroads and shipping pressed their case with the government as powerful established interests. But, apart from the large banks' limited stake in the cement industry, the groups with much to gain from highway construction were relatively new and weak.[25]

For Guadalhorce and Calvo Sotelo, however, highways were a needed infrastructure investment capable of stimulating economic growth.[26] In February 1926, soon after their appointment to the civil government, the dictatorship established a National Highway Authority (Patronato del Circuito Nacional de Firmes Especiales) to oversee construction and maintenance of 7,000 kilometers of reinforced concrete roads.[27] This system consisted of fourteen interconnecting roads. At its heart was Madrid, with major arteries leading north and east from the capital. Important routes were also located along the northern, eastern, and southern coasts. These roads led from the French border to sea resorts to encourage tourism. Relatedly, the regime restored historical sites, sponsored local folklore festivals, and hosted two international expositions.[28]

The civil government invested 455.8 million of an originally profected 600 million pesetas in its highway program.[29] Since that expenditure was beyond what could be provided routinely from tax revenues, the regime resorted to debt emissions as part of its extraordinary budget. As with the Railway Funding Agency, the government looked to several sources to pay the service charge on the debt. These included 14 million pesetas from the national budget, 4 million from provincial and municipal governments, and 20 million from license taxes.[30]

The dictatorship also announced prizes for the town councils that most distinguished themselves in road repairs. New legislation encouraged provincial governments to band together for this purpose. A loan of 255 million pesetas in May 1928 underwrote the efforts of 38 provinces to improve old roads and build new highways.[31] During the dictatorship an annual average of 1,576 kilometers of highway were constructed, producing a total of 77,418 by 1929.[32] Of equal importance to new highway construction were improvements in existing roads. Unfortunately, no reliable statistics have been tabulated here. There seems little question, however, that the dictatorship's highway program contributed to the national increase in cement consumption from 431,881 tons in 1923 to 1,773,946 tons in 1929.[33]

Less positively, the highway program had a negative, if unavoidable, effect on the railroads. Major road construction took place between Madrid and Barcelona and between each of those cities and France. These routes had previously been among the railroads' most lucrative, and the loss of revenue hurt them. There is another problem of cost effectiveness. Highways are a state responsibility. Nonetheless, the scope of the dictatorship's program might have been imprudent. As with the railroads, the dictatorship's investments in highways contributed to a short economic boom. But that spurt was not self-sustaining. High debt and maintenance charges placed a continuing burden on government finances that worked against long-term economic growth. In subsequent decades the state had difficulty even maintaining Primo's highways, as is attested by the nostalgia of foreign travelers for the dictatorship's road system.[34]

Energy

The dictatorship's energy programs suffered from similar defects and were only somewhat more successful. The regime was particularly concerned with electric power. In 1923 there was a general consensus about that sector's needs.[35] First, the vicious circle of high costs and low consumption had to be broken. Second, any solution to this problem should be compatible with the welfare of the coal industry, which was suffering from analogous problems. Third, a uniform, integrated electric grid should be constructed out of the patchwork quilt of small, inefficient units dotting the country. In dealing with these problems, the dictatorship benefited from the prosperity of the mid and late 1920s, which kept money flowing throughout the economy. There were also a host of new domestic and industrial applications for electricity.

As with the railroads, the electric companies did not receive the regime's initial actions well. The Municipal Statute in March 1924 granted limited power over rate changes to local government. An April decree further limited the ability of companies to make rate changes. Previously, utilities used rate reductions to encourage conversions to electricity. To the displeasure of consumers, these reductions were generally quickly followed by upward revisions. The dictatorship's restrictions on rate changes ended this abuse, but were widely criticized by the industry.

Again, however, as with the railroads, the regime quickly decided that it was better to work with, rather than against, the power companies. In short order it enacted an expanded version of the 1917 industrial aid law and other beneficial legislation.[36] In April 1925 the state agreed to pay half of the construction costs incurred by the Guadalquivir Canal and Power Company (Sociedad Canaliza y Fuerza Guadalquivir). This company had been established the year before to develop the hydroelectric and irrigation potential of the Guadalquivir River. In addition to that outright grant, the dictatorship offered an advance of 40% on the company's remaining expenses. In August 1926 similar aid was extended to the Hispano-Portuguese Electric Company (Sociedad Hispana—Portuguesa de Transportes Eléctricos) to develop hydroelectric power on the Duero River. Among the other companies to benefit from such agreements were Iberian Electrical Metallurgy (Electro Metalúrgica Ibérica) on the Alberche River and the Spanish Explosives Company (Unión Española de Explosivos) on the Carrión River.

These arrangements were enormously lucrative and virtually assured the companies involved of quick, high profits with minimal initial capital outlay. With so much money involved, rumors soon circulated of bribes, kickbacks, and other illegal activities involving high officials of the regime.[37] Head of the company developing the Alberche River project was Primo's minister of war, the duke of Tetuan. According to *Hojas Libres,* that company had been founded, "like so many others, void of capital and full of appetites, a device designed to devour millions."[38] It received large state subsidies despite expert technical opinion that its industrial benefit could never compensate for its high cost.

About the same time, an Urquijo-backed hydroelectric company ran into financial difficulties only to be bailed out by large government handouts.[39] One of the directors of the Guadalquivir company was Guadalhorce himself.

Matters were no better with the hydrographic confederations, the dictatorship's greatest stimulus to electric-power development. Shortly after being named development minister, Guadalhorce called on Manuel Lorenzo Pardo, a leading civil engineer, to draft a comprehensive plan for hydraulic development. Lorenzo Pardo worked on this project in January and February of 1926 with Guadalhorce and other members of the cabinet. The result was the March 1926 decree establishing the Ebro Hydrographic Confederation. Electrical power, irrigation, and improved river transport were major purposes of this legislation. Reforestation and soil erosion projects were secondary considerations. This coordinated approach to the problems of a river system was similar to the Tennessee Valley Authority in the United States. In each case a quasi-governmental agency was created to pool public and private resources. Similar legislation was passed in August 1926 for the Segura River, in June 1927 for the Duero River, and in September 1927 for the Guadalquivir River. A comprehensive act for all hydraulic confederations was adopted in May 1928.

This legislation gave representation to all those affected by the development of a particular river system, from farmers to towns concerned about their water supply to manufacturers wishing cheaper electricity. On the twin assumption that these interests had the best understanding of their area's needs and the most to gain from its development, much of the planning and cost was made their responsibility. In practice, however, the hydrographic confederation's potential for grass-roots democracy and initiative was undermined by the dictatorship's top-heavy bureaucracy and the ability of local elites to place themselves in charge of the confederation's administration.[40] High-priced, noncompetitive contracts and well-paid sinecures charcterized the program.

The regime defined its role as filling the gap between local resources and the requirements of the plan. The government sought maximum return for a minimum expenditure, preferring to guarantee loan issues of the confederation rather than extend outright grants. In the period 1926–27 the state contributed 52,500,000 pesetas directly to the Ebro confederation, while guaranteeing another 125,000,000 pesetas in bonds. This program contributed to an increase in national electrical production from 701 million kilowatt hours in 1923 to 1,096 million kilowatt hours in 1929.[41]

The dictatorship made several attempts to improve coordination of electrical production. In April 1926 it called a meeting of industry representatives to discuss planning between energy suppliers and consumers. Present at this gathering were the Permanent Spanish Electrical Commission, the Association of Producers and Distributors of Electricity, the Spanish Coal Consortium, and the Society of Industrial Assemblers. Their conflicting needs and ideas, however, provided little basis for government action. In April 1928 the government renewed its call for suggestions. This time it entrusted policy formulation to its own General Office of Commerce, Industry, and Insurance. Little emerged from this body due to the same welter of interests that had frustrated action in 1926.

In April 1929, however, the regime offered any organization representing 70% of electric-power production in the country legal standing as an "official chamber" *(camara oficial)* of the government with advisory powers on matters affecting hydroelectric production and related industries. The government also offered special concessions for connecting links between existing systems.[42] The beneficiary of the legislation was the Association of Producers and Distributors of Electricity, the industry's largest trade organization, dominated by hydropowered producers. In return for the advantages gained from membership, the producers committed themselves to the eventual integration of the industry.

Given the economies of scale involved in electrical production, the dictatorship's reliance on large producers had a clear rationale and did not go unrewarded. While energy output increased 134% from 1922 through 1929, transmission losses increased only 80%.[43] But the favoritism and catering to special interests that characterized the regime's programs here was not always consistent with maximum productivity. At 15 centimos/kilowatt hour, the cost of electricity in 1929 was considerably in excess of Guadalhorce's goal of 6 centimos/kilowatt hour.[44]

The greater part of increased electrical production in the 1920s came from water power, not coal. Coal interests were also sacrificed to the dictatorship's enthusiasm for railroad electrification. Arguments of economic efficiency could be advanced for the regime's policies. Nonetheless striking is the strength of the hydroelectric companies' ties, and the corresponding weakness of the coal producers' ties, with the economic and financial elites close to the government.[45]

Coal, however, was too important to be altogether neglected. Traditional international payments problems and Primo's economic nationalism inclined the government to substitute domestic output for imports. But, though abundant, Spain's coal was low grade.[46] Geological difficulties made it expensive to extract. Mining's fragmentation into a number of small companies, many only working marginal deposits, further raised coal's cost.

The directory temporized over these problems by naming several study commissions in 1924 and 1925.[47] With impetus from Guadalhorce, the civil government quickly followed the path laid by the regime's other transportation and energy programs. In January 1926 the government appointed the National Council for Combustible Fuels (Consejo Nacional de Combustible), composed primarily of coal and oil representatives, with lesser numbers of representatives from consuming interests, the military, and fuel-industry workers. Subsequent legislation, climaxing with the Coal Statute in August 1927, gave the council broad powers.

One of the council's responsibilities was ensuring industry compliance with its revamped guidelines for domestic coal consumption.[48] Railroads, for example, were required to use 85% Spanish coal on their express trains and 90% on all others. Steel and other metallurgical operations were required to use 50%, and in some cases all, domestically produced coal. The level for textile, sugar, cement, thermal electricity, and most other industrial plants was 80%. The council was also to see that less-productive coal fields were abandoned for those with higher yields. Helping it perform these functions was a central sales office established in 1926 as the intermediary for all transactions between producers and consumers. Still more important was creation of a bond-issuing Combustible Fuel Funding Agency (Caja Combustible del Estado) as a source of short-term operating and long-term investment capital.

These efforts brought mixed results.[49] Large coal producers grew at the expense of small, reflecting the dictatorship's propensity to identify the well-being of the economy as a whole with that of its dominant interests. On the other hand, because high-priced coal was inconsistent with the interests of many other economic sectors and a bottleneck to economic development generally, the dictatorship was content to let the price of that commodity fall 12% from 1927 to 1929, reaching the lowest level since World War I.[50] That price drop derived more from the end of the British coal strike and from the operators' ability to impose, with government backing, increased work loads with lower wages on its labor force than it did from increased mining efficiency. Indeed, from the beginning a basic problem with the dictatorship's coal program was that its encouragement of monopolistic trends militated against the competition needed for increased productivity.[51]

Coal's problems were, in part, those of a subsector without strong connections with other economic elites. How influential those elites, especially in high finance, could be with the government was evident in CAMPSA, the national oil monopoly and the dictatorship's most enduring legacy. Spain has no significant oil reserves, and until 1927 distribution of petroleum products there was dominated by Shell and Standard interests. As noted, those companies' profits made them an irresistible nationalization target for the financially pressed dictatorship. CAMPSA, however, was not established as a simple state monopoly, but as a quasi-public corporation.[52] The state retained shares worth only 45 million out of an initial capitalization of 195 million pesetas. The rest was subscribed by a large banking consortium and Sabadell y Henry, an independent refiner.[53] Although the state reserved a place in CAMPSA's management, effective control remained with the large bankers. Calvo Sotelo wished CAMPSA to invest in new exploration and refining and transport capacity. The bankers, however, opted for immediate maximization of profits, the course followed for most of CAMPSA's history since then. With 261.4 million pesetas from CAMPSA from 1928 through 1929, the state's share in these profits was clear. But no less clear was the fact that, despite the government's increased revenue, it had handed the greater part of the management and the profits from the new monopoly over to a small group of financiers.[54]

This course fit the pattern of the dictatorship's other transportation and energy initiatives. Infrastructure investment was important to modernization and was intended to pay for itself ultimately through greater economic growth. Nonetheless, the dictatorship gave disproportionate support to interests tied to the existing structure of privilege. Policies of this sort further distorted an already top-heavy economy. Certainly there was a logic in reducing redundancies and increasing economies of scale in transportation and energy. But reliance on government-sponsored concentration for these purposes rather than an acceleration of competitive pressures promoted short-term profits more than the improved productivity needed for better living standards and lasting growth.

NOTES

1. For banker support for development programs using Spanish capital, see chap. 5. For the 1924 proposal of the Federation of National Industry (Federación de Industrias Nacionales), see Aguilar, "La actividad," p. 93. Grass-roots support for extensive construction projects is evident in a 1924 Badajoz province petition; see AHN Leg. 1, Exte. 152.

2. On the origins of the railroads' problems, see Nadal, "The Failure," pp. 549–53.

For their situation at the beginning of the dictatorship, see Canals, *La cuestión ferroviaria,* and *Las Finanzas* 3, no. 96 (30 October 1923): 1465–66.

3. For a private 3 October 1923 letter from leading bank directors to Primo, see AHN Leg. 318, Exte. 3518 (13 June 1924). For the editorial opinion of a prominent banking publication, see *Las Finanzas* 3, no. 94 (16 October 1923): 1423–35.

4. Bankers were more heavily represented on the boards of directors of rail companies in 1921 than they were on the boards of all other economic sectors except electrical power and mining companies; Roldan et al., *La formación* 2:250–51. For more on the linkage between banks and the railroads, see Velarde, *Sobre la decadencia,* pp. 284–86, and Tuñón de Lara, *La España* 1:87.

5. The text of the statute is contained in Ceballos Teresi, *Historia económica* 5:244–82.

6. These statistics are from a press release issued on 25 March 1930 by Leopoldo Matos Massieu, the finance minister for the Berenguer government. They are quoted in ibid., p. 227. See Machimbarrena, "La mejora," p. 261, for more on this point.

7. Velarde, *Política económica,* pp. 75–76.

8. Ceballos Teresi, *Historia económica* 7:233.

9. Wais San Martín, *Historia general,* pp. 336–38.

10. INE, *Principales actividades,* p. 100.

11. See the Santander-Mediterranean Company's concession to build a rail line from Ontaneda to Calatayud; Ortega, *España encadenada,* pp. 298–300; AHN Leg. 47, Exte. 8637 (3 January 1928), and Leg. 492 (18 October 1924); and *Hojas Libres,* April 1927, pp. 46–47.

12. Oliveros, *Asturias,* pp. 248–49, and Machimbarrena, "La mejora," p. 260.

13. Ceballos Teresi, *Historia económica* 7:232.

14. On the fall of the railroad share prices and rumors of an impending change in government policy during the dictatorship's last days, see AHN Leg. 51, Exte. 10465 (28 January 1930). A major fear in railroad circles in 1929 was that the regime would enact a new railroad statute limiting state subsidies and placing the companies under greater government control; Iglesias, *Política de la dictadura,* pp. 70–71.

15. Roldan, *La formación* 2:54–60 and 251. For general background on shipping, see Pedro Gual Villabi, *Curso de política económica contemporanea: Libro 3: Política del comercio y de los transportes* (Barcelona: Juventud, 1950), pp. 790–97.

16. Ramos Oliveira, *El capitalismo,* pp. 90–91.

17. Ibid., p. 89. See also *Hojas Libres,* November 1927, pp. 11–12.

18. It is possible that the Transmediterranean might also have benefited from the king's holding 3,000 of its shares; Ortega, *España encadenada,* p. 301. The close ties between the regime and the shipping companies were attacked especially strongly in ibid., pp. 238–40. One of the first critics of the dictatorship's shipping policies was the marquis of Cortina; Ramos Oliveira, *El capitalismo,* p. 86. On the company's soliciting favors from the dictatorship, see AHN Leg. 34, Exte. 2128.

19. Ceballos Teresi, *Historia económica* 7:370–73.

20. It is true, however, that the 1922–23 budget provided for 25% of the cost of local road repairs. The dictatorship extended this legislation and used it as the basis of its own April 1924 legislation; García-Nieto et al., *La dictadura,* p. 246.

21. On 20 September 1923 the directory ordered "the General Office of Public Works [to] study and prepare a plan for the distribution of funds for the construction and repair of highways, with attention to the need for fleshing out the national and poorest means of communication"; las Heras, *Auxiliar,* p. 62.

22. Maura Gamazo, *Bosquejo* 1:154.

23. García-Nieto et al., *La dictadura,* pp. 246–47. For the local impact of this program, see Valverde, *Memorias,* p. 33.

24. These statistics are from Calvo Sotelo, *Mis servicios,* p. 456.

25. Roldan et al., *La formación* 2:250.

26. The growth in this need is evident in an increase from 37,169 to 111,765 in licensed moter vehicles between 1923 and 1926; *Anuario estadístico: 1928,* p. 493.

27. Pemartín, *Los valores,* pp. 289–99. For detailed information on the National Highway Authority, see AHN Leg. 48, Exte. 9218.
28. Ceballos Teresi, *Historia económica* 7:383.
29. Calvo Sotelo, *Mis servicios,* pp. 445–46.
30. Velarde, *Política económica,* p. 54.
31. Ibid., p. 56, and Pemartín, *Los valores,* p. 302.
32. Ceballos Teresi,*Historia económica* 7:383.
33. José Luis Escario, "Política de obras públicas," pp. 20–21.
34. For a less sanguine contemporary assessment of the regime's achievement, see Percy F. Martin, "Roads of Spain," *Roads and Road Construction* 8, no. 79 (1 July 1929): 275–76.
35. Sintes Olives and Vidal Burdils, *La industria eléctrica,* pp. 445–62.
36. Ibid., pp. 499–548, contains the text of this legislation.
37. See, for example, *Las Finanzas* 10, no. 377 (18 February 1930): 153.
38. *Hojas Libres,* April 1927, pp. 47–49, and June 1928, pp. 65–70.
39. Ibid., May 1927, pp. 65–66.
40. Velarde, *Política económica,* pp. 27–43; Maura Gamazo, *Bosquejo* 1:183–84; *Las Finanzas* 10, no. 378 (4 March 1930): 209; and *Hojas Libres,* November 1927, pp. 7–10.
41. INE, *Principales actividades,* p. 84.
42. Sintes Olives and Vidal Burdils, *La industria eléctrica,* pp. 420–23.
43. INE, *Principales actividades,* pp. 84–85.
44. The actual cost of electricity is from Serrano, "La racionalización," p. 8, and Guadalhorce is quoted to this effect in Ceballos Teresi, *Historia económica* 7:18. For a less positive view of the dictatorship's electricity "mania," see L. Sánchez Cuervo, "El problema de la energía elétrica en España," *Revista de Obras Públicas* 74, no. 2463 (15 October 1926): 450–53, and 74, no. 2466 (1 December 1926): 510–14.
45. Roldan et al., *La formación* 2:250–51. The weakness of ties between coal producers and government was relative, not absolute. Among the prominent financiers with stakes in coal were Victor Falgueroso González, Claudio López Brú, Elías Masavéu Rivell, José María San Martín, and the count of the Gaitanes, José Luis Ussía Cubas. For more on this point, see David Ruiz González, *El movimiento obrero en Asturias* (Oviedo: Amigos de Asturias, 1928), pp. 163 and 166.
46. On the abundance of coal, see Moore, *Economic Demography,* p. 279. On the problems of that sector, see Antonio de Miguel, *El potencial económico de España* (Madrid: Gráfica Admisistrativa, 1935), pp. 162–63.
47. For the dictatorship's coal policies, see Pemartín, *Los valores,* pp. 250 and 256–257, and Ceballos Teresi, *Historia económica* 5:383–84 and 496–504.
48. Velarde, *La política económica,* p. 97. The original guidelines for compulsory domestic coal consumption date from October 1921 and were made more extensive in December 1923. After February 1926 the guidelines were loosened only to be reimposed in April 1927 with the exemptions cited.
49. On the impact of the regime's policies, see Antonio L. Oliveros, *Asturias en el resurgimiento español* (Madrid: Juan Bravo, 1935), pp. 247–48.
50. INE, *Principales actividades,* p. 146. In contrast to the regime's solicitude for other transportation and energy subsectors, subsidies to coal producers were actually cut 10 million ptas. over the same two-year period; Pemartín, *Los valores,* pp. 256–57.
51. *Las Finanzas* 7, no. 267 (1 March 1927): 5428.
52. Calvo Sotelo, *Mis servicios,* pp. 193–229, is a detailed account by the minister most deeply involved in the establishment of CAMPSA.
53. Particularly prominent in the consortium were the Hispanic American, Urquijo, Biscay, Spanish Credit, Arnus, and Central banks; Ceballos Teresi, *Historia económica* 6:291–92.
54. May 1934 Cortes debate over Primo's fiscal record produced repeated accusations of corruption in CAMPSA and of the dictatorship's failure to receive sufficient revenue from the monopoly; *Diario de las Sesiones,* 18 May 1934, p. 2971; 22 May 1934, pp. 3008–9; and 23 May 1924, p. 3054.

7

Industry, Agriculture, and the Dictatorship's Economc Legacy

Primo devoted considerable attention to industry and agriculture in his effort to increase national wealth. Uncertain about how to translate his aspirations into concrete programs, he relied on large producers for help.[1] Many producers benefited in the short term. However, those gains were neither evenly distributed nor always in the long-term interest of the economy as a whole.

Industry

The dictatorship's commitment to industrial development was evident in comprehensive legislation in 1924 and 1927. These laws provided subsidies, production bonuses, and tax exemptions for expansion and modernization. The dictatorship extended the Industrial Credit Bank's funding and lending authority. The government also increased its patronage of Spanish manufacturers and used high tariffs and other measures to encourage the country's producers to rely more on each other.

However, Primo quickly absorbed the fears of manufacturers haunted by the postwar recession.[2] Every measure he undertook for increased production was accompanied by legislation guarding against surpluses. Economic corporativism was his primary defense against overproduction. He organized special regulatory committees for one industry after another. These committees had antecedents in the bodies established by the constitutional regime to deal with the economic dislocations brought by World War I. Each committee was composed primarily of producer trade organization representatives.[3] Suppliers, customers, and organized labor were frequently represented in smaller numbers. Government officials and occasionally academic experts also took part. Each committee functioned as a government-sponsored cartel, assuring the profitability of its industry through production ceilings and price minimums. After October 1926 final authority in matters of plant expansion and relocation was entrusted to the Regulating Committee for Industrial Production (Comité Regulador de la Producción Nacional). This committee was also formed on a corporative basis. It was part of the National Economic Council, the dictatorship's principal advisory body on economic and trade matters.

Primo's own ingenuous statement on the council's founding suggests how vulnerable he was to influence from the interests represented in that body.

> When in the course of government matters, I had to intervene in international affairs, I suffered from the defects of action that result from acting almost alone. The difficulty of forming an opinion on such important matters . . . without having at hand all the advisers, statistics, information, and the facts, in sum, made me understand that in order to strengthen my weakness [in this area], I had to provide myself with an agency that I never believed would prove to be so perfect or that would bring together persons of such value and merit. On contemplating it now, a certain peace of mind returns to me and the uncertainties that had plagued me are dissipated. Now we can penetrate to the heart of the problem of commercial treaties. . . .[4]

Primo had denounced the old politicians as corrupt because of their close ties with manufacturers as well as financiers. The weight of large manufacturers in economic decision making, however, actually increased during the dictatorship. Under the constitutional regime producers exercised their influence informally and were counterbalanced by the landed classes. But the suspension of the Cortes, and especially the Senate, undercut the political strength of traditional nonindustrial elites. The dictatorship's corporative machinery, on the other hand, formally institutionalized the policy role of large manufacturers while largely bypassing their smaller competitors.

The advice Primo received from the National Economic Council contributed to his conviction that the nation's economic health was synonymous with that of its major producers. He had originally intended that the council accomplish in economics the decentralization and revival of citizen and interest-group initiative sought in his early political reforms. But what resulted was economic decision making concentrated in fewer hands and industry's increased dependence on government. The promptings of the industrial elite were reinforced by support from protectionist groups and even organized labor for government aid to business.⁵ Close ties between government and industry produced allegations of favoritism and corruption similar to those surrounding the regime's hydraulic program and its dealings with railroad, shipping, and banking elites.⁶ Money and cronyism were not the only avenues to the dictator's favor. A businessman who left the calling card of an attractive woman from Madrid's demimonde might also hope to benefit from Primo's gratitude.⁷

Protection, production controls, and expanded banking activity brought benefits to most manufacturing sectors. The long-term well-being of consumer-oriented Catalan industries might have depended on expanded purchasing power in the interior of Spain. Still, the influx of capital, decline of competition, and protection of the home market provided by the dictatorship mitigated some of the alienation engendered by the regime's hostility to Catalan regionalism.⁸ Basque heavy industry profited even more, due largely to Primo's public-works expenditures. By 1930 steel supplanted textiles as the second major industry after construction. If the regime accelerated a shifting balance form agriculture to industry, within the industrial sector the equilibrium was tilting from light to heavy production. That was an ironic outcome for a dictator whose own basic values remained rooted in an older, preindustrial society.

The regime was particularly successful in protecting manufacturers from overproduction and the decline in European prices in the period. From 1923 to 1930 the price index for imported goods declined 15.4% in Spain, despite the dictatorship's high tariffs.⁹ Nationally produced goods, however, actually increased a marginal 0.6% in the period. This evidence suggests the support that industrial profits received from a

Index of Common Share Quotations of Leading Spanish Manufacturers
(1914 = 100)

Manufacturer	1923	1926	1928
United Spanish Explosives (Unión *Española de Explosivos*), mining and chemicals	146.9	181.2	498.4
General Sugar (*General Azucarera*), food processing	184.0	217.0	309.6
Duro-Felguera Metallurgy (*Metalúrgica Duro-Felguera*), metallurgy and chemicals	121.7	114.6	167.0
Paper Products (*Papelera*), paper	128.5	153.1	259.8
Blast Furnaces (*Altos Hornos*), steel	33.4	40.9	57.2

SOURCE: Tuñón de Lara, *La España*, vol. 1, p. 171.

price policy that retarded the expansion of purchasing power, an approach attacked by the Catalan industrialist and politician Francesc Cambó.[10]

There was, then, a deep contradiction underlying the dictatorship's economic program. Artificial price floors contributed to high profits in the short term but eroded the incentives necessary for the regime's long-term goal of increased productivity. Another problem with the dictatorship's industrial program was its acceleration of the movement toward economic nationalism that had begun under the constitutional regime. The dictatorship relied on the National Economic Council, as the representative of producers, for foreign trade recommendations.[11] Since council members came from virtually every sector of the economy, they had conflicting interests.[12] Coal producers, for example, required substantial tariff protection, while the steel industry wanted greater access to cheap, high-grade British coal. For textile manufacturers the need was cheap foreign cotton, for cement manufacturers modern imported machinery, for food processors inexpensive tinplate, for shipping companies British ships, and for construction firms Portuguese wood. But in each of these, and virtually every other industry, individual companies had more to lose from a reduction in the duties protecting their particular products than they had to gain from any parallel reduction in duties on the materials they required. The only conceivable basis for agreement under these circumstances was high tariff protection for every major economic sector. Strong protectionist currents ran throughout Southern and Eastern Europe in the interwar period. But the extreme protectionism emanating from the council alarmed much of the newspaper-reading public and particularly merchants.[13]

The dictatorship did not follow all of the council's recommendations.[14] Primo did yield, for example, against the wishes of competing national manufacturers, to a military request that purchases of brass be made from a reliable foreign manufacturer.[15] Nonetheless, he renounced a number of trade agreements signed under the constitutional regime and followed a highly protectionist course during his first five years.[16] Tariffs rose by one-third over their prewar levels.[17] From 1923 to 1929, Spain's share of world trade declined by the same proportion.[18]

Andes and Calvo Sotelo disagreed with Primo's contention that Spain had the potential for a high degree of self-sufficiency.[19] Their arguments slowly made an impression on the dictator. Primo had always been interested in using agricultural exports to eliminate the country's trade deficit and to earn capital for economic development. He also subsidized textile exports and hoped that international expositions in Barcelona and Seville would stimulate foreign demand for Spanish goods. But he was forced to recognize that Spain's restrictions on imports limited access to foreign markets. By the end of 1926, Primo declared that tariffs should be based on some form of comparative advantage and that not every sector of the economy could be protected from foreign competition.[20]

Unfortunately, trade policy was still the responsibility of the National Economic Council. Throughout the latter half of 1927 the council worked on a comprehensive tariff reform. Its deliberations were complicated by its rapid growth.[21] From 1924 to 1927 the council grew from 147 to 756 members. There were 125 members in its tariff section alone. This collection of interests could operate with neither efficiency nor judiciousness. Its proposal entirely disregarded Primo's appeal for selectivity and called for a considerable increases in almost every category of duty.[22]

Primo was frustrated and disillusioned. As part of a governmental reorganization in November 1928, he stripped the council of much of its autonomy and put it under the supervision of a newly established ministry of the national economy headed by Andes. The ministry was entrusted with drafting a new tariff reform. However, the regime was too preoccupied with political and other economic problems during the next year to devote much attention to this complex issue. As a result Primo never succeeded in making major changes in the autarkic policies of the first years of the dictatorship.[23]

Primo was no more successful with foreign investment. The 1920s saw, in particular, a considerable influx of American capital. Among the American and European firms attracted by the social peace brought

General European Tariff Levels, 1927

Bulgaria	67.5%
Poland	53.5
Spain	49.0
Romania	42.3
Yugoslavia	32.0
Czechoslovakia	31.3
Hungary	30.0
Italy	27.8
France	23.0
Germany	20.4
Sweden	20.0
Austria	17.5
Switzerland	16.8
Belgium	11.0

SOURCE: Hertz, *The Economic Problem*, p. 72.

by the dictatorship were ITT, Standard Electric, General Electric, General Motors, Nestlé, Iberian Potassium (Potasas Ibéricas), Iberian Nitrogen (Sociedad Ibérica del Nitrógeno), Pirelli, Phillips Ibérica, and Spanish Aluminum (Aluminio Español).[24] High officials, including possibly Primo himself, were directly implicated in scandals involving these companies.[25] The taint of corruption obscured the increasingly hard line taken by the dictatorship on foreign capital. The single most visible legacy of the dictatorship in Spain today is CAMPSA, the state oil monopoly created in 1927 by the nationalization of foreign oil companies in the country. At the same time that Primo established CAMPSA, he enacted legislation facilitating the takeover of other foreign operations by Spanish interests. This legislation produced few results, due partly to the ability of foreign companies to camouflage themselves behind influential Spaniards.[26] In any event, the issue of foreign investment became moot after the oil nationalization and increase in political and economic instability in 1928.

The dictatorship's industrial policies did little to alleviate Spain's basic economic problems. Production limits and artificial price floors constricted the expansion of purchasing power with adverse linkage effects extending from consumer textiles to industrial machinery.[27] The absence of demand for high-volume production militated against capital intensification needed for modernization. Even with the stimulus from the dictatorship's public works programs, for example, steel productivity did not climb as rapidly as might have been expected in an industry noted for its entrepreneurial talent.[28] Newer industries also failed to develop. By the early 1920s Spain had demonstrated sufficient technical ability to produce aircraft and automobiles. But isolation from world markets and dependence on high-priced, often barely extant, domestic suppliers placed a substantial handicap on these emerging sectors.[29]

Primo learned too late that autarkic policies linked every sector of the economy into an interdependent chain. When shortages and high costs affected key sectors, the consequences were felt throughout the economy. As two business writers observed shortly after the fall of the dictatorship,

> small industrial manufacturers endure a precarious existence originating in the high cost of their products. These products are made still more expensive by the high cost of their component parts and materials. Unable to survive on their own, the manufacturers constantly solicit the favor of the state in plaintive voices.[30]

In the end the dictatorship's program contributed to industry's chronic inefficiency and dependence on the state. By expanding the constitutional regime's policy of promoting the short-term interests of industrialists, the dictatorship undermined the economy's long-term interests as industry generally failed to undertake the modernization needed for meeting international competition and for boosting domestic purchasing power through higher wages.[31]

Agriculture

The dictatorship's agricultural policies followed a similar pattern. Agriculture was closely linked to the regime through the National Economic Council. Primo sought foreign exchange by promoting products competitive in international markets, primarily oranges, olive oil, almonds, and wine.[32] Price floors and import restrictions protected wheat, sugar, and other uncompetitive crops as import substitutes. Primo also regarded such crops as mainstays of internal purchasing power and, ultimately, of national wealth. José Pemartín, the regime's semiofficial propagandist, summarized the government's position on wheat:

> The cereal problem, of which wheat is the principal part, is a problem of balance in Spain. Spain produces wheat at an expensive price compared with Canada and Argentina; but, on the other hand, at present price levels, it is difficult to achieve significant agricultural profits and to satisfy the needs of the rural workers, who receive the smallest share of the overall income.
> The government cannot, nonetheless, allow the price of wheat to increase without limit, as this would be counterproductive. Enriching the price of subsistence goods would work against the national economy and even those workers themselves.[33]

Primo himself declared, "Even in the most modest Spanish home, a rise of two or three centimos in the price of bread has little effect; but those two or three centimos are the basis of the countryside's continued purchasing power and of the general prosperity of all Spaniards."[34] Primo's support of internationally uncompetitive crops paralleled Mussolini's "Battle of the Wheat" in much the same way that his ill-starred peseta defense paralleled the Italian dictator's "Battle of the Lira." The agricultural policies of Spain and most other southern and eastern countries were clearly no exception to the general lack of governmental economic sophistication in the 1920s.[35]

Price-level maintenance was occasionally difficult, as in 1925 when there was overproduction of wheat and sugar.[36] Poor harvests, on the other hand, required a carefully controlled increase in imports.[37] The Commodity Committee (Junta de Abastos) regulated these imports and food prices generally. Merchants and chambers of commerce criticized the committee.[38] High prices for agricultural, as well as industrial, products militated against the mass purchasing power on which their own livelihoods depended. And with agricultural products, in particular, they were caught between high wholesale and inelastic retail prices.

Agricultural producers themselves occasionally divided over the regime's programs.[39] Valencia fruit growers wished to import inexpensive wooden crates from Portugal, but lumber producers in Soria sought protection from that important market. Winemakers argued for restrictions on shipment of Spanish cork to France, while livestock raisers wanted cheaper feed-grain sources. In general, producers for international markets inclined toward freer trade, and producers more dependent on the home market were protectionist.

Conflicts also existed between agricultural and industrial sectors.[40] Olive oil producers asked repeatedly for freer importation of tinplate used in packaging. Rice growers complained with some justification that they were damaged by the dictatorship's restrictions on agricultural machinery and fertilizer imports. Particularly controversial was the protection given domestic nitrogen and phosphate products, an industry in which military defense considerations coincided with the financial interests of Catalan bankers and the Urquijos.

Industrialists had their own complaints about agriculture, with manufacturers of synthetic alcohol pitted against grape growers.[41] An infant brewing industry also resented its dependence on high-priced domestic barley. Milling companies generally opposed the opening of new processing facilities, while wheat growers saw such measures increasing the competition for their product. At the same time, textile manufacturers sought curbs on the export of Spanish wool. Along with the industrialists in the National Economic Council, however, most agriculturalists felt that they had more to gain in the end from continued protection of their commodity than from lessened protection for needed production inputs. Indeed, agricultural price levels suggest that while domestically dependent wheat did well under the dictatorship, olive oil and wine—although still export oriented—also derived some benefit from a protected home market during the period.

Primo had political as well as economic reasons for tending to the interests of agricultural producers.[42] His immediate predecessor, Spain's last Liberal cabinet, had lost support in the countryside by

Agricultural Price Indices
(1913 = 100)

Year	General	Wheat Flour	Olive Oil	Wine
1923	171	159	183	115
1924	183	154	194	122
1925	195	173	193	88
1926	183	172	191	98
1927	182	175	222	159
1928	176	179	177	133
1929	180	178	181	124

SOURCE: INE, *Principales actividades,* pp. 32, 37, 52, 146, and 150.

proposing increased agricultural taxation. The new dictator was himself forced to back down over a similiar measure. Shortly after taking power Primo reached out to the rural propertied classes in two major speeches, in Medina del Campo on 29 May 1924 and in Seville on 20 June 1924. In response to landowner complaints, he also curtailed in April 1925 the Cadrastal Survey begun under the constitutional regime. His efforts did not go unrewarded. The CNCA, led by large landowners and supported by small cereal producers in the north, provided important support for the Patriotic Union. Agriculture might not have been the dominant interest in the 1920s that it had been at the turn of the century, but, as rural producers had periodic occasion to remind Primo, agriculture was still the social and economic backbone of the country and the interests of its elite classes could only be ignored at grave political peril.

The dictatorship assisted agriculture in other ways besides favorable tax treatment, price supports, and tariff protection. Indeed, in their main features, Primo's agrarian policies prefigured Franco's attempt to develop the rural economy without directly challenging its underlying social structure. Central to that effort was irrigation. The regime's major project, the Ebro Hydrographic Confederation, improved existing irrigation systems on 109,136 hectares, but was responsible for only 72,163 hectares of new irrigation.[43] Much of this development was poorly planned. The dictatorship's fears about the genuine democracy promised by its hydrographic legislation, together with the influence of established elites in local areas and Madrid, resulted in contracts let out on the basis of special relationships rather than rational purposes.[44] Projects were launched helter-skelter. Dams were frequently built where they could be only of marginal utility, while many areas were neglected that could have benefited substantially from them. There are few reliable statistics on state irrigation expenses, due in part to the complex financing. However, the 52.5 million pesetas in state subsidies granted to the Ebro Hydrographic Confederation amounted to slightly more than 40% of its total expenses. Overall, it appears that the dictatorship's irrigation investment averaged approximately 40 million pesetas per year.[45] This was a small expenditure compared with the 80 million pesetas per year spent during the first two years of the republic and the 158 million pesetas spent in 1933, times of less prosperity than the dictatorship.

Primo also recognized the need for improved credit.[46] Before the dictatorship the principal sources of agricultural credit were underfinanced municipal institutions, the *positos,* and Catholic cooperatives in the north central provinces.[47] In 1923 the *positos* issued loans totaling 23.1 million pesetas, a very small sum for a predominantly agricultural nation of 22.1 million.[48] In October of that year the dictatorship appointed a Junta for the Study of Agricultural Credit (Junta Consultiva del Crédito Agricola). A large wheat harvest, which made marketing difficult, and the junta's recommendations led it to establish the National Agricultural Credit Service (Servicio Nacional de Crédito Agricola) in March 1925.[49] The service began by providing wheat farmers with short-term loans to see them through the harvest and marketing periods. Over the next two years its loans were extended to other crops and for such wider purposes as capital improvement and feed purchases. From 1923 to 1929 the worth of loans made by the service grew from 4.5 to 37.2 million pesetas. The service also increased the funding of the *positos.* From 1923 to 1928 the loans made by the *positos* rose from 26,009,000 pesetas to 32,027,000 pesetas.[50] Real as this progress was, agricultural credit was still altogether inadequate at the end of the dictatorship. In 1931, the overall value of the major crops produced in the country totaled 9.6 billion pesetas compared to a total of slightly less than 32.2 million pesetas in loans made by the national service and 30.9 million pesetas in loans made by the *positos.*[51] In other words, less than 7/10 of 1% of the value of agriculture production had been supported by state-sponsored credit that year.

The dictatorship also promoted agricultural wealth through reforestation.[52] Over the centuries Spain's forests had been depleted for fuel, building material, and farm acreage. By the 1920s what remained was largely in mountainous areas, protected more by transport difficulties than government policy. This meant that Spain lacked forest cover to preserve water tables and protect the soil from wind and water erosion.

Reforestation was a long and costly process. Moreover, Spain still needed wood for building and paper. These competing pressures frustrated political action, despite a general recognition of the problem. A December 1924 edict against indiscriminate cutting was difficult to enforce. Corporative organizations of wood producers and consumers, such as the Resin Consortium *(Consorcio Resinero)* provided little help. Wood users argued for freer importation, and producers sought to preserve their highly priced market.[53] The only basis for compromise was to limit imports while allowing continued large-scale forest cutting. This approach protected the directly affected interests but neglected the public interest. Another problem was the government's shortage of funds. In 1926 the dictatorship pledged 100 million pesetas to reforestation. But that was not enough to prevent a decline in total forest acreage.[54]

The dictatorship sought improved agricultural education.[55] What little legislation the constitutional regime had passed languished before Primo took over. In 1924 the dictatorship instituted a number of services, including improved education for agricultural technicians. In 1926 it established the National Agronomy Institute. In 1926 and 1927 the regime also promoted better livestock education and appointed twelve itinerant instructors for this purpose. However, the number of students enrolled in the elite university agricultural education program actually declined.[56]

The dictatorship's protectionism, and the limited results of its development policies, placed a handicap on its effort to boost agricultural exports.[57] Primo sought to "maintain a large volume of exports in order to compensate for the imports that weigh so heavily against us in the battle of the balance of trade."[58] According to Pemartín, agricultural exports were "indispensable, in fact, in our country for the development of the national economy."[59] The corporate economic entities attached to the National Economic Council established and monitored quality-control programs for principal agricultural exports. The Orange Junta (Junta Naranjera) was particularly active in this area after a severe frost damaged much of the 1927 crop. The Combined Olive Oil Commission (Comisión Mixta del Aceite) performed similar functions and used a one-centimo-per-kilogram tax on olive oil to promote that product's sales in foreign markets. In order to preserve foreign-market shares during difficult production years at home, producers successfully petitioned the government to reduce the duties on olive oil destined for reexport. These policies contributed to a substantial increase in agricultural exports similar to the gains made by other southern and eastern European states during the period.

Less successful than export promotion were the dictatorship's land-reform efforts. As Malefakis has noted, the dictatorship limited itself during its first three years to a modest effort "to eliminate obvious anachronisms and rationalize existing institutions."[60] In June 1926, however, it instituted a program of *foro* redemption for the northwest. This program did little in itself to end the fragmentation of peasant holdings, which was the basic economic problem in that region. But it was a preliminary step for future parcellary concentration. The dictatorship also enacted legislation giving more stability to tenant leasing arrangements.

However, its most significant action was revamping of the constitutional regime's internal colonization program in July 1926.[61] This reform did not help impoverished day laborers, but it did benefit some tenant farmers. In all, 4,202 peasants acquired 21,501 hectares of land.[62] Although this was a substantial improvement over the constitutional regime's record, it was not enough to have a significant impact on either the economic or social structure of the countryside.[63] Primo considered more extensive change and even declared that 1929 would be the year of agrarian reform. But the landed classes had had little trouble in forcing retreats on attempted increases in rural taxation twice before when Primo had enjoyed widespread support. They had even less trouble dissuading him from this last, most fundamental challenge to their interests during the dictatorship's final months of decline. The result was one of the dictatorship's greatest failures and another example of its means defeating its ends. In underwriting agricultural profits and leaving untouched a large pool of landless labor, the regime took away much of the incentive to invest in more capital-intensive farming.[64]

The dictatorship's agricultural record was mixed at best. Increased exports were beneficial, but affected only limited regions and sectors. Meanwhile, the dictatorship failed to carry out improvements in agricultural infrastructure and transformations in land tenure needed to raise rural living standards and to make the countryside a motor for wealth rather than a brake on the national economy. This failure was partially obscured by the regime's artificially supported agricultural price levels. Behind that facade productivity stagnated.

The Dictatorship's Economic Legacy

By many outward signs the dictatorship was a time of prosperity. But the regime suffered from a flawed economic vision and the contradictions in its own base of support. It did not alleviate underlying problems, but compounded them by greatly enlarging on the constitutional regime's economic nationalist precedents. High tariffs, production

Mean Annual Agricultural Productivity for Three Year Periods

Crop	Years	Area (thousands of hectares)	Production (millions of metric quintals)	Yield (quintals/hectare)
Wheat	1907–08	3,609	33.0	9.15
	1917–19	4,175	37.0	8.85
	1927–29	4,318	38.2	8.84
Oats	1970–09	1,467	11.6	7.91
	1907–19	1,822	14.0	7.68
	1927–29	2,309	17.6	7.62
Barley	1907–09	4,252	44.1	10.37
	1917–19	5,046	54.5	10.80
	1927–29	5,420	59.1	10.90
Rye	1907–09	2,644	22.5	8.51
	1917–19	2,198	19.2	8.74
	1927–29	1,972	16.7	8.47
Olives	1907–09	4,170	7.0	1.70
	1917–19	4,630	10.3	2.22
	1927–29	5,320	15.1	2.84
Wine	1907–09	4,083	41.7 million	10.21 hectoliters/
	1917–19	3,931	66.9 hectoliters	17.02 hectare
	1927–29	4,309	75.4	17.50

SOURCE: INE, *Principales actividades*.

ceilings, and fixed prices protected weak and inefficient producers. These measures enhanced immediate profits but reduced purchasing power. This problem was not apparent as long as the government continued to pump money into the economy. Well before the depression, however, Primo exhausted his capacity to borrow. His economic legacy to the republic consisted of artificial distortions, a large debt, and a host of unfinished projects.

Spain was not alone in this. Frederick Hertz concludes his examination of the Danubian states in the period by declaring:

> Our study examines economic development in the new states by means of copious statistical material. It shows that all the efforts to foster, by an extreme protectionism, either the rapid increase of agricultural production or that of industrial output had only a very limited success.[65]

He later adds,

> Economic nationalism has often been defended . . . on the ground that it was the only means of accumulating sufficient capital for the further develoment of a country's resources and the employment of

an increasing population. This argument, however, is not confirmed by the facts. The Danubian States were driving protectionism to extremes. But the formation of capital was everywhere extremely slow and insufficient. . . .[66]

He also offers this cautionary observation:

It is necessary to warn against the cheap argument that all this was merely due to the world crisis. This event had certainly a disastrous influence in bringing about the collapse and the protracted depression, but its effects would never have been so devastating if the Danubian States had been able to cooperate. Moreover, the world crisis itself was to a very great extent the fruit of economic nationalism.[67]

Primo relied on economic development as an alternative to social change. In that respect his dictatorship mirrored other technocracy-minded authoritarian regimes in the interwar years. If less well endowed than some more developed states in northwestern Europe, Spain nonetheless possessed more hydroelectric potential, coal, iron, and other ores than most other southern and eastern European states. Under those circumstances Spain might reasonably have been expected to have exceeded the growth rates of those other late developing countries.[68] Similarly, the low base from which Spain started in 1923 might have been expected to have contributed to larger percentage increases in economic activity than those achieved in the more developed states. But Spanish growth rates were not appreciably different from those of either group of countries, despite the dictatorship's policies. Indeed, those policies constitute the explanation for Spain's mediocre performance. Economic nationalism was endemic to southern and eastern Europe but was carried to an extreme in Spain. Promoting development while constricting purchasing power and restricting interchange with the international economy was tantamount to pressing an automobile's accelerator and brake pedals simultaneously. Exhaustion ensued. Ironically, too, because this overheating of the domestic economy failed to narrow the distance from more advanced countries, the trade deficit rose significantly despite the dictatorship's protectionism.[69]

The mistakes and negative consequences of Primo's policies are clear. What else could have been done? First, the regime should have been more selective from the beginning in its support of national producers. Branches of production that were potentially self-sustaining should have been encouraged, but branches without that potential should never have been allowed to hamper economic development.

Second, it should have realized that its restrictive corporative machinery meant that more stimulus had to be given the economy than otherwise would have been necessary. And if there had been less stimulus, fewer safeguards against overproduction would have been needed. Less ambitious programs might have accomplished more at lower cost and been supportable for a longer period. Third, the social dimension of economic development should have been taken more fully into account. The dictatorship's attempt to promote development from above did not accomplish the desired results. The regime might have been more successful had it devoted more attention to increasing purchasing power and less to the short-term interests of producers. Hugh Seton-Watson argued for this approach in the eastern European states suffering from severe agricultural overpopulation:

> Industrialization is one of the principal cures for agricultural overpopulation, but it will not make progress unless it is planned in accordance with the needs of the country rather than those of foreign capital, unless it makes use of the resources of the country and unless it can supply an increased internal market. Everything must begin from government action to raise . . . purchasing power. . . .[70]

Certainly more could have been done along these lines in Spain, where the population problem was less pressing. One way to increase purchasing power would have been to lessen the regime's price-support policies and autarkic program. Social reform would have been another.

NOTES

1. On Primo's lack of clarity in economic thinking, see Carlos Velasco Murviedro, "Concentración e intervención en la dictadura: Hechos y ideas," in *Economía política de la dictadura de Primo de Rivera*, ed. idem, p. 160.

2. Velarde, *Política económica*, pp. 89–90.

3. The corporate system was more developed on paper than in practice. Coal, textile, and agricultural interests were particularly active; Belford, "El sistema bancario," p. 229. Nonetheless, the eagerness with which membership in the corporate bodies was sought is striking. See, for example, AHN Leg. 34, Exte. 2308, and Leg. 139, Extes. 309, 317, 387, and 390. On the work of the council itself, see Florensa Palau, "Economía y comercio exterior," pp. 475–78.

4. Pemartín, *Los valores*, p. 273. Primo's early economic views are outlined in García-Nieto et al., *La dictadura*, pp. 76–77 and 81–82.

5. On the protectionist Economic Study Society (Sociedad de Estudios Económicos) in Barcelona, see AHN Leg. 139, Exte. 435. On the Patriotic Union, see *Unión Patriótica*, 15 January 1927. For labor's protectionism, see AHN Leg. 33, Exte. 1863.

6. On such criticism see, Maura Gamazo, *Bosquejo* 1: 184–85; Iglesias, *Política de la dictadura*, pp. 72–101; and Ortega, *España encadenada*, pp. 301–3. Typical favors sought from the regime are detailed in AHN Leg. 1, Extes. 38, 805, and 890; Leg. 30, Exte. 656; Leg. 33, Exte. 2074; Leg. 34, Exte. 2218; Leg. 138, numerous Extes., especially 42, 125,

235, and 264; Leg. 139, numerous Extes.; and Leg. 524, "Zubiria, Conde de"; *Hojas Libres,* October 1927, pp. 68–78; and Ciges Aparicio, *España bajo la dinastía,* pp. 446–47.

7. Cánovas Cervantes, *Apuntes históricos,* p. 63.

8. Gómez Navarro et al., "Aproximación," pp. 197–200, and Velarde, *Sobre la decadencia,* p. 197. On the problems that Catalonia nonetheless experienced, see *Hojas Libres,* May 1927, pp. 19–24.

9. INE, *Principales actividades,* p. 149.

10. Purchasing power and conditions of life among different social sectors during the dictatorship are discussed in chap. 11. For Cambó's criticism, see his *La valoración de la peseta* (Madrid: M. Aguilar, n.d.).

11. The National Economic Council's role in foreign trade policy formulation is treated by Elli Lindner, *El derecho arancelario español* (Barcelona: Bosch, 1934), pp. 74–90.

12. Member organizations of the council are listed in Velarde, *Política económica,* pp. 100–107, and Román Perpiñá Grau, *De economía hispana, infraestructura, historia* (Barcelona: Ediciones Ariel, 1974), pp. 65–67. Indicative of the requests for lower tariffs are AHN Leg. 36, Exte. 3651; Leg. 37, Extes. 4298 and 4313; and Leg. 138, Extes. 88, 135, and 155. Export curbs were even sought on occasion as in the case of the Barcelona Metallurgical Union's (Unión Metalúrgica de Barcelona) 1924 request regarding copper; AHN Leg. 36, Exte. 3896. On the countervailing demand for higher tariffs, see AHN Leg. 138 generally and, especially, Extes. 32, 51, and 126; and Leg. 139, Extes. 327, 328, 338, 352, 422, 440, 447, 546, 556, and 651.

13. On the protests of individual merchants and chambers of commerce, see AHN Leg. 27, Extes. 306–9; Leg. 34, Extes. 2125, 2134, and 2297; Leg. 37, Extes. 4514 and 4528; and Leg. 138, Exte. 16. On the general alarm occasioned by the council's deliberations, see Florensa Palau, "Economía y comercio exterior," pp. 476–77. On the autarkic sentiment in Spain, see Velasco Murviedro, "Concentración e intervención," pp. 169–79.

14. See, for example, Maura Gamazo, *Bosquejo* 1:149.

15. AHN Leg. 2, Exte. 1012. Even here, however, the military inclined more in the end toward protectionism than free trade. In June 1929, two years after this May 1927 incident, a military conference declared support for national brass manufacturers to be in the interest of national defense; AHN Leg. 139, Exte. 352.

16. Lindner, *El derecho arancelario,* pp. 79–81, and Ramos Oliveira, *Politics, Economics, and Men,* pp. 194–95.

17. Federick Hertz, *The Economic Problem of the Danubian States* (London: Victor Gollancz, 1947), p. 72. Additional information is contained in Lindner, *El derecho arancelario,* pp. 168–71.

18. Banks, *Cross-Polity,* p. 198.

19. Maura Gamazo, *Bosquejo* 2:318–19, and Calvo Sotelo, *Mis servicios,* pp. 256–59.

20. *Unión Patriótica,* 1 November 1926, pp. 1–2. See also the statement of S. Castedo, the vice-president of the National Economic Council; ibid., October 1926, pp. 23–24.

21. Lindner, *El derecho arancelario,* pp. 75–84, and Velarde, *Política económica,* pp. 92–94.

22. Typical of criticism of the council's work was *Hojas Libres,* January 1928, pp. 67–68.

23. Part of his problem was that despite growing frustration in this area, he never altogether lost his protectionist sentiments, as is evident in a 22 July 1929 letter to Andes; AHN Leg. 139, Exte. 415. In fact, the around-the-world flight of the *Jesús del Gran Poder* appears to have temporarily revived those feelings; Rubio, *Crónica,* p. 393.

24. Campillo, *Las inversiones extranjeras,* pp. 173–74 and Tuñón de Lara, *El movimiento,* p. 751.

25. See, for example, Anthony Sampson, *The Sovereign State of ITT* (London: Stein & Day, 1973), p. 24; *Diario de las sesiones,* 8 May 1934, pp. 2672–73; Ramos Oliveira, *El capitalismo,* pp. 206–24; Ossorio, *Mis memorias,* pp. 138–39; and Saldaña, "El famoso

'affaire.' " Particularly criticized was the regime's relationship with the ITT controlled telephone monopoly. For a complaint about tax fraud involving the monopoly, see AHN Leg. 50, Exte. 9744. For the monopoly's requests for state favors, see AHN Leg. 39, Exte. 5698; Leg. 47, Extes. 8613 and 8636; and Leg. 50, Extes. 9847 and 9993. For French complaints about Spanish protection of the lucrative telephone equipment market, see AHN Leg. 1, Exte. 178.

26. The original governing board of ITT's Compañia Telefónica Nacional de España (CTNE), for example, consisted of Julián Cifuentes y Fernández and Amadeo Alvarez y García, associated with the Hispanic American Bank, and Valentín Ruiz Senen associated with the Urquijo Bank as well as the marquis of Perijáa and Gumersindo Rico González. Quickly named president of the new monopoly was the marquis of Urquijo himself; Robert Carballo Cortina, "El capital extranjero y la dictadura: La ITT en España," in *Economía política de la dictadura de Primo de Rivera, Cuadernos Económicos de I.C.E.*, ed. Carlos Velasco Murviedro, 10 (1979): 582–85. For a similar situation at Pirelli, see Tuñón de Lara, *Poder,* p. 121 n. 3. In general, see Jellinek, *The Civil War,* pp. 71–74.

27. On textiles, see Ramos Oliveira, *El capitalismo,* pp. 28–71, and Miguel, *El potencial,* pp. 79–94. On machinery, see Nadal, "La economía," pp. 401–5.

28. For general background on the steel industry as well as its development under the dictatorship, see Higinio Paris Equilaz, "Problemas de la expansión siderúrgica en España," *Anales de Economía* 12, nos. 47–48 (July–December 1952): 271–384; Luis Barreiro, "La industria minera-siderúrgica española," *Revista Nacional de Economía* 30, no. 89 (January–February 1930): 69–78; and Ronald H. Chilcote, *Spain's Iron and Steel Industry* (Austin: University of Texas Press, 1968).

29. Particularly striking is the example of aviation; see "The 50th Anniversary of Spanish Civil Aviation," *Spain Today* 19 (January 1972): 65–70, and Pemartín, *Los valores,* pp. 536–62.

30. Sintes Olives and Vidal Burdils, *La industria eléctria,* p. 136.

31. For a more general European perspective, see Rothschild, *East Central Europe,* p. 271.

32. See, for example, *Unión Patriótica,* 1 November 1926): 1–2. On Primo's purposes for agriculture more generally, see Duarte, *España: Primo de Rivera,* pp. 43–64.

33. Pemartín, *Los valores,* pp. 318–19. Further information on wheat is contained in Nadel, "La economía," pp. 381–85, and AHN Leg. 138, Extes. 126 and 204.

34. Velarde, *Política económica,* p. 121.

35. For general discussion of agricultural policies and the circumstances shaping them in southern and eastern Europe, see Hugh Seton-Watson, *Eastern Europe between the Wars,* 3d ed. (New York: Harper & Row, 1967), pp. 75–122; Moore, *Economic Demography,* pp. 99–117; Rothschild, *East Central Europe,* pp. 22–24, 66–68, 122–24, 140–42, 267–72, 290–92, and 328–31; and Friedrich Hertz, *The Economic Problem of the Danubian States* (London: Victor Gollancz, 1947). For more detailed discussions of individual countries, see Henry L. Roberts, *Rumania: Political Problems of an Agrarian State* (New Haven: Yale University Press, 1951), pp. 3–85; Ferdinand Zweig, *Poland between Two World Wars* (London: Secker and Warburg, 1941), pp. 125–57 passim; Antony Polonsky, *Politics in Independent Poland* (Oxford: Oxford University Press, 1972), pp. 24–27, 65–68, 79–89, and 347–53; Tomasevich, *Peasants,* pp. 242–60, 308–472, and 601–80.

36. The government's role in sugar overproduction was pronounced, but still typical of its policy toward internationally uncompetitive crops; see John S. McGee, "Government Intervention in the Spanish Sugar Industry"; Joaquín Sánchez de Toca, *Interviú sobre actualidades sociales y económicas* (Madrid: El Financiero, 1921), pp. 16–23; and Miguel, *El potencial,* pp. 109–28.

37. Manuel de Torres, *El problema triguero y otras cuestiones fundamentales de la agricultura española.* (Madrid: Consejo Superior de Investigaciones Cientificas, 1944), pp. 108–9.

38. On the committee and its detractors, see AHN Leg. 34, Exte. 2452; Leg. 35, Exte. 2889; Leg. 36, Exte. 4141; Leg. 37, Exte. 4468; Leg. 51, Exte. 10377; Leg. 138, Exte. 3; and Leg. 416 generally.

39. For general complaints concerning economic regulation, see AHN Leg. 138, Extes. 304 and 368. On the importation of wooden crates, see AHN Leg. 38, Extes. 4782 and 4834. On the importation of feed grains, see AHN Leg. 34, Exte. 2603. On fruit growers' concern for exports, see AHN Leg. 30, Exte. 473.

40. On tinplate importation, see AHN Leg. 33, Exte. 1994. On chemical fertilizer imports see, for example, AHN Leg. 138, Exte. 15, and Tamames, *Estructura*, p. 398. On the problems of rice producers, see Hernández Andreu, "Algunos aspectos," pp. 383–93.

41. On the alcohol controversy, see AHN Leg. 36, Exte. 3382; Leg. 37, Extes. 4492, 4524, 4551, 4553, 4578, 4579, 4594, and 4599; and Leg. 139, Exte. 576. On brewer requests for imported barley and oats, see AHN Leg. 37, Extes. 4268 and 4353. On the debate over factory openings, see AHN Leg. 138, Extes 30, 31, 37, 86, 133, 138, 149, 166, 187, 213, 214, 223, 237, 258, and 259. On the request of textile and other clothing manufacturers, see AHN Leg. 34, Extes. 2274 and 2444; Leg. 37, Exte. 4358; and Leg. 39, Extes. 5620, 5621, and 5627. Disputes over specific policies notwithstanding, the interest of most agricultural organizations in working within the dictatorship's corporative framework is evident in AHN Leg. 34, Extes. 2414, 2421, 2422, 2432, 2433, 2443, 2472 and 2473; Leg. 35, Extes. 3031–38 and 3047–53; and Leg. 139, Exte. 362.

42. On the controversy over taxation of rural wealth, see Velarde, *Sobre la decadencia*, pp. 203–5; and Malerbe, "España," p. 60. By 1929 tax collectors were to work "with," not against, rural producers; AHN Leg. 139, Exte. 570. On Primo's campaigning for agrarian support and on the backing given the Patriotic Union by the CNCA, see Tuñón de Lara, "En torno," pp. 19 and 26. On the continuing influence of rural elites, especially in the latifundia provinces, see Gómez Navarro et al., "Aproximación," pp. 192–95. On the extent to which members of the regime derived private advantage from favorable treatment for agriculturally related activities, see *Hojas Libres*, November 1927, pp. 7–17 passim.

43. The statistical information on this point is not consistent. For the variety of opinion, see Velarde, *La política economica*, p. 47; Arespacochaga, "La política hiráulica," pp. 170–73; Jorge Nadal Oller, "La economía española," pp. 385–89; Banco Central, *Estudio económico*, p. 46; Ramos Oliveira, *Politics, Economics, and Men*, p. 212; and Manuel Lorenzo Pardo, *La conquista del Ebro*, p. 39. I have cited the figures provided by Pardo and accepted by Velarde as the most likely. These are also approximately the same as those of Arespacochaga.

44. Sintes Olives and Vidal Burdils, *La industria eléctrica*, p. 428, and Ortega, "Política hidráulica y política colonizadora," pp. 360–73.

45. Malefakis, *Agrarian Reform*, p. 234.

46. *Unión Patriótica* (1 enero 1927), pp. 1–3.

47. Agricultural credit at the time Primo took power is described by Luis Redonet y López Dóriaga, *Crédito agrícola: Historia, bases y organización* (Madrid: Calpe, 1924).

48. INE, *Principales actividades*, p. 51.

49. José López de Sebastián, *Política agraria en España 1920–1970* (Madrid: Guadiana de Publicaciones, 1970), pp. 52–53.

50. Velarde, *Política económica*, p. 118. A partial listing of the legislation governing the *positos* in this period is contained in las Heras, *Auxiliar indicador*, pp. 709–12, cxl, and clxxiv.

51. López, *Política agraria*, p. 52, and INE, *Principales actividades*, pp. 30 and 51. Commercial banks under the dictatorship were less likely to lend directly to producers, especially small landowners, than they were to seek indirect benefit from the agricultural prosperity of the period by opening offices in rural areas and by investing in agricultural machinery and fertilizer manufacture; Belford, "El sistema bancario," pp. 242–43.

52. Miguel, *El potencial*, pp. 183–98.

53. Tamames, *Estructura*, 3d ed., pp. 216–17. See also Ceballos Teresi, *Historia eco-*

nómica 5:524–25; 6:422–23; and 7:45–46; and Fernández Díez, "La economía castellana," p. 125.

54. Miguel, *El potencial*, p. 189.
55. Pemartín, *Los valores*, pp. 329–34.
56. In 1923 there were 835 students enrolled in agricultural education programs and 31 degrees awarded. In 1929 there were only 131 students and 19 degrees. It may be argued that much of this drop was due to the university disorders in 1928 and 1929. Nonetheless, in 1927 there were only 872 students and 10 degrees. INE, *Principales actividades*, p. 168.
57. On agricultural exports generally see Ceballos, *Historia económica* 7:50–52, and Pemartín, *Los valores*, pp. 262–65 and 271–72. For the requests of producers for export subsidies and for the occasional domestic opposition to such requests, see AHN Leg. 34, Extes. 2100–2393 passim; Leg. 36, Exte. 3864; and Leg. 45, Exte. 8207. For additional information relevant to agricultural exports, see AHN Leg. 139, Extes. 365 and 566. For statistice, see INE, *Comercio exterior*, pp. 74–80.
58. Pemartín, *Los valores*, p. 262.
59. Ibid.
60. Malefakis, *Agrarian Reform*, p. 436.
61. On the importance Primo attached to internal colonization, see *Unión Patriótica*, 1 January 1927, pp. 1–3.
62. Cristóbal de Castro, *Al servicio de los compesinos* (Madrid: Javier Morata, 1931), p. 199.
63. Indeed there is even some question whether the five hectares per colonist awarded under this legislation provided enough land for viable holdings. Spain has many climatic and topographic similarities with Yugoslavia. In that country research on agriculture in the interwar period has indicated that holdings that size were only marginally viable; Tomasevich, *Peasants*, pp. 392–97.
64. The negative impact of a surplus labor pool on agricultural investment was also evident in Poland; see, for example, Rothschild, *East Central Europe*, p. 67.
65. Hertz, *The Economic Problem*, p. 220.
66. Ibid., p. 222.
67. Ibid., p. 220 Hertz's conclusions are supported by other studies of the period. Different aspects of industrial development and purchasing power are discussed by Tomasevich, *Peasants*, pp. 246–54 passim and 683–702; Seton-Watson, *Eastern Europe*, pp. 116–17; and Roberts, *Rumania*, pp. 73 and 75–85 passim.
68. For further comparison of Spain's economic potential with other southern and eastern European states, see Moore, *Economic Demography*, pp. 122–35.
69. Government statistics showing a decrease in the trade deficit from 1,400 million to 629 million ptas. from 1923 to 1929 have long been known to be inaccurate. More reliable are the estimates of Juan Antonio Vandellós made in 1931. According to Vandellós, Spain's trade deficit more than tripled, from 200 million to 728 million ptas., between 1923 and 1929; Florensa Palau, "Economía y comercio exterior," p. 487. For more on the problematical nature of trade statistics, see above, p. 9–10 n. 1.
70. Seton-Watson, *Eastern Europe*, p. 117. Stalin's industrialization drive has been regarded as a successful example of development pursued on the opposite basis, by the extraction of investment capital through forced reductions in consumption. The high social cost of Stalin's program is widely recognized. There has been a recent tendency to question it on economic grounds as well; see Robert C. Tucker, "Stalinism as Revolution from Above," in *Stalinism*, ed. idem (New York: W. W. Norton, 1977), pp. 87–89. The current vogue of "supply side economics" notwithstanding, there is a growing awareness that increased purchasing power fuels the capital formation needed for improved productivity, rather than drains from it. See, for example, "Europe in the 1980s," *The Economist* 275, no. 7134 (24 May 1980): 94–95.

Part Four

SOCIAL REFORM

8
Palliatives

Primo's conservative paternalism resulted in a number of social reforms, but it did not extend far enough to produce significant change in the life and work of the laboring classes. Primo and Martínez Anido harassed the communists and the anarchosyndicalist CNT. But the dictator offered the Socialists a voice on social policy in exchange for their not challenging the regime politically. The Socialists insisted on being the sole labor representatives on any governmental body they were appointed to. When Primo allowed the Catholic trade unions and the free syndicates *(sindicatos libres)* representation on the National Economic Council, the Socialists refused to participate. Primo also repeatedly, if unsuccessfully, challenged the Socialists' claim that they, and not the government, decide which of their members should sit on governmental boards. These tensions did not prevent the Socialists from serving on the Supreme Court of the finance ministry, the Superior Railroad Council, the Combustible Fuel Commission, and a number of municipal town councils.[1] In 1924 the directory replaced the Social Reform Institute with a new Superior Labor Council, more directly subordinated to the labor ministry. But the same Socialist representatives that served on the old body continued on the new. The Socialists also represented Spain at the International Labor Office. From such positions they promoted a variety of social reforms. As a member of the Council of State, Largo Caballero pursued special advantages for the UGT. The Socialists' greatest opportunity came in November 1926 with Aunós's establishment of the Corporate Labor Organization, a labor-management arbitration system in which the UGT served as the almost exclusive representative of the working class.

The Socialists had been greatly impressed by the Labor party's strong showing in Britain's December 1923 election and the subsequent formation of the Lib-Lab cabinet. With institutionalization of their own role, albeit a secondary one, in government policy making and with virtual elimination of competition from more radical worker organizations, some Socialists aspired to a position as the government's left leg, helping the UGT organizationally while promoting reforms beneficial to the working class as a whole. Their moderation was evident in the statement of principles advanced by Largo Caballero in 1925, downplaying the movement's past political goals and emphasizing step by step progress for social and economic reform.[2] The failure of this tempered approach cannot be attributed either to a lack of opportunity to present the Socialist case or even to a lack of goodwill on Primo's part. Primo did indeed show an interest in the welfare of the working classes, especially when confronted with specific hardships or injustices. But at bottom he held much the same hierarchical vision of society as the well-entrenched elites to whom he was beholden. By themselves the Socialists could not have provided Primo with an independent base for his regime, even had he been inclined to look to them for such support. But their weakness, even in the temporarily and artificially favorable circumstances that prevailed after 1923, meant that social reform for Primo would never be a matter of social restructuring, but remained cultivation of a new set of attitudes through symbolic gestures and palliatives. That orientation produced greater progress than had been achieved under the constitutional regime, but not enough to meet the reform needs of a highly inegalitarian society.

Labor Legislation

Labor legislation had a late start in Spain.[3] It received attention for the first time in the modern era in five brief articles in the 1889 Civil Code on "the service of domestic servants and salaried workers."[4] Little else was added before 1900. After that date successive governments enacted laws on collective bargaining, the right to strike, industrial accidents, apprenticeship, and women's working conditions. This legislation, however, was not always consistent. Moreover, important sectors of the economy were left unregulated. The Social Reform Institute sought to remedy these deficiencies, and a wide range of politicians supported its effort to fashion a comprehensive law governing the labor contract. But little was accomplished before 1923.

The directory largely confined itself to incidental changes in legislation on overtime pay and railroad labor contracts. After the establishment of the civil government, one of Aunós's immediate concerns was labor legislation.[5] Within nine months he announced his Labor Code to the public, systematizing and supplementing existing law. What allowed him to act so quickly was the Social Reform Institute's preparatory work. The Labor Code had four parts. The first dealt with contractual obligations between employers and workers, collective bargaining, the rights of foreign companies and workers, conditions for the termination of a contract, standards to be fulfilled in government contracts, and the role of the courts in labor disputes.

The second part of the code concerned apprentice contracts, establishing minor changes in the 1911 apprenticeship law. The third part dealt with accidents. Here Aunós did not institute significant innovation as much as he systematized existing law on liability, the extent of obligation, and professional retraining. The last section attempted to reform the industrial tribunal system. The basic problem was that the legislation creating the tribunals in 1912 did not require knowledge of labor law on the part of employer and worker members. That act had attempted to insure representativeness, but had resulted in many decisions that were appealed into the regular court system. Aunós dealt with this situation by modifying the selection of the juries and by limiting appeals of tribunal decisions to matters involving more than 2,500 pesetas.

There were many areas where the code failed to produce innovation. Other areas, such as sickness, industrial hygiene, and agricultural labor, either received only vague treatment or were neglected entirely. A more complete and up-to-date compilation had to wait until the republic's Labor Contract Law of November 1931. Nonetheless, the Labor Code was a step forward. It was the first such compilation in modern Spanish history, and it helped make labor law more relevant by making it more systematic and comprehensible.

Women

The government's policy toward women was at once emancipatory and protective. During the 1920s Spain shared in the general liberalization of European attitudes toward women. Smoking, cosmetics, knee-length skirts, and the freedom to visit night spots previously unfrequented by "respectable" women signified changes in the way women perceived themselves and were perceived.[6] Primo supported women's increased participation in public life. The Municipal Statute extended the franchise to many women. That same act also granted them the right to serve on town councils. In November 1926 women were authorized to participate in the newly established corporate labor organization, and the legal restriction barring them from the Royal Academy was removed. In February 1927 widows of bureaucrats gained the right to a position in the same branch of public service as their deceased husbands. Primo was proud that fourteen women were invited to be members of the National Assembly. He declared of one of these members, "[that woman] is a symbol for us, not only of a very important sector of the national population, but [also] of a sector that represents the firm determination that we have of giving participation to the Spanish woman in the majority of national activities."[7] The Patriotic Union had a women's section, and its journal discussed ways that women could contribute to the dictatorship's national regeneration effort.[8]

Primo did not, however, regard women as men's equals. According to one critic, in fact, his "ostentatious feminism" was colored "with a trace of masculine and even more specifically, military galantry of a freudian type which antagonizes sincere proponents of equality far more than frank anti-feminism."[9] Liberal opponents accused Primo of proclaiming himself a champion of women in an attempt to appear modern, but of failing to understand that women *(mujeres)* were more than essentially domestic creatures *(hembras)*.[10] Some of Primo's conservative supporters were still more chauvinist, declaring that the hearth was the "sacred temple that no woman should abandon for the sake of immersing herself in the affairs of the world."[11] A few even criticized use of lipstick.[12] The regime made it clear that many areas of public life would continue to be all-male preserves. In April 1924 women were declared unqualified to perform notary-public responsibilities. In December of that same year they were prohibited from serving as tax collectors, and in March 1925 they were prohibited from holding provincial office. This attitude explains why most significant women's legislation dealt with factory conditions, pregnancy, and family subsidies rather than with rights and opportunities. In February 1925 the directory announced that it would inspect working conditions for women in shops run by charitable organizations. In 1926 the civil government initiated several important labor reforms, most of which owed their inspiration to the International Labor Office.[13] In February women and children were disqualified from working with lead paints. In July the regime began regulating and inspecting conditions in cottage industries. It was particularly concerned with rest periods for needle workers. In August the dictatorship issued its compilation of labor legislation, which strengthened the safeguards for women and child labor. In December the labor ministry issued new, restrictive guidelines on the employment of women and children on Sundays. In August and September 1927 still more extensive legislation was adopted governing rest periods for women in various occupations.

The dictatorship was as concerned as population conscious France and Italy with the health of pregnant women and their newborn children. Primo inherited momentum here from the constitutional regime.[14] In July 1923, Spain ratified an International Labor Organization convenant on employment before and after childbirth.[15] The following month the government announced a program of 50-peseta grants to women who did not abandon their newborn children and placed themselves under a doctor's care before and after giving birth.[16] In October Primo announced his support for these programs. More than 3,300,000 pesetas in maternity subsidies were dispensed from 1923 through 1930.[17] In 1929 the dictatorship embraced the principle of compulsory maternity insurance, which was later implemented by the republic. The regime also adopted legislation allowing women to leave work for an hour each day to nurse their new child.[18] The impact of these measures is reflected in a decline in the infant mortality rate, from 14.8% to 11.7% between 1923 and 1930.[19]

Primo also encouraged large families.[20] In July 1926 the regime announced with much fanfare a modest program of financial aid to families of workers and government employees with more than eight children. Organizational problems delayed implementation well into the next year, and it was not until August 1928 that the program assumed final form.[21] Direct cash subsidies ranged from 100 pesetas per year for families with eight children to 1,000 pesetas per year to families with eighteen children. These awards were supplemented by tax exemptions and small grants of state bonds. The amounts provided by this program were not sufficient to cover the costs involved in having extra children, but they were substantial enough to help many large families. Nonetheless, a decline in the Spanish birthrate had begun long before the dictatorship and persisted well after, little affected by this legislation.[22]

In the end, the most significant changes in the status of women occurred independently of any political initiative. From 1923 through 1927 the percentage of women in the university population nearly doubled, rising from 4.7% to 8.3%.[23] Women's participation in the active population increased 8.7% between 1920 and 1930.[24] The percentage of women among skilled workers grew from 22.6% to 26.7% between 1925 and 1930.[25] Over the same period, the percentage of women in apprentice programs increased from 32.6% to 36.4%.[26] Most significantly, women's wages rose faster than men's.[27]

Apprentice and Child Labor

The dictatorship was far less active in regulating child labor than women's, despite the fact that the two concerns had traditionally been linked.[28] The regime perfunctorily ratified the recommendations of various ILO conferences, excepting those governing agricultural labor. By 1930 Spain had acquired a reasonably comprehensive system of laws in this area. No child under ten years of age could work at all, unless it was for his immediate family. Children between ten and fourteen were allowed to work six hours per day, but only if provision was made for at least two hours of study per day toward completion of their primary education. Youths from ten to eighteen were protected against night and overtime work and were excluded from hazardous occupations, such as interior mining or working with lead-based paints and inflammable materials. But even today Spain has an uneven enforcement record for child-labor legislation, and during the 1920s governmental commitment was less than now.[29]

Still less was done for apprentices. The dictatorship missed an opportunity for legislative innovation here with its Labor Code in 1926. It may have been, however, that market conditions alone were sufficient to better the fortunes of this underpaid and neglected segment of the labor force. Declining demand for highly skilled, artisan labor contributed to increased demand for semiskilled, less highly paid apprentices. Their wages rose faster than most skilled and unskilled workers.[30]

Housing

Primo inherited rent controls and programs for new housing from the constitutional regime. The dictatorship never escaped the contradiction between those policies. Its declared goal was "restoration of the balance between supply and demand."[31] From the beginning, however, it was forced to acknowledge the large body of opinion in favor of rent control. A June 1924 decree declared that "continuation of the current system of urban rents" was more "imposed than accepted."[32] Its desire to restore "normality" in this area by reestablishing "the freedom of contract to urban leases" had to be "temporarily subordinated to the extraordinary pressure of the majority of citizens' insistence on the extension of the existing" legislation.[33]

The dictatorship even extended controls to all towns of more than 6,000 population, compared with towns of 20,000 or more covered by earlier legislation. On the other hand, the regime liberalized portions of the controls. A December 1925 decree exempted luxury apartments leased for more than 6,000 pesetas per year. Apartments renting for less were eligible for graduated increases. This act did not placate landlords. Residential property continued to lose desirability as an investment. The only sector to attract much interest was luxury building.³⁴ In reaction to declining earnings, landlords let their properties deteriorate. The dictatorship was forced to devote increasing attention to urban "ruins" in its last years.³⁵

The government attempted to counter the tendency toward declining housing for low-income groups through new construction.³⁶ In October 1924 it introduced several modifications in previous legislation.³⁷ A fixed cash grant replaced earlier continuing subsidies. The government also offered low-interest building loans. The loans could amount to seventy percent of construction costs, while the cash bonuses could amount to another twenty percent. Much of the government's largesse was underwritten through special bond issues. This legislation was supplemented by efforts to harness the resources of local town councils and the National Insurance Institute.³⁸

A July 1925 law extended subsidized housing to lower-middle-class incomes.³⁹ According to Aunós, the principal beneficiaries were artists, journalists, intellectuals, and lower-paid government employees. In August 1927 another measure designed primarily to benefit civil servants was enacted, with a similar law adopted in February 1928 for military personnel. The rapid growth of housing programs called for a centralized mechanism for dispensing state funds. To meet this need the government established the Small Property Development Bank in August 1928. Operating funds were to come through bond issues and establishment of savings-bank offices. The latter half of 1928, however, was neither economically nor politically propitious for initiatives of this sort.

The multiplicity of the dictatorship's programs and its administrative decentralization make difficult direct comparison of its record with that of the constitutional regime. Nonetheless, Cotorruelo Sendagorta estimates that from 1911 through 1932 approximately 15,000 housing units were constructed with government help.⁴⁰ If the 2,585 units constructed prior to 1924 are subtracted from that total, one is left with more than 12,000 units built with the dictatorship's legislation.

Government housing expenditure through 1924 has been estimated at 8,670,127 pesetas, an investment matched by 25,661,181 pesetas from other public and private sources.⁴¹ From 1924 through 1929 the dictatorship spent approximately 110,000,000 pesetas on housing.⁴² Both the dictatorship's financial commitment and its results surpassed those of the constitutional regime. The only area where comparison does not favor the dictatorship is cost efficiency. Under the constitutional regime new housing units were constructed at an approximate mean cost to the state of 3,400 pesetas, compared with 9,100 pesetas during the dictatorship.

The dictatorship took pride in its housing programs.[43] Not all of its satisfaction seems warranted. Its surpassing of the constitutional regime's record suggests more about the limited achievement of its predecessor than any positive accomplishment of its own. Even had all 15,000 housing units constructed in the two decades after 1911 been built in Madrid alone, they would have constituted only a small improvement in that one city's needs. Worse, much of the new construction proved too expensive for the low-to-moderate income groups it was intended for.[44]

Much of the blame can be placed on the cumbersome state bureaucracy. Applications for matching grants were discouraged by endless paperwork, a myriad of small requirements, and long delays.[45] But the wheels of government turned very quickly for the well-connected. While sincere applications were snarled in red tape, there were rumors of corruption and sizable profits made by a few contractors.[46] Here lies part of the explanation for the greater cost of housing units during the dictatorship.

The ultimate source of failure, however, was the fact that the regime did little to transform housing itself into a profitable investment. It passed onto the second republic the same inconsistency it had inherited from the constitutional regime between rent controls and new housing. With this problem unresolved, it was unable to disburse all the matching grants it made available for housing.[47] Spain still suffers the consequences.

Public Health and Social Insurance

The dictatorship inherited a rudimentary public-health system from the constitutional regime. By 1923 a health bureaucracy and guidelines on the responsibilities of the state and local government had been established. The dictatorship's accomplishment was less one of major changes in the system and more one of infusing it with a new spirit.[48] The regime increased the funding of services that had been financially starved under the constitutional regime.[49] The total amount spent on public health during fiscal year 1920–21 was 4,032,000 pesetas. In fiscal year 1929 the total was 11,780,000 pesetas. Money spent on infants' health rose from 65,000 pesetas to 1,325,000 pesetas. Public charity expenditure rose from 2,362,000 pesetas to 4,693,000 pesetas.

Public health was one of Martínez Anido's responsibilities at the interior ministry.[50] He oversaw the establishment of the Central Anti-Malaria Commission and the National Public Health School in 1924.

The latter trained public-health inspectors and administrators. It was the first such institution in Spain. In 1925 the National School of Child Health and Welfare was established to train youth workers and child-health-care specialists. During the same year the National Testing Institute was established to monitor the quality of commercial pharmaceutical products. Before the dictatorship victims of leprosy were generally warehoused in poorly maintained, underfinanced centers. The regime built new facilities in Granada, Orense, Alicante, and the Canary Islands and established a National Leprosy Institute for overseeing the care of patients. A later innovation was the 1927 merger of separate health agencies into a single National Health Institute.

However, the same rivalry for political and personal advantage that plagued other branches of government under the dictatorship also afflicted public health.[51] Dr. Francisco Murillo Palacios, head of the health system, found his authority repeatedly challenged by his subordinate, Dr. José Alberto Palanca, who had ties with Martínez Anido. Conflict between them impeded the system's functioning and did not end until Martínez Anido sacked Murillo in 1928.

The government delegates were an early instrument for public health.[52] But many *pueblos* saw little need to alter traditional health and sanitation practices. The problems raised by the delegates concerning water purity, waste disposal, or filthy slaughter houses and laundry facilities were often not seen as problems by the local people. Moreover, the delegates were frequently handicapped by their inexperience and unfamiliarity with the areas assigned to them. They either set unrealistic or unobtainable goals or resigned themselves passively to conditions they were meant to master. In each case they became irrelevant to the local people and lost effectiveness as agents of change.

More successful was systematization and recompilation of existing law. The constitutional regime's legislation was frequently sound. But lack of administrative follow-through and neglect had created uncertainty as to the responsibilities of different branches of government. Typically, when the dictatorship was confronted with a particularly confused situation concerning state aid for local water-system improvements, it sorted through past legislation on the matter and reissued the principal parts of it as a single comprehensive act.[53] In many instances the dictatorship also mandated greater local responsibilities.[54]

Much of its legislation remained, nonetheless, incomplete, inadequately funded, or more a statement of intent than of action. Still, more progress was made in public health than in most other areas during the dictatorship. The death rate due to malaria fell between 1924 and 1927 from 5 per 10,000 to 0.5 per 10,000.[55] From 1923 through 1930 the infant mortality rate fell fourteen percent.[56] The death rate also fell at approximately the same rate.[57]

Government-sponsored social insurance began with establishment of the National Insurance Institute in 1908.[58] The retirement program with which the institute started was not a substitute for existing cooperative and private insurance-company programs.[59] Instead the institute intended to reach out to the large numbers of Spaniards not yet covered by any pension program. Enrollment was limited initially to those with incomes below 4,000 pesetas per year. The institute's function was as much educational as insurance. The mortality rate had fallen from 32.0 per 1,000 in 1890 to 23.5 per 1,000 in 1908. More people were living beyond their peak productive years.[60] At the same time, increased geographic mobility brought a decline in traditional community and family supports for the elderly. These facts pointed to a need to inculcate the idea of saving for retirement, as well as to provide an easily understood program allowing working-class wage earners to do so. The institute sought to meet these needs through voluntary insurance. Employee contributions were supplemented by government and employer contributions. The program was administered through local savings and insurance centers. Nearly thirty percent of the proceeds were invested in socially useful projects, such as low-income housing, hospitals, agricultural loans, and electrification.[61] Most of the remaining capital was invested in government securities, with lesser amounts placed in industrial issues, real estate, and loans to private individuals. Employee contributions, however, were modest, and the program continued for nearly a decade more as a catalyst for saving than as a comprehensive retirement system in itself.

Invalid, widow, and orphan benefits were initiated in the final years of the constitutional regime.[62] The institute began subsidizing cooperative unemployment insurance schemes in 1919. A retirement fund was also established for children. Its purposes were to keep assessments down by beginning payments at an early age and to inculcate in the young the idea of saving for old age. Another modification was the "system of improvements," whereby a worker could make extra contributions in return for a larger pension, an earlier starting date for benefits, or a larger estate for his heirs. The institute was also intrusted in 1923 with the state's new program of 50-peseta maternity grants. The most important change made before the dictatorship in the institute's original program, however, was compulsory participation in the retirement program in 1921.[63]

Those additional responsibilities meant that the institute was experiencing growing pains when Primo took power. The compulsory-retirement insurance program faced employer opposition and worker apathy.[64] Other programs, such as the maternity grants and system of improvements, had only just begun. Social insurance was not an immediate priority for Primo. By the time of the civil government, however, Primo had become an enthusiastic advocate of old age insurance and occasionally even appeared at promotional "Homages to the Aged" organized by the institute.[65] The dictatorship also established a separate retirement fund for employees of the pension system and its various affiliates. Throughout the dictatorship the institute studied ways to extend social insurance. It was particularly concerned with cottage industries, the merchant marine, and agriculture. Planning meetings were also held for maternity and unemployment insurance. In this sense, the dictatorship was less a time of innovation than of consolidation and preparation for future advances.

By 1923 government sponsored social insurance was relatively new. As late as 1927 the institute viewed itself as a back-up for the programs of private companies and cooperative organizations.[66] By the end of the dictatorship this situation was reversed. The institute's program had grown so quickly in numbers and capital that the government itself had become the principal provider of social insurance.[67] Still, it is important to note that the program's capitalization only amounted to approximately 15 pesetas per person in the country in 1930.

Clearly, the dictatorship did institute social reforms bettering the life of the working classes. In many areas the dictatorship achieved more than the constitutional regime. Nonetheless, the social reform record of Spain's self-proclaimed iron surgeon was disappointing in much the same way as Europe's other rightist dictatorships in the period.[68] Most of the dictatorship's legislation originated elsewhere, either with the constitutional regime or the International Labor Office. The dictatorshop realized improvements in relatively uncontroversial areas such as public health and social insurance. But it backed away from eliminating the rent controls underlying the housing problem in the same way that it sidestepped rural land reform. In general, Primo tried to influence, rather than basically alter, the course of social development. When that flow was in a positive direction, as with women and apprentices, his government was little more than a benign irrelevance. But when that flow was negative, as with housing, his government did little to improve the situation. Part of his disinclination for strong action stemmed from reluctance to antagonize his conservative backers. But Primo himself was also motivated by the conviction that Spain was, as constituted, an essentially healthy and united country. As such, he lacked the vision and sense of purpose needed for fundamental reform.

NOTES

1. Tuñón de Lara, *El movimiento,* p. 776.
2. Andrés Gallego, *El socialismo,* pp. 130–31.
3. On labor legislation before the dictatorship, see Alfonso R. de Grijalba, *El contrato de trabajo* (Madrid: Francisco Beltrán, 1922).
4. The history of legislation on the labor contract is given briefly by Alejandro Gallart Folch, *Derecho español de trabajo* (Barcelona: Editorial Labor, 1936), pp. 43–51.
5. Aunós discusses the Labor Code in *La política social de la dictadura* (Madrid: Real Academia de Ciencias Morales y Políticas, 1944), pp. 47–51.
6. José Luis Aranguren, "La mujer de 1923 a 1963," *Revista de Occidente* 1, 2ª epoca, nos. 8–9 (1963): pp. 31–43; and Anabel González, Amalia López, Ana Mendoza, and Isabel Urueña, *Los orígenes del feminismo en España* (Madrid: Editorial Zero, 1980), pp. 109–55. The extent of these changes should not be overstated. The degree to which even "emancipated" women continued to see their role in traditional terms is evident in María Martínez Sierra, *La mujer ante la república: Conferencias leídas en el Ateneo de Madrid en los días 4, 9, 11, 15 y 18 de mayo de 1931* (Madrid: Tipográfia Artística, 1931).
7. Miguel Primo de Rivera, *Intervenciones en la Asamblea Nacional del General Primo de Rivera* (Madrid: Sáez Hermanos, 1930), p. 67.
8. Carmen Ferns de Zaracondegui, "Actuación femenina en la vida nacional," *Unión Patriótica,* 15 November 1926, p. 8, and E. Rodríguez Sadia, "La mujer y la paz," ibid., 1 December 1926, p. 4.
9. Maura Gamazo, *Bosquejo* 2:96.
10. *Hojas Libres,* January 1928, pp. 82–84.
11. *Heraldo de Panadés,* 21 December 1929, p. 1.
12. Ibid., 14 September 1929, p. 2.
13. The ILO's role as a shaper of much of Spain's labor legislation for women and children is discussed in Gallart, *Derecho,* pp. 261–67.
14. Private organizations and local and provincial governments had also been active in encouraging pre- and postnatal care as well as the building of maternity hospitals; José Bordiu, *Los municipios y los seguros sociales* (Madrid: Imprenta Municipal, 1927), p. 581.
15. Gallart, *Derecho,* p. 262.
16. Bordiu, *Los municipios,* pp. 60–61.
17. Instituto Nacion de Previsión, *Memoria 1934,* p. 109.
18. Temma Kaplan, "Spanish Anarchism and Women's Liberation," *Journal of Contemporary History* 6, no. 2 (1971): 103.
19. Nadal, *La población,* p. 188.
20. Aunós, *La política social,* pp. 52–53 and 82. A different system of family subsidies was enacted by the Franco regime; Michael Kenny, *A Spanish Tapestry* (London: Cohen and West, 1961), p. 182; and Posada, *Los seguros sociales,* pp. 163–202.
21. Supplemental legislation to the 1926 act is listed in las Heras, *Auxiliar,* pp. 317–18 and 688. The 1928 act is discussed in Ceballos Teresi, *Historia económica* 6:457.
22. In 1860 the birth rate was 26.5/1,000; in 1900, 33.8; in 1920, 29.3; in 1930, 28.2; and in 1960, 21.6; Nadal, *La poplación,* pp. 129–30.
23. These percentages are computed on the basis of figures in INE, *Principales actividades,* p. 165. The growth in absolute numbers over the same period was from 1,194 to 3,285. Student disorders and campus closures distort enrollment figures for the re-

maining years of the regime. By 1930 total enrollment had fallen to 33,557 from 39,719 in 1927. Women's enrollment over the same period fell from 3,285 to 1,744. Women's attendance did not rise significantly during the republic. Total women's enrollment reached its peak at 2,980 in 1935. The highest percentage of women in the university population during the republic was 8.9.

24. In 1920, 9.2% of the active population was composed of women and in 1930, 10.0% was so composed; Francisco Sánchez López, "Movilidad social en España (1900–1930)," *Revista de Estudios Políticos* 119 (1961): 49.

25. Ministerio de Trabajo y Previsión, *Salarios y jornadas de trabajo, 1914–1930* (Madrid: Sobrinos de la Sucesora de Minuesa de los Ríos, 1931), p. 127.

26. Ibid.

27. Wages for skilled women rose from an index of 82 (1914 = 100) to 124 in 1925 and 153 in 1930. Over the same period wages for skilled males rose from 86 to 116 in 1925 to 114 in 1930. Wage increases for men and women apprentices were approximately equal. Women's wages had traditionally been less than men's. Women were also less represented by trade unions. This suggests that part of the increase in their wages might have resulted from employer efforts to take advantage of the weak position of organized labor in the period by replacing relatively expensive male workers with less expensive females; ibid., p. 33.

28. On child labor legislation in the period, see Gallart, *Derecho,* pp. 261–66 passim.

29. On recent child labor conditions, see "Menores en el trabajo," *Cuadernos para el Diálogo* 119 (May 1973): 44.

30. Ministerio de Trabajo, *Salarios y jornadas,* p. 33.

31. This quotation is taken from the preamble to the 8 December 1926 decree on rents, as reprinted in Ceballos Teresi, *Historia económica* 6:535.

32. Cotorruelo, *La política,* p. 48.

33. Ibid.

34. Iglesias, *Política,* pp. 100–191.

35. This concern is evident in the regime's 15 December 1924 decree on rents. Relevant portions are quoted in Ceballos Teresi, *Historia económica* 6: 278.

36. Summaries of housing legislation from the period are contained in las Heras, *Auxiliar,* pp. 71–74, 195, 378, 510–11, 30, 49, 130, 142, and 81, and Miguel Carazony de la Rosa et al., *Legislación española: Leyes sociales* (Madrid: Editorial Lex, 1934), pp. 795–956.

37. The text is quoted in *Boletín Oficial del Ministerio de Trabajo,* 15 August 1924, p. 36.

38. Bordiu, *Los municipios,* pp. 31–32, and Aunós, *La política social,* p. 54.

39. Aunós, *La política social,* p. 42.

40. Cotorruelo, *La política,* pp. 55–56. Cotorruelo himself derived this figure from a 1932 report of the Real Estate Social Policy Patronate (Patronato de Política Social Immobilaria).

41. Ibid., pp. 51–52.

42. Overall 91,468,049 ptas. were spent on workers' housing *(casas baratas).* Another 20,000,000 ptas. was raised through debt emission for other low- to middle-income housing. Ibid., p. 54.

43. *Unión Patriótica,* 1 October 1926, pp. 6–8, and 15 October 1926, pp. 4–5.

44. Cotorruelo, *La política,* p. 55.

45. Iglesias, *Política,* p. 101.

46. Maura Gamazo, *Bosquejo* 2:130–37.

47. Iglesias, *Política,* p. 101.

48. A listing of public health legislation is contained in las Heras, *Auxiliar,* pp. 453, 835–42, and 195–96. The dictatorship's goals and accomplishments are discussed by Isidro S. Fígueroa, *Unión Patriótica,* 1 October 1926, pp. 30–31; 15 October 1926, pp. 23–25; 1 November 1926, pp. 19–23; 15 November 1926, pp. 25–26; and 25 December 1926, pp. 13–20.

49. The following totals are from Calvo Sotelo, *Mis servicios,* p. 481.

50. Oller Piñol, *Martínez Anido*, pp. 184–93.
51. The fate of the dictatorship's "new men" and their programs for public health is detailed in Rico-Avello, *Notas*, pp. 21–25.
52. An account of the activities of a governmental delegate in public health is contained in E.T.L., *Por pueblos*, pp. 101–8, 117–18, and 121–26.
53. de Ucelay, "Las obras municipales," p. 183.
54. This trend was particularly evident in municipal water supply and sewage disposal matters. José María Cano Rodríguez, "La actual legislación sanitaria y sus modificaciones convenientes," *Revista de Obras Públicas* 77, no. 2535 (15 October 1929): 390–91; 77, no. 2536 (15 November 1929): 431–36; 78, no. 2546 (15 April 1930): 159–64; and 78, no. 2552 (1 June 1930): 323–26.
55. Oller Piñól, *Martínez Anido*, pp. 184–93.
56. Jordi Nadal, *La población española* (Barcelona: Ediciones Ariel, 1917), p. 188.
57. Ibid., p. 130.
58. The early history of the institute is detailed in Instituto Nacional de Previsión, *¿Qué es el Instituto Nacional de Previsión?* (Madrid: Instituto Nacional de Previsión, 1927), pp. 3–16; Inocencio Jiménez, *El Instituto Nacional de Previsión* (Madrid: Instituto Nacional de Previsión, 1930), pp. 9–60; and Carlos G. Posada, *Los seguros sociales* (Madrid: Revista de Derecho Privado, 1943), pp. 3–38 and 113–42.
59. Instituto Nacional de Previsión, *Qué es*, pp. 3–4.
60. Nadal, *La población*, p. 129.
61. At the end of 1929, the institute's 324,164,332 ptas. in investments were distributed as follows: 155,677,991 ptas. in state bonds, 8,432,843 ptas. in local government bonds, 68,052,584 ptas. in railroad and industrial securities, 48,001,607 ptas. in various secured loan notes, 840,565 ptas. in loans to various official corporations, 24,931,476 ptas. in loans to various social organizations, 8,459,554 ptas. in loans to different individuals, and 9,767,712 ptas. in real estate. Altogether, a total of 94,871,050 ptas. from these different categories was invested for social purposes. Jiménez, *El Instituto*, pp. 57–60. See also *Boletín Oficial del Ministerio de Trabajo*, 15 August 1924, pp. 35–36.
62. José Bordiu, *Los municipios*, pp. 79–94 passim; and Gallart, *Derecho*, p. 40.
63. See Instituto Nacional de Previsión, *Régimen obligatorio de retiros obreros* (Madrid: Calpe, 1925).
64. Jiménez, *El Instituto*, pp. 13–14 and 16–17, attests to resistance to the program, particularly in less modern areas of the country.
65. Jiménez, *El Instituto*, p. 37.
66. Instituto, *Qué es*, p. 4.
67. For two different views on how well this ssytem has functioned recently, see Perceval, *The Spaniards*, p. 183, and "Developmental Social Security," *Spain Today*, 16 March 1970, pp. 31–32.
68. Particularly striking is the analogy with Italy, where "government-sponsored insurance systems against unemployment, old age, accident, and invalidity were for the most part legacies from the era of the much-maligned Giolitti or from the semi-revolutionary year 1919. What Mussolini did was to rationalize them and extend their range while simultaneously whittling down other workers' rights that were already in existence"; H. Stuart Hughes, *The United States and Italy* (New York: W. W. Norton, 1968), p. 88.

9

Corporate Labor Organization

The dictatorship's corporate labor organization was one of its most ambitious reforms. Based on individual labor-management arbitration committees, it regulated many labor matters. Aunós traced corporativism's origins to the nineteenth century.[1] However, it was early-twentieth-century industrial growth and social conflict that produced general interest in institutionalizing labor-management cooperation. Spaniards were aware of arbitration committees in other parts of Europe.[2] The Social Reform Institute was established in Spain in 1903 with representatives of trade unions and employer associations. One of the institute's earliest functions was to mediate labor conflicts.[3] The industrial tribunals had been established in 1912. They were presided over by a lower-court judge from the national judiciary and included worker and management representatives as the jury. As law courts, the tribunals were enmeshed in legalism and appeals. They were not well suited to deal with the upsurge in labor conflict in the 1910s.

The politicians' failure to cope with the challenges of these years led some employers and workers to search for new methods of bridging the gap between them. This search produced the first mixed arbitration commission in Barcelona, consisting equally of worker and employer representatives.[4] Special acts of the Cortes in October and November 1919 lent the commission legal backing, but this particular experiment was doomed from the start. Barcelona was Spain's most revolutionary city, and it was then passing through its most turbulent period before the civil war.[5] What hurt the commission most, however, was its generic aspect. Since it was not limited to any one industry, it lacked the representative quality needed for labor and employers to entrust their disputes to it.

A second spontaneous attempt at labor-management cooperation was more modest. The Mixed Commission for Commercial Labor in Barcelona was limited, as its name implied, to commercial trade. It received government recognition in April 1920. That act authorized separate joint committees of employer and worker representatives for banking, transport, wholesale trade, and retail trade. Each committee, in turn, chose representatives to sit on a higher mixed commission chaired by a magistrate of the Barcelona court. The latter body had a general supervisory function. This experiment enjoyed a measure of success, despite the polarized labor relations at the time.

International developments reinforced this momentum. In 1908 the Lucerne Congress of the International Association for Labor Legislation had endorsed arbitration committees as a means of resolving wage disputes. During the war several countries resorted to this device to gain labor's cooperation in maintaining production. After the war fear of revolution and recognition of the need for social reform led to its extension.

Socialist members of the Social Reform Institute also encouraged state action.[6] In 1919 the government established a mixed commission to arbitrate construction wages in Madrid. A similar act that year established regulatory juntas to intervene in harvest strikes. A 1922 act encouraged provincial governments to create mixed commissions. The committee system was extended to certain sectors of government service in August 1923.

The directory showed little interest in carrying forward the constitutional regime's progress. Its inactivity stemmed, in part, from preoccupation with political reform and the fighting in Morocco. Employer resistance to "worker control" was a factor as well.[7] Aunós, however, was greatly impressed by Mussolini and visited Italy in April 1926 when the Italian Labor Charter was unveiled.[8] Scarcely a month later Belgium announced its arbitration system. Aunós tested the waters in Spain with a July 1926 decree on cottage industries, containing a provision for labor-management committees.

In November 1926, Aunós proclaimed the National Corporate Organization (Organización Corporativa Nacional). His declared goal was social peace based on a working together of labor and employers.[9] Aunós also intended a sense of shared enterprise to lead to increased productivity. These goals were conservative in that they presupposed, along with the dictatorship's other programs, working within rather than transforming the social order. At the same time, Aunós was neutral concerning the thrashing out of differences of opinion between labor and management that would take place within the corporate structure. In this sense, he was more sincere than his Italian counterparts.

Aunós claimed much originality for the scheme, notwithstanding his drawing on foreign models and Spanish precedents.[10] Belgian and Italian systems contained government controls over committee membership. But in Spain committee selection rested with trade unions and employer associations. The basis of the system was a "free union in an obligatory corporation."[11] With the Socialist UGT as the only mass trade union still functioning, its predominance in the corporate organization was assured. That fact made the system attractive to UGT leaders as a means of building their own strength as well as of achieving concrete gains for the working class.

There were four principal levels to the organization: the local labor-management committee *(comité paritario)*, the mixed commission *(comisión mixta)*, the council of the corporation *(consejo de corporación)*, and the delegate commission of the councils of the corporations *(comisión delegada de consejos)*.[12] At the low end of the scale, the local labor-management committee for a particular industry in a given area was composed of five worker and employer representatives each. Presiding over it were a president and vice-president appointed by the ministry of labor on the provincial governor's recommendation. The president and vice president's salaries were paid through assessments levied on the committee, particularly the employers. To ensure that the president and vice-president were nonpartisan, they were chosen from some other occupational category than that governed by the committee. This measure also contributed to their reliability as government agents. Each committee regulated labor conditions, enforced labor law, mediated disputes, and ran local employment offices. It had authority to petition lower court judges to impose fines of up to 1,000 pesetas against violators of its accords. The local committee's decisions could be appealed to higher levels of the corporate structure.

The next highest level was the mixed commission. It was composed of three worker and three employer representatives elected by the separate labor-management committees under its jurisdiction. Here, too, the labor ministry appointed a president and vice-president. The commission supervised and coordinated the activities of mixed committees in a particular branch of the economy, generally on a provincewide basis. In less developed provinces, where there was less immediate interest in corporativism, the labor ministry could appoint mixed commissions without the prior establishment of local labor-management committees. In these instances the mixed commission propagandized on behalf of the system.

Directly above the mixed commissions were the councils of the corporations. This level integrated nationally the labor-management committees and mixed commissions representing a particular industry.

Each council consisted of eight worker and eight employer representatives elected by the local labor-management committees. Again, the government appointed the president and vice-president. Each council was responsible for laying down general labor guidelines for its industry. It was also responsible for reviewing the activities of individual committees and commissions, and for adjudicating appeals. Each council was charged with advising the government on legislation as well as promoting productivity.

The highest corporate level was the delegate commission of the councils. The delegate commission was composed of seven employer and worker representatives each, chosen in an election in which two electors from each of the twenty-seven councils participated. At this level the state bureaucracy and corporate hierarchy merged. The director general of labor and social action and the inspector general of labor were ex officio members of the delegate commission, and the ministry of labor could take part in its deliberations as well. The delegate commission was the last appeal for a decision of a local labor-management commission, and it was the starting place for implementation and enforcement of much labor legislation.

Aunós conceived this structure as a transmission belt between the government and employers and workers. Ideas and problems requiring solution were to flow up and policy implementation down. Government technical personnel were authorized to advise at every level. While appeals could be made easily, the presidents of the local committees were government appointees carrying out state policy. Success in appealing a decision in which they had taken part was not easy.[13]

Aunós's system was enormously ambitious. It divided the national economy into twenty-seven separate corporations. Two of these—mining and fishing—were classified as "primary production." Sixteen additional corporations were listed as "secondary production": electricity, gas, and water; metallurgical processing and manufactures; construction material processing, including wood, cement, brick, and glass; construction and new buildings; furniture; textiles; clothing and hats; luxury goods, such as jewelry, games, and watches; scientific and electrical material; graphic arts, including printing, bookbinding, and photography; chemical-related industries such as pharmaceuticals, fertilizers, explosives, paper, celluloid, and leather goods; baked goods; canned foods; other food and candy processing; sugar and alcohol products; and the press and publishing. There were nine service-industry corporations: land transport; air and sea transport; telecommunications; public entertainment; hotels, restaurants, and taverns; hygienic services such as baths, barber shops, laundries, shoe shining, and public lavatories; commerce; banking; and any industry not included in the other twenty-six corporate categories.[14]

The obstacles to instituting such a grandiose project were formidable. Spain lacked the administrative resources necessary for rapid implementation of Aunós's plans. Far more seriously, the system required that labor and employers' divisions were small and readily negotiable. Few workers or employers shared that view, even in the relatively prosperous mid-1920s. Not surprisingly, the program's success was incomplete. It was slow to penetrate beyond the larger industrial centers, and even in Barcelona and Asturias it had few roots by 1929.[15]

These shortcomings are understandable. What is surprising is that the program succeeded as well as it did. On the basis of figures provided by Aunós, Stanley Payne has estimated that by May 1929 fifteen percent of the Spanish work force and somewhat less than half of the industrial workers were covered by the system.[16] Many labor-management committees existed largely on paper, but others had concrete accomplishments. The textile committee in Calella, for example, introduced a minimum weekly salary of 45 pesetas and established a local employment office.[17] The newspaper committee in Madrid established written contracts, up to a year's sick leave at reduced salary, twenty days vacation per year, and a generous severance-pay schedule. Cotton workers in Barcelona instituted old age and sickness pensions of 50 pesetas per week and introduced new guidelines for pay and working conditions. Catalan committees petitioned the government on maintaining wine-export markets.[18] At a higher level, many mixed commissions were also active. Overall, in 1929 and 1930 more than 1,000 accords were reached within the corporative structure.[19]

Through December 1930 in the first region—the provinces of Madrid, Cuenca, Ciudad Real, Guadalajara, and Toledo—20,346 disputes were presented to corporative entities.[20] Of these, 70.7% originated from labor-law infractions, 27.5% from disagreements over layoffs and dismassals, and 1.8% from strikes or lockouts. In the 14,399 disputes over points of law, local committees reached a clear-cut decision in 5,280 cases. In 4,574 instances fines or other sanctions were imposed. On the 359 occasions when strikes and lockouts were brought before corporate committees, there was successful adjudication 308 times. Nationally, 26% of all strikes in 1929 were resolved by corporate committees.[21] The system had similar success in arbitrating employee-dismissal disputes. Of the 5,598 complaints brought before corporate bodies, a mutually satisfactory settlement was achieved in 3,115 instances. Only 405 of 2,473 decisions returned in favor of one party or the other were appealed. Another measure of the system's effectiveness is the 13,531 inspection visits in the first region to monitor enforcement of corporate accords and labor laws. All but 48 of these inspections were made in Madrid, however, suggesting that the system had little penetration outside the capital. Nonetheless, the system was sufficiently established to provide a basis for the republic's mixed juries (*jurados mixtos*).[22]

In general, there was greater awareness of the system's shortcomings than its achievements. Business was particularly critical, complaining that the system subordinated economic life to political considerations.[23] Employers lost some of their freedom to make personnel and salary decisions. Within the corporate structure they were frequently outvoted by government and worker interests.[24] Cost was another negative factor. Most administrative expenses, including the salaries of the president, vice-president, and secretary of each committee and mixed commission, were paid for assessments and fines levied against employers.[25] Employers petitioned Aunós concerning these grievances in December 1928. Two years later they were still making the same remonstrances.[26] Primo himself speculated that discontent over the corporative organization alienated business from him.[27] Labor's attitude toward the system confirms some employer complaints. The UGT actively supported the scheme as benefiting workers and its own organization. Even elements of the proscribed CNT in Catalonia advocated participation.[28]

If labor found the corporate structure convenient for pursuing class interests, it had its own complaints.[29] Once a labor representative had been elected to a committee, he was totally independent of his rank-and-file constituency. As with the employer representatives, he could neither be recalled nor replaced. The Socialists complained that their representatives were often manipulated by the government-appointed committee officers. Some feared that corporatism would do away with unions altogether. Rank-and-file dissatisfaction, in fact, denied the Socialists much of their hoped-for organizational benefits. Although the Socialists held a near monopoly of worker positions in the corporate organization outside of Catalonia, they were unable to extract sufficient concessions from employers to generate strong worker interest in the system or to attract new members for the UGT. The Socialists actually experienced membership declines in the mining and industrial centers of Asturias and Vizcaya, two of their strongest provinces before the dictatorship and areas where the corporate system remained weak.[30]

Even the regime's principal propagandist acknowledged that the system was excessively complicated.[31] The marquis of Guad el Jelu, who worked under Aunós in the labor ministry, also voiced reservations.[32] He declared that it was not well thought out, and that continuing legislative "rectifications" eroded public support. Poor planning was particularly evident in the overlap in the authority of the local committees with the industrial tribunals. After Aunós's reform of the tribunals in August 1926, they confined themselves largely to questions of law. Many committees, on the other hand, lacked legal knowledge. They frequently announced decisions that belonged to judges, not arbitration boards. The improvised quality of the system was made more pronounced by the ongoing elections held for worker and employer representatives on new labor-management committees.

Clearly the corporate system was not as well conceived as it might have been. Equally apparent, its penetration was still incomplete at the fall of the dictatorship. Nonetheless, the system achieved more than it was often given credit for. That it was widely held in low esteem is partly attributable to Spain's class divisions. The dictatorship had intended that corporativism bridge class lines. Through it labor and capital were to resolve their differences and work for economic growth that would benefit them both. But, as seen, few workers or employers shared that goal. Most workers valued corporativism only to extract concessions from factory owners. Employers opposed the system from the beginning and showed little willingness to make concessions in return for the economic favors granted them by the regime.

Under these circumstances the corporative system could only function as a transmitter of large and irreconcilable differences. The state sought to condition this transmission process through its tutelary role in the system. But the gulf between labor and management was too wide for the dictatorship to bridge easily. Both sides feared and misunderstood its intervention. Their mutual suspicions, in turn, frustrated the work of the organization and limited its growth.

NOTES

1. Aunós, *La política social,* pp. 59–60. Corporativism's nineteenth-century antecedents are also discussed by Gabriel Maura Gamazo, *Jurados mixtos para diminuir las diferencias entre patronos y obreros y para prevenir o remediar las huelgas* (Madrid: Asilo de Huerfanos del S.C. de Jesus, 1901), pp. 230–35.

2. French experiments with corporativism are discussed briefly by Peter N. Stearns, "Against the Strike Threat: Employer Policy toward Labor Agitation in France, 1900–1914," *Journal of Modern History* 40, no. 4 (1968): 497–98.

3. Maximiano García Venero, *Historia de los movimientos sindicales españoles* (Madrid: Ediciones del Movimiento, 1961), pp. 310–11.

4. Gallart, *Derecho,* p. 165.

5. Thus, the CNT as the most important labor federation in the city only briefly supported the commission; Jon Amsden, *Collective Bargaining and Class Conflict in Spain* (London: London School of Economics and Political Science, 1972), p. 17.

6. The background to the dictatorship's corporative legislation is described by the count of Altea, "National Corporate Organization in Spanish Industry," *International Labour Review* 14, no. 6 (June 1927): 828–41. Increased strike activity and social tension after World War I also played a role in state support for arbitration committees. Additional information on this point is contained in Instituto de Reformas Sociales, *Avance estadístico de huelgas: Correspondiente al primer semestre de 1922* (Madrid: Editorial Bética, 1922), pp. 19–20 and 30; Instituto de Reformas Sociales, *Avance estadístico de huelgas: Correspondiente al primer semestre de 1923*, p. 28; and Grijalba, *El contrato*, pp. 251–54.

7. See, for example, Asociación constituida por los Vocales de Representaciones Patronal en el Instituto de Reformas Sociales, *El "Control" Obrero* (Madrid: Establecimiento Tipográfico de las Sucesoras de Rivadeneyra, 1923), pp. 20–63.

8. Aunós, *La política social*, pp. 58–59.

9. Ibid., p. 64.

10. Ibid., pp. 63–64.

11. Ibid., p. 64.

12. The formal structure of the corporate system is described in ibid., pp. 64–69.

13. Emilio Novoa, *Comités paritarios* (Madrid: Editorial Reus, 1931) pp. 35–40.

14. The corporate system was extended to agriculture in 1927. However, agricultural labor-management committees were far more restricted in their authority and little was done to implement them. In October 1927 a half-hearted attempt was made to provide a corporative framework for urban tenant-landlord relationships, and in October 1928 earlier corporate legislation governing cottage industry was strengthened. Nonetheless, the basic thrust of corporativism remained toward urban industry and commerce; Aunós, *La política social*, pp. 70–72, and Velarde, *La política economica*, pp. 154–55.

15. Ruíz González, *El movimiento obrero en Asturias*, pp. 196–97, and Santiago, *La Unión General de Trabajadores*, pp. 35 and 45.

16. Stanley Payne, "Spanish Fascism," p. 7; Carr, *Spain*, p. 571, estimates that by 1929 more than a million workers were affected by contracts negotiated by corporative committees.

17. The following examples are taken from Aunós, *La política*, pp. 73–77. Additional evidence of the efficacy of the system is contained in Santiago, *La Unión General de Trabajadores*, pp. 32–35, and Ministerio de Trabajo, *Estadística de las huelgas 1930–1931*.

18. AHN Leg. 139, Exte. 675.

19. Santiago, *La Unión General de Trabajadores*, pp. 33–37.

20. *Anuario estadístico 1930*, p. 605. Statistics have not been collected on other regions.

21. Ministerio de Trabajo y Previsión Social, *Estadística de las huelgas 1930–1931*, p. 29.

22. Amsden, *Collective Bargaining*, p. 26, and Gallart, *Derecho*, pp. 131 and 166–67.

23. The negative response of employers is detailed in Simone Comes, *L'Organisation Corporative de L'Industrie en Espagne* (Paris: Libraire de Jurisprudence Ancienne et Moderne, 1937), pp. 144–48.

24. Writing with unusual prescience in 1930, Gabriel Maura Gamazo foresaw the day when the dictatorship's corporate system might become the tool of a leftist government and militant trade unions; *Bosquejo* 2:34.

25. It would be interesting to know more about the identity of the state representatives in the corporate system. To what extent, for example, did the government attempt to use the corporate organization as patronage? Emilio Novoa, *Comités*, pp. 5–41 passim, provides indirect evidence on this point.

26. Comes, *L'Organisation Corporative*, pp. 147–48; and *Las Finanzas* 10, no. 373 (28 January 1920): 80.

27. Maura Gamazo, *Bosquejo* 2:196–97.
28. Tuñón de Lara, *El movimiento obrero,* p. 779–80.
29. Labor criticism is detailed in Novoa, *Comités,* pp. 5–41.
30. Andreś Gallego, *El socialismo,* pp. 150–51.
31. Pemartín, *Los valores,* pp. 383–84.
32. His critique is contained in Aunós, *La política social,* pp. 97–144.

10
Education

The dictatorship made important improvements in education. Its goal, as with the corporative labor organization, was to unify and modernize the country. However, its policies ultimately inspired wide opposition. The basic characteristics of Spanish education were well established at the beginning of the present century. The system was underfinanced, rigidly bureaucratized, out of touch with the rest of Europe, and riven by anticlerical and regional linguistic disputes. It produced more lawyers and professionals than the backward economy could absorb, but it did not produce enough technicians to modernize the country. In these respects education mirrored and reinforced Spain's backwardness more than it contributed to development.

Attempts were made to reform the system in the late nineteenth and early twentieth centuries. A number of would-be modernizers came from the Liberal party. They sought to increase the study of science and modern languages. These proposals were coupled with efforts to secularize state-supported education and to institute state inspection and control over church-supported schools. The clericals were strongest in the Conservative party. They favored maintaining traditional humanist-school curricula. They also advocated increased religious content in public education and continued autonomy for church schools. There was a fairly even balance between clerical traditionalists and secular modernizers. Unlike France, the conflict between them did not end in a decisive victory for either, but continued intermittently throughout the nearly half-century of the constitutional regime. With perception of educational reform distorted through contrasting lenses of clericalism and anticlericalism, it was almost impossible to reach consensus on measures to improve education per se.

Financial problems also existed. Educational reform, as with almost every other type of social and economic improvement, was handicapped by the limits of public and private capital. Politicians had little alternative to continued church and local-government control of education. Equally serious was the lack of public interest in education. In the early twentieth century discussion of education centered in a small, largely urban middle-class group. These journalists, academicians, and politicians divided on the specifics of reform, but they generally agreed that improved education was vital to Spain's regeneration. Luís Bello documented in considerable detail that their concern was not echoed in many Spanish *pueblos*.[1] What was taught in the schools had little relevance to the traditional lives of many parents. There were economic disincentives as well. School books were a burden on many family budgets. Each day a child attended school could mean a lost day of income from his labor. The low level of instruction and poorly maintained facilities of most primary schools did little to inspire attendance. In their apathy toward these conditions, local governments reflected their communities.[2]

The dictatorship had two general educational goals: expansion of the system at every level and its infusion with religious and patriotic spirit.[3] On one level, these objectives could be regarded as good politics. Every effort before and after the dictatorship to expand public education had been eyed with suspicion by the church. But by linking that expansion with measures favorable to the church, the regime could hope to win support for its educational programs from secular reformers and the church alike. This approach to reform, however, greatly overestimated the potential for consensus. In fact, the regime's clericalism generated so much discord that it detracted from most other aspects of its educational program. Specific mistakes in execution exacerbated this problem.

That education was so controversial was due in large measure to Eduardo Callejo, the civil government's minister of public instruction. Callejo was conscientious, hard working, and dedicated to Primo. Unfortunately, he lacked political judgment and experience. Time and again his clumsy application of Primo's religious and nationalist ideas

Educational Expenditures

1920–21	134,214,000 ptas.
1923–24	151,924,000 "
1924–25	162,186,000 "
1925–26	163,884,000 "
1927	173,643,000 "
1928	185,778,000 "
1929	212,700,000 "

SOURCE: Calvo Sotelo, *Mis servicios*, p. 479.

placed the regime in untenable positions and stirred controversy. Worse, Primo's sense of personal loyalty often amounted to a vice. Rather than undercut his embattled minister, Primo placed his government's prestige behind a series of questionable decrees.

Where Callejo was least controversial and most effective was primary education. State involvement at this level had long been accepted. At the same time, much required doing. Spain already had twelve national universities, and approximately the same percentage of university students as France, Germany, and Britain.[4] But illiteracy was far greater in Spain than in the more developed countries of north central and northwestern Europe.[5]

The importance of primary education was evident in the ninth of the Patriotic Union's ten commandments, a call "to contribute to the extent of my ability to the noble end that every Spaniard will by his eleventh year know to read and write as well as know God and love his country."[6] As early as 1924, Primo had committed primary education to moral, religious, and patriotic purposes. A February royal order called for suspension of teachers who advanced "doctrines opposed to the unity of the country or offensive to religion, or who acted with such little enthusiasm for these principles that it could be presumed that they held contrary views." Primo advocated the adoption of a single, national textbook for each level and area of instruction in order to promote his educational objectives. His plans for the single text, however, did not take final form at this time. Under the directory, improvement of primary education was largely a matter of exhortation. Local government was encouraged to make fuller use of its resources and the state matching grants originated by the constitutional regime. The governmental delegates were also asked to enforce required attendance laws and to rally local support for education.[7]

After this slow beginning the regime realized significant improvements. The number of state-sponsored elementary schools expanded from 27,080 in 1923 to 33,446 in 1930, an increase of 23.5%. Many older school buildings were either expanded or replaced. More than 8,000 primary schools were constructed in their entirety or received additions.[8] Over the same period the number of primary teachers increased 19.9%, from 28,924 to 34,680. This additional capacity provided for a growth in primary school attendance from 1,691,331 in 1924 to 2,078,696 in 1930.[9] The 22.9% jump in attendance from 1924 through 1930 exceeds the 16.4% increase achieved by the republic from 1931 through 1935. The regime also improved the quality of primary education. Minimum teacher salaries were raised to 2,500 pesetas per year and, in some instances, to 3,000 pesetas per year.

Primary Education

Year	Number of Schools	Number of Teachers	Number of Students
1923	27,578	28,924	—
1924	27,080	28,924	1,691,331
1925	27,684	29,661	1,727,980
1926	27,883	31,874	1,764,639
1927	27,883	33,518	1,800,008
1928	28,890	32,480	1,818,364
1929	30,904	33,518	1,836,720
1930	33,446	34,680	2,078,696
1931	35,989	35,680	2,148,978
1932	37,072	36,680	2,221,844
1933	38,499	49,168	2,262,140
1934	40,830	52,954	2,397,562
1935	42,766	46,805	2,500,391
1936	42,741	47,945	1,502,322

SOURCE: INE, *Principales actividades*, p. 163.

Meager as those amounts were, they represented an improvement in a country where teacher salaries as low as 1,500 pesetas were reported. These figures suggest that progress in primary education was one of the dictatorship's most significant contributions.[10]

If the dictatorship has not received the credit it deserves, part of the reason is the controversy resulting from its secondary and university education reforms.[11]

The potential for conflict was greater over secondary than primary education. The church controlled most secondary education. Curriculum emphasized the humanities and frequently reflected the church's views on political and social as well as religious questions. Secondary education also catered to the elite. Only a small percentage of the population benefited, and for most of that privileged number it was preliminary to university study.

Callejo attempted to improve the quality of secondary education and to increase its accessibility. The government established twelve state secondary schools from 1923 through 1930, bringing the total to 94. Enrollment at these schools increased from 57,679 to 70,876 over the period. Under the dictatorship, business schools also increased enrollment, from 7,233 in 1923 to 13,071 in 1930.[12]

Callejo would have done well to limit himself to quantitative increases. Instead he embarked on a major change in the content of instruction. He attempted to increase the amount of scientific and technical training offered and to require preuniversity specialization at an earlier age. He defended both measures as bringing Spain into line with more advanced European countries. Callejo was too much a friend of the church to receive much opposition from that quarter, despite the fact that his reforms were at variance with traditional Catholic education. But the measures were retroactive. Students already well into their secondary education were suddenly faced with new requirements before they could enter a university. Discontent resulted among middle-class parents to whom the regime looked for much of its support.

Callejo provoked still more controversy by requiring a single text throughout the country for each course of study. A desire to upgrade instruction and reduce its cost inspired this reform.[13] As seen, Primo had earlier promoted this measure as a means of inculcating civic and moral virtues. It was the reform's propoganda dimension that generated the greatest discontent. Many teachers also saw the single text as stifling their creativity.

The most controversial educational measures, however, affected the universities. At no other level were the regime's contradictions more apparent. One of its earliest promises was administrative decentralization. Three months after the Municipal Statute and eight months before the Provincial Statute, a June 1924 decree committed the dictatorship to university autonomy. Since the nineteenth century, academicians had sought greater curricular and financial freedom. The dictatorship hoped to win their support and improve instruction through increased flexibility in those areas.

However, after the brief euphoria following Primo's coup had subsided, criticism from intellectuals repeatedly stung Primo. By mid-1924 the relationship between the regime and the university community had become paradoxical. On the one hand, grants of autonomy continued until September 1929, when the Civil Engineer School was awarded that status. On the other hand, the dictatorship actively repressed academic dissent. Unamuno was the best known but not the only professor to face jail or exile. Other repressive acts included the required carrying of student identification cards and purging of the moderately leftist Junta for Further Study.

Primo's record was equally contradictory in linguistic matters.[14] He pledged local cultural autonomy. At the same time, he was committed to an integral Spain and declared that one of the country's worst threats was Catalan separatism. In recognition of what he regarded as legitimate regional aspirations, he expanded the Royal Academy in November 1926 to include eight specialists in Basque, Catalan, and Galician languages as well as several regional dialects. His government, however, discouraged regional languages in the schools. In December 1925, in fact, conflict on this matter between the ministry of public instruction and the Medical School of the University of Barcelona reached the point where the school was temporarily closed.

In education, as elsewhere, the dictatorship instituted sweeping personnel change. Political and patronage considerations, however, motivated this turnover as much as concern for learning. Worse, Primo and Callejo did not always make good use of even the few talented "new men" that they did attract. The Council of Public Instruction was the official advisory body for higher education. Callejo reorganized it in June 1926 to include nearly forty academicians, but he neither sought its advice nor included it in any significant way in decision making.[15] It was shortly thereafter that he purged the European oriented Junta for Further Study of a "sectarianism [that was] exotic and contrary to the Spanish spirit."[16] He replaced its members with sycophants who contributed little to that elite body.

The basic problem that the dictatorship had with the university community was that, as an authoritarian regime, it was incompatible with the spirit of liberal academic life. Primo and Callejo never understood that contradiction. They looked at the universities in a simple quantitative way as a needed service sector. The more students and professors there were, the more modern the country would become. In 1923 an all-time high of 25,690 students were enrolled. By 1928 the total had risen to 45,463.[17] Had it not been for the campus disorders of that year and the next, the student population might well have increased still further rather than falling to 41,229 in 1929. The dictatorship sought to make room for this expansion through construction of University City. The project had become a national cause even before Primo's coup. It was publicly identified with Alfonso, and benefited from private contributions as well.[18] What was intended was an entirely new campus for the University of Madrid, providing for one-fourth of the country's total university population. The dictatorship supported the project with 130,000,000 pesetas budgeted for its completion.[19]

The dictatorship also established residential colleges, imitating the British system, at the Universities of Salamanca, Zaragoza, and Valladolid. Another innovation was the Social School.[20] Aunós was the force behind this idea. He hoped to use the resources of his ministry for serious study of social problems. Settlement houses and social work had been developing for a half-century elsewhere in western Europe and North America. Aunós intended the school to achieve similar objectives in Spain.

In general, the dictatorship brought building and institutional innovation. More Spaniards benefited from university education than ever before. It is therefore more than simply ironic that conflict with students and professors became the most visible factor in Primo's downfall. This is partly explained by the regime's shortcomings, inconsistencies, and authoritarian clumsiness. However, these factors had been present before 1928, and only after that date did the relationship between them become fully polarized.

What drove the academic community into unremitting opposition was the extension of degree-granting authority in May 1928 to two Catholic institutions, the Jesuits' Deusto College and the Augustinians' El Escorial College.[21] The inspiration for this act came from the church. Callejo and his director of secondary and higher education, Wenceslao Gonzáles Oliveros, viewed the church's ambitions sympathetically. They submitted a proposal to this effect to a special committee of the National Assembly. When the committee rejected the plan, Primo disregarded its objections and enacted the proposal by decree.

From the dictatorship's perspective, this act did not directly attack the prerogatives of the national universities. Indeed, all that was intended was to extend to the church a share of the period's general growth in education. But in a country where there had always been a shortage of professional opportunities, the measure was viewed as a blow to the employment prospects of an already greatly expanded student population. For professors, opposition to the act was motivated less directly by self-interest. They had benefited from the expansion of education. Moreover, before any student at a nonstate university could qualify for a degree, he had to be examined by a professor from a national university. But what did matter to many academicians was that by extending degree-granting authority to Catholic schools, the regime upset the uneasy balance between secular and church interests.

University opposition was also likely related to the increasing debility of the regime.[22] By 1928, Primo had lost much of his direction, and it was evident that he was casting about for a way to leave office. Dissipation of the regime's support left it vulnerable and led to the clerical issue serving as a focal point for academic grievances that had been accumulating since 1923. When the dictatorship took action against university disorders in 1928 and 1929, it was taken aback to discover how much public opinion had shifted to the opposition. The government imprisoned the leader of the student radicals José María Sbert, as an example.[23] But that action only further inflamed the dissidents. Dissent from the universities was not enough to bring the dictatorship down by itself, but it distracted the regime and depreciated its public standing.

Education parallels the dictatorship's other social reforms. The regime demonstrated energy and ambition after a slow start under the directory. But it underestimated the difficulty of mending deep social and political divisions with rhetoric and administrative fiat from Madrid. Primo presumed that his good intentions provided sufficient middle ground for contending factions to unite. Mistakes in execution were certainly made. But the root of the regime's difficulties lay with its facile perception of the problem. Improvements in educational capacity and technical training were contributions to the modernization of the country. But the constitutional regime's experience had demonstrated that educational reform was potentially one of the most controversial questions before the country. Primo and Callejo failed to heed that lesson, and their record was diminished by needless conflict.

NOTES

1. Luís Bello, *Viaje por las escuelas de España,* vols. 1, 2, 3 (Madrid: Magisterio Español, 1926, 1929), and vol. 4 (Madrid: Compañía Ibero-Americana de Publicaciones, 1929).
2. Ibid. 1:34–35.
3. The dictatorship's educational reforms are reviewed in Pemartín, *Los valores,* pp. 449–80.
4. Banks, *Cross-Polity,* pp. 217–18, 230, and 233; and *Diario de las Sesiones,* 23 March 1932, p. 4689.
5. The definition of illiteracy is elusive; see Carlo M. Cipolla, *Literacy and Its Development in the West* (Harmondsworth: Penguin Books, 1969), pp. 11–18. On illiteracy in Spain, see María Dolores Samaniego, "El problema del analfabetismo en España (1900–1930)" *Hispana* 33, no. 124 (May–August 1973): 375–400.
6. *Heraldo del Panadés,* 7 September 1929, p. 1. On the Patriotic Union's views of the nationalist purposes of education, see also *Unión Patriótica,* 1 December 1926, p. 8.
7. E. T. L., *Por pueblos,* pp. 139–79. The delegates were particularly important to the dictatorship, given the absence of an efficient bureaucracy to enforce the regime's educational reforms. On this point, see Roberto Dottrens, *El problema de la inspección y la educación nueva* (Madrid: Espasa Calpe, 1935).
8. Calvo Sotelo, *Mis servicios,* p. 480.
9. Attendance statistics are lacking before 1924.
10. For a less positive view, see Rodolfo Llopis, *La revolución en la escuela* (Madrid: M. Aguilar, 1933).
11. For a partisan critique of the dictatorship's record in secondary education, see Marcelino Domingo, *Le escuela en la república* (Madrid: M. Aguilar, 1932), pp. 100–101.
12. Aunós, *La política social,* pp. 40–41 and 89.
13. On the seriousness of the textbook problem, see Domingo, *La escuela,* pp. 120–23.
14. Ibid., 61–63.
15. Pemartín, *Los valores,* pp. 462–63, and Maura Gamazo, *Bosquejo* 1:181–82.
16. Pemartín, *Los valores,* p. 464.
17. INE, *Principales actividades,* p. 165.
18. Beyond providing for expanded student numbers, another goal of Alfonso and Primo in constructing University City was to undermine the considerable influence that the Junta for Further Study had long exercised among academics. Among the private

contributions made to the project was 500 ptas. from the Chamber of Commerce in Alicante; AHN Leg. 2, Exte. 1133.

19. Pemartín, *Los valores,* p. 470.

20. Aunós, *La política social,* pp. 43–44; Gallart, *Derecho,* pp. 412–22 passim; and Pedro Sango y Ros de Olano, *Principios y realizaciones del servicio social* (Madrid: M. Minuesa de los Ríos, 1934), pp. 23–24.

21. For additional information on this issue, see Fernández Almagro, *Historia del reinado,* pp. 526–29 passim. The regime's clericalism affected the universities in other ways as well. In March 1928, for example, the government canceled a public forum on eugenics sponsored by the Medical School of the University of Madrid; Rubio, *Crónica,* p. 328.

22. It is interesting to note how summarily the regime dealt with an earlier outburst of campus discontent in spring 1926 through the arrest and exile of such prominent dissidents as Jiménez de Ásua and Álvarez del Vayo. When the Ateneo in Madrid protested, the government simply closed it as well; Maura Gamazo, *Bosquejo* 1:167–68.

23. AHN Leg. 138, Exte. 246.

11
The Social Situation at the End of the Dictatorship

Six and one-half years of "revolution from above" did little to alleviate social tensions. Under the dictatorship the upper classes grew more prosperous. A 1930 U.S. Department of Commerce report attested to their increased disposable income, finding that Spain was "a steadily rising" market for "foreign merchandise of a luxury or semi-luxury character."[1] American automobile exports to the country did, in fact, rise from $6,193,000 in 1926 to $11,112,000 in 1929.[2] Spain's own production of cars increased from 21,855 units in 1925 with a value of 110 million pesetas to 36,928 units in 1929 with a value of 270 million pesetas.[3] By 1930 the total of motor vehicle licenses issued had climbed to 238,547, an increase of 165% over the figure of 89,910 for 1925.[4] Figures on automobiles are paralleled by telephones. From 1923 to 1930 their number increased 129% from 91,800 to 210,300.[5]

Whereas these figures support the popular conception of the dictatorship as an era of prosperity for the established classes, the condition of the working class was less positive. The weakened position of organized labor and the dictatorship's price-support policies contributed to a 2.6% drop in real wages from an index of 106.6 to 103.8 between 1 January 1925 and 1 January 1930.[6] Nominal wage indices demonstrate that this deterioration had an uneven impact. The largest sectors, skilled males and unskilled workers, showed hourly wage declines for 1925 to 1930. Much of the increase in women and apprentice wages resulted from employers hiring them in place of higher salaries, skilled males. Women's wages advanced from one-third to one-half those of males. It is unlikely that much of the increase from 1920 to 1925 was due to the dictatorship. Partial figures compiled by the International Labor Office indicate that real wages from 1923 to 1925 in the building trades fell from an index of 111 to 104 for bricklayers and from

Nominal Hourly Wage Indices for Different Labor Categories
(1914 = 100)

Year	Skilled Workers		Unskilled Workers	Apprentices	
	Men	Women		Men	Women
1920	86	82	89	100	112
1925	116	123	117	142	150
1930	114	153	103	158	162

SOURCE: Ministerio de Trabajo, *Salarios y jornadas*, p. 33. No separate breakdown exists for male and female unskilled workers. The wage statistics are for nonagricultural occupations. Much less is known about agricultural labor, but it appears that a day's wage for unskilled agricultural labor was slightly less than half the national income average in the years before the First World War, less than a third that average following the inflationary war years, and somewhere between one-third and one-half the national average at the end of the dictatorship. Thus, agricultural labor probably experienced some short-term benefits from the prosperity of rural Spain in the 1920s but still did not improve its relative situation over the prewar period. See Malefakis, *Agrarian Reform*, pp. 100–102.

Asturian Coal Field Daily Peseta Wage

Year	Interior Work	Exterior Work
1923	11.25	8.79
1924	11.25	8.79
1925	10.99	7.68
1926	10.50	7.92
1927	10.72	7.90
1928	10.36	7.89
1929	10.50	7.94

SOURCE: Ministerio de Trabajo, *Salarios y jornadas*, 72.

an index of 133 to 108 for unskilled laborers.[7] Over the same period in the metal trades, the drop was from 104 to 90 for fitters, while the change was from 157 to 158 for unskilled workers. Asturian coal mining, for which yearly wage figures are available, mirrors the downward trend.

The wage decline was particularly pronounced in more developed provinces.[8] Nominal wages for skilled workers fell between 1925 and 1930 from an index of 233 to 224 in Barcelona, from 207 to 200 in Madrid, from 146 to 140 in Santander, from 192 to 188 in Málaga, from 190 to 188 in Cadiz, from 152 to 150 in Oviedo, and from 143 to 133 in Valencia. Exceptions to the trend for skilled workers were Vizcaya, the leading industrial province and always something of an anomaly, where wages climbed from an index of 273 to 295, and Seville, where wages increased from 219 to 225. Unskilled wages followed a similar pattern. They fell in Valencia from an index of 243 to 193, in Barcelona from 253 to 236, in Seville from 200 to 191, and in Zaragoza from 261 to 217. An exception to this trend was Madrid, where unskilled wages rose marginally from an index of 224 to 226.

There is some evidence that working conditions may also have deteriorated during the period. As noted, wages for interior and exterior mine work in Asturias declined by nearly 7% and 10% respectively from 1923 to 1929. During the same period, output increased by almost 27% with a nearly constant labor force.[9] Improved technology may have been partly responsible for increased productivity here, but accident statistics suggest there might have been a national tendency toward increasing work loads.[10]

There were bright spots in working-class life. Wages for clerical, paper, and railroad workers showed improvement. The eight-hour day provided leisure time for many workers. Movies, spectator sports, radio, and the popular press all made advances. Nonetheless, available evidence indicates that during a time of increasing prosperity for the well-to-do, most workers were losing ground. The unenviable position of Spanish labor is underscored by international wage and price statistics. These circumstances alienated far more workers from the regime than its social reforms won back.

Wage and Living-Expense Indices, 1 January 1930
(United Kingdom = 100)

Nation	Wages	Food	Heat, Light, and Soap
United States	259	132	131
Canada	203	122	123
Australia	173	114	117
Denmark	121	109	108
Sweden	121	106	107
Ireland	105	107	109
United Kingdom	100	100	100
Netherlands	85	85	98
Germany	81	106	106
Czechoslovakia	65	85	88
France	56	95	97
Austria	53	98	102
Poland	51	74	78
Italy	50	100	116
Spain	46	94	102
Estonia	32	70	72

SOURCE: Ministerio de Trabajo, *Salarios y jornadas,* pp. 173–74. The original source of this data was the International Labor Office.

The radicalization of labor under the dictatorship is demonstrated by the Socialists.[11] UGT trade-union leaders had opted, against the arguments of some PSOE leaders, for limited cooperation with the dictatorship. And certainly their appointment to a variety of governmental advisory and regulatory positions brought them closer to the center of political power than they had been under the constitutional regime. Still, the corporate organization disappointed UGT hopes for increased urban industrial membership. The union grew from approximately 217,386 to 258,503 between 1925 and 1929, with much of its growth coming from the nonindustrial areas of New Castile, Extremadura, Granada, and Aragon.[12] That increase was not insignificant. Neither was it particularly impressive for the sole national workers' organization in a nation of more than 23 million. Indeed it was probably not much more than one-fourth of the CNT's strength during its peak years before the dictatorship.

Such organizational considerations, however, were largely irrelevant to the rank and file. As seen, traditional Socialist strongholds in the northern industrial cities and mining areas gave little support to corporativism. Some Socialist workers began to look to the illegal Communists for leadership. In October 1927 workers in Bilbao went out on a 24-hour general strike against the regime. At about the same time, the Socialist leadership was cajoling Asturian miners to accept the dictatorship's plan to aid mine workers by working an additional hour every day without any increase in pay. The miners resisted this effort in a bitter month-long strike. Communist gains in the building trades in Seville in 1927 and 1928 further jolted the leadership.

The National Assembly was the issue over which rank-and-file dissatisfaction came to a head. Proposed participation in the assembly was cooly received in local Socialist meetings.[13] In October 1927 a special party congress repudiated not only representation in the assembly, but every other form of cooperation with the regime as well. Shortly before the June 1928 party congress, Primo attempted to bring the Socialists back into line by declaring,

> One could make a single exception, namely, in regard to the Socialist Party, if they had directed their activity to the study and solution of economic questions, particularly of the question of production. . . . But the leaders of this movement in Spain have proved to be disturbers of order and, with a few exceptions, have aimed rather at embittering the spirit of the workers and hindering production than at finding genuine solutions. . . . Therefore, the dictatorship cannot grant them any specially favored treatment as a party.[14]

The Socialist leadership was in a difficult position. The dictatorship had shown a consistent willingness to crack down on Socialist dissidence. With increased restiveness below and official intimidation above, the leadership equivocated. The regular party congress in June and the trade union congress in September declined to disassociate themselves from the regime. But the Socialists never did take part in the National Assembly. When the assembly's constitutional proposal was announced in 1929, the dictatorship's days were clearly numbered. The Socialists cautiously moved toward the opposition by calling for the prompt return of democratic government.

Other sectors of the labor movement also became more radical. Segui's murder in March 1923 had dealt a severe blow to the possibility of the CNT's evolving along reformist lines.[15] But as of 1924 it was still not certain that the confederation would become totally revolutionary. The CNT leadership called for a general strike to topple the dictatorship. The lack of rank-and-file support for the strike can be seen as resulting from either a realistic assessment of the dictatorship's strength or the weariness of labor generally after five years of bitter conflict. But in either case, the strike's failure demonstrates a lack of congruity between the rank and file and the radical leadership. Possibly under a government with greater sensitivity to labor, Ángel Pestaña and other moderates could have led the movement in a reformist direction. But labor did not fare particularly well in the 1920s, and driving the CNT underground in 1924 only reinforced the radicals. In 1927, Buenaventura Durruti, Francisco Ascaso, and Grigorio Jover formed the Iberian Anarchist Federation (FAI) to control the CNT and keep it on a revolutionary course. They never lost their grip on the confederation after that.

The Communists were decimated by the dictatorship's persecution and imprisonment of union leaders. Communist policy itself never deviated significantly from the Comintern's hard line. It was that militant stance which attracted disgruntled Socialists. Interestingly, the Catholic unions failed to grow significantly. Their failure can only partly be explained by the regime's support for the Socialists. More basically, the Catholic unions were premised on a belief in social cooperation inconsistent with labor's leftward drift in the 1920s.

Repression brought surface calm to labor relations. Strikes, in particular, were down considerably under Primo. Nonetheless, strikes jumped dramatically in 1930 after his fall. This increase cannot be attributed to the depression. Overall industrial activity in 1930 was ahead, if only marginally so, of 1929.[16] Unemployment does not appear to have risen significantly until 1931.[17] What this suggests is a failure of the dictatorship. The regime's economic program was generally seen as contributing to business prosperity benefiting the upper classes. Primo's social reforms were inadequate as a complement for these

Strikes

Year	Number	Days Lost	Workers
1922	488	2,672,567	119,417
1923	458	3,027,026	120,568
1924	165	604,512	28,744
1925	181	839,934	60,120
1926	96	247,223	21,851
1927	107	1,311,891	70,616
1928	87	142,698	70,024
1929	96	313,065	55,576
1930	368	3,745,360	247,460
1931	610	3,843,260	236,177
1932	435	3,489,473	269,104

SOURCE: *Anuario estadístico,* successive editions.

Barcelona Province Labor Exchange Activity

Year	Job Requests	Job Offers	Placements
1927	5,145	2,134	2,016
1928	5,337	2,206	2,070
1929	6,494	2,581	2,163
1930	6,265	2,058	2,010
1931	15,835	1,759 (sic)	1,941 (sic)
1932	7,561	1,385	1,355

SOURCE: González-Rothvoss, *Anuario español,* p. 46.

policies. They did not provide labor with either the material benefits or sense of security to alleviate class conflict.

NOTES

1. Philip M. Copp, "Spain: An Agricultural and a Growing Industrial Power," *Commerce Reports* 52 (29 December 1930): 772.
2. Ibid., p. 771.
3. Calvo Sotelo, *Mis servicios,* p. 261.
4. *Anuario estadístico 1930,* p. 509.
5. Banks, *Cross-Polity,* p. 198. Rates of increase in other European countries were 70% for the United Kingdom, 90% for France, 31% for Germany, 31% for Sweden, 87% for Switzerland, and 48% for the Netherlands. Many of the states with rates of increase similar to Spain came from late developing countries in southern and eastern Europe: 150% for Poland, 126% for Hungary, 103% for Austria, 142% for Italy, and 162% for Greece. It may be argued that the high rates of growth experienced by those countries signify only their late start and the small base from which they began. Still, the telephone was something of a luxury in most developed countries and even more of a luxury in relatively underdeveloped countries.
6. Ministerio de Trabajo, *Salarios y jornadas* pp. 154–55. The ministry compared wages at approximate five-year intervals–1914, 1920, 1925, and 1930.

The Social Situation at the End of the Dictatorship 229

7. *The Europe Yearbook 1926*, pp. 556–57.

8. Ministerio de Trabajo, *Salarios y jornadas*, passim. The human dimension of the problem posed by these statistics is discussed in *Hojas Libres*, 1 May 1927, pp. 19–24.

9. Ibid., p. 72, and Tuñón de Lara, *El movimiento*, p. 76.

10. The two sources on accident statistics in the period are the government and the private insurance companies and mutual organizations. Government figures show a dramatic increase in accidents, from 21,350 to 160,714, between 1921 and 1930. However, much of this increase was likely due to simple improvements in recording procedures. The unreliability of government figures is discussed in successive editions of the official *Estadística de los accidentes*, issued from 1904 to 1921 by the Social Reform Institute and thereafter by the labor ministry. See especially the volumes for 1922, pp. 8–10, and for 1923–24, pp. 7–9. More reliable appear to be the statistics of the private insurance companies and mutual organizations. They show an increase from 1923 to 1930 in accidents from 130,116 to 225,988 and in accident deaths from 337 to 652; Mariano González-Rothvoss, *Anuario español de política social 1934/35* (Madrid: Sucesores de Rivadeneyra, 1934), p. 1686.

11. General treatments of the Socialists in this period include Andrés-Gallego, *El socialismo*, and Harry Feldman, "The Socialist Movement in Spain (1917–1930)," (Master's thesis, Columbia University, 1958).

12. Tuñón de Lara, *El movimiento*, p. 775, and Payne, *The Spanish Revolution*, p. 78.

13. The position of the Socialist leadership in 1927 and 1928 is discussed in Feldman, "The Socialist," pp. 78–81.

14. *International Press Correspondence* 8 (1928): 676.

15. An anarchist perspective on the CNT is Murray Bookchin, *The Spanish Anarchists* (New York: Free Life Editions, 1977), pp. 204–24.

16. According to the *Anuario estadístico 1934*, p. 270, industrial production in 1930 had an index of 111.45 compared with 110.11 in 1929. Electrical production increased more in 1930 than it did in 1929; INE, *Principales actividades*, p. 84.

17. Unemployment statistics only began to be gathered systematically at the end of the dictatorship and then only in limited areas. According to Ministerio de Trabajo, *Estadística de las Huelgas 1930 y 1931*, pp. 46–50, there was a slow increase in unemployment for men from 3.29% in the first quarter of 1930 to 3.67% in the last quarter of 1931 in Barcelona province. Over the same period male employment fell from 322,097 to 319,258 but the number of those listed as unemployed only increased from 10,582 to 11,561. This discrepancy suggests a tendency for the unemployed to drop out of the labor market where they were statistically "lost." For more on the problem of unemployment and unemployment statistics in the period, see Joaquín Guichot y Javier Ruíz Almansa, *El paro involutario y estadísticas del mismo* (Madrid: Consejo Superior de Trabajo, Comercio y Industria, 1925); Luis Jordana de Pozas, *La previsión contra el paro forzoso* (Madrid: Sucesora de M. Minuesa de los Rios, 1928), pp. 15–16; Instituto Nacional de Previsión, *Compilación de disposiciones legislativas, estatuarias y reglamentarias del INP* (Madrid: Espasa Calpe, 1932), pp. 433–43 and 677–706; Instituto Nacional de Previsión, *La previsión contra paro forzoso* (Madrid, 1928), pp. 21–32; Instituto Nacional de Previsión, *Caja nacional contra el para forzoso* (Madrid, 1934), pp. 3–20 and 57–65; Anselmo Sanz Serrano, *Resumen histórico de la estadística en España* (Madrid: Instituto Nacional de Estadística, 1956), pp. 199–200; and Carlos Caamano, "El problema del obrero," *Blanco y Negro* 45, no. 2289 (2 June 1935).

Conclusion

Spain suffered the characteristic problems of late developing countries in southern and eastern Europe during the early twentieth century. Economic backwardness and social inequality reinforced each other. Closely tied to the structure of privilege, Spain's parliamentary politicians pursued policies advantageous to narrow elite interests. Those policies deepened inequalities and perpetuated backwardness. The politicians' failure aggravated and, in some instances, underlay the period's conflicts over class relations, regionalism, religion, the monarchy, and the military. Their failure also contributed to a crisis of political legitimacy, which left parliamentary government no defense when a difficult colonial war turned the army against it.

As dictator, Primo intended more than serving as the military's avenging angel. His goal was nothing less than national regeneration. He brought to government qualities that had been largely absent during the last years of the constitutional regime—energy, confidence, and an intense if somewhat ill-focused ambition for his country's future. Nonetheless, he too failed. His economic policies produced only a short-lived, unevenly distributed spurt. He expanded on the constitutional regime's social reforms but left office with class rifts as deep as before. His greatest failures, however, were political, where he tried and needed most to succeed. The Patriotic Union attracted more place seekers than patriots, and the National Assembly generated more divisions than it healed. The regime's constitutional proposal was so unworkable that Primo could not even use it to withdraw from power.

So great a failure had many origins. Bungling and inexperience were not the least. The sheer magnitude of Primo's objective, an all-encompassing revolution from above, also played a role. In February 1930 the economist Pedro Gual Villabi wrote of the fallen dictator:

> His great power of assimilation, the very rapidity of his mental reactions, and his dynamism—qualities which all recognize—led him to throw himself into every problem before the government. . . . To help him . . . he appointed ministers, who were too young and

perhaps a little too bright, and who also wished to have a great legislative impact. Out of these circumstances originated an enormous, fantastic legislative effort, which shook up everything, . . . and which, in the end sowed more dissent and criticism than it raised appreciation and praise.[1]

More basic to Primo's downfall, however, was a fundamentally flawed view of society and its reform needs. The Spain in which he was emotionally rooted was a country of small towns and prosperous farms. In that small-scale society the better elements and those who depended on them still knew and worked with each other face to face, not yet divided by extremes of wealth. That society, however, no longer existed, indeed never had. After six years in power Primo recognized as much himself in a speech in Toledo.

> I, who do not share an enthusiasm for building great cities, would be pleased to have all 22 million Spaniards living in 4,000 small towns of 5,000 people each (with the exception of a few capitals, manufacturing centers, and ports) with a very strong rural life, enjoying good communications and having a well distributed share of good, small, low cost industries, complemented by agricultural, forestry and livestock production, in which case there would not be large fortunes, but many small ones, and everyone would have to work to live; I have in mind a village life—moral, pure, civilized, healthful, and pleasant—in which the mayor, the judge, the priest, the military commander, the doctor, the schoolmistresses and schoolmasters, and the more educated citizens would be the leaders of each town, maintaining the principles of faith and church, morals, justice, patriotism, discipline, health, and citizenship. The support of a government promoting great irrigation works and transport facilities, and our capable artisans producing well and cheaply for markets which commercial instinct should seek and dominate—that would make Spain a prosperous and happy Arcadia.[2]

Primo's tragedy, and that of Spain, was that it was to this Arcadia that he had addressed himself on taking power. This image of an essentially consensual society led him to think of reform in terms of personalities and attitudes rather than social and economic structures. This mind-set gave him an exaggerated sense of the ease with which basic change could be effected through rhetoric and decrees from Madrid. In this mythic society resided his *neutra masa* to whom he directed his early political reforms—the governmental delegates, the municipal and provincial statutes, the Patriotic Union, and the Somatén.

Those efforts failed to produce a new civic compact. Rather than modify his political prescription, Primo sought to make Spain fit it through the economic and social programs of the civil government. That modernization drive, however, was flawed by Primo's basic conservatism as much as his political reforms had been. It presumed that quantitative social and economic improvements were both possible and sufficient without major structural changes. Constraints exercised by established classes and institutions also precluded Primo's following a more transformative course. Nor was he immune to the pleasures and profits proffered by the rich and powerful.

The civil government's activism did, however, briefly maintain the dictatorship's momentum. But, because it catered to short-term elite interests rather than to the long-term welfare of the nation, it was rapidly self-exhausting. As Primo tired of governing and Spain tired of him, the need for a political formula became urgent. But no basis had been laid for it. The irrelevance of Primo's vision was fully revealed in his final months in the large gap between his constitutional proposals and the political realities of the country.

To say that Primo failed, however, is not to say that he did not have a fundamental impact. His traditional conservatism made him a ready tool of Spain's new financial and industrial plutocrats. His development policies amplified the constitutional regime's unfortunate precedents. They widened that most fundamental social division between rich and poor and left the government in a deep fiscal crisis on the eve of the great depression. Primo's mishandling of regional and religious issues only aggravated the general crisis that forced Alfonso's abdication a year after his own departure and that plagued the republic that followed them both.

Spain in 1931 was far more troubled and difficult to govern than in 1923. Primo's own political reforms may have failed, but he had nonetheless succeeded in laying the basis for the mass political mobilization of the 1930s by discrediting the old political elite and by disrupting its local base of operation. When the dictatorship collapsed in 1930, few could or would put the pieces of the old regime together again. The second republic's own constitution had a number of safeguards against *caciquismo* and established a government far more reflective of its society than had been the case of either the dictatorship or the constitutional regime. This central strength of the republic was also its greatest weakness. After 1931 widely divergent opinions were transmitted clearly and directly to the center of the political arena. The very imperfection of the constitutional regime as a political intermediary, on the other hand, had allowed it to function as a buffer between contending factions.

Worse, the failure of the dictatorship's social and economic policies

Conclusion

meant that the republic had to deal with more threatening conditions than the monarchy. The depression exacerbated the situation. Under those circumstances the very representativeness of the republic resulted in the expression of strongly opposed views that furthered the politicization and division of the country. The republic reaped the whirlwind but could fall back on no store of political legitimacy to sustain itself. In this sense the dictatorship was no mere "parenthesis" in political evolution, but a revolutionary break in continuity well beyond the country's subsequent ability to accommodate.

That became clear as the republic attempted to formulate reform policies of its own. Manual Azaña, Marcelino Domingo, Indalecio Prieto, and other republican reformers committed blunders as political novices comparable to those of Primo's new men. That, however, was less the source of their failure and of the ensuing civil war than their attempt to enact meaningful, if moderate, social reform. Certainly the republic was a catalyst igniting revolutionary expectations in traditionally aggrieved groups. But the main thrust of its two center-left governments was less revolutionary than it was to reverse the dangerous precedents set by the dictatorship and constitutional regime. By 1931, policies catering to short-term elite interests had proven counterproductive to the country's long-term needs. But the polarized country bequeathed by Primo left the republic with little middle ground on which to enact moderate reform. Legislation insufficient to satisfy the left inflamed the right, contributing to the final split of July 1936.

Franco came to power after a three-year civil war wearing the internationally fashionable trappings of his fascist allies. Franco's fascism, however, was only slightly less ambivalent than Primo's. His support, too, ranged from established elites to the *clases medias*. The experience of the republic and civil war, however, cowed and united Franco's supporters behind him more than Primo's had ever been. Giving credit where due, Franco was also better at manipulating them by playing one faction against another.

Franco's policies also bore a resemblance to those of his authoritarian predecessor. Behind a showy corporatist facade, with the Falange substituting for the Patriotic Union, autarkic development continued to substitute for structural social change. Not surprisingly, those policies left Spain poor and divided. Poverty, though, had advantages of its own and became, to an extent, self-correcting. After autarky had reached its inevitable dead end in 1959, foreign tourists flocked to the country's cheap resorts, foreign investors came seeking low wages, and emigrants sent large portions of their pay home from more developed European countries.

Against the backdrop of an expanding economy and middle class, Spain welcomed the return of democracy after Franco's death in 1975. This time, too, democracy appeared ill-omened. Its arrival coincided with the developed world's stagflation, much as the second republic had been born into the world depression of the 1930s. Regional tensions, terrorism, and an aborted military coup also revived memories of earlier troubles.

Despite these disturbing parallels, Spain was a far different country in the late 1970s and early 1980s than it had been a half-century earlier. The economic growth of the late Franco years had helped to produce a broad middle-class society. A sense of material well-being trickled down to large sectors of labor. These circumstances, together with a general determination to avoid the mistakes of the past, laid the basis for the consensual politics of the past decade. New democratic governments of both right and left have had a difficult time with the regional disputes, structural economic problems, and social inequities that eluded Primo and Franco, but they have tackled them with more common purpose, respect for each other, and, indeed, greater prospects for long-term success than any previous Spanish regime in this century. The burden of a troubled past that Primo had inadvertently added to appears to be lifting at last.

NOTES

1. *Las Finanzas* 10, no. 377, (25 February 1930): 177.
2. Miguel Primo de Rivera, "Prologo," in *Curso de Ciudadania,* ed. Junta de Propaganda Patriótica y Ciudadania C. (Madrid, 1929), pp. 10–11.

Bibliography

GENERAL

Government Publications

Diario de las Sesiones

Instituto Nacional de Estadística. Principales actividades de la vida española en la primera mitad del siglo xx. Madrid: Instituto Nacional de Estadística, 1952.

Books

Acedo Colunga, Felipe. *José Calvo Sotelo.* Barcelona: Editorial AHR, 1957.

Alba, Santiago. *Para la historia de España.* N.p., 1930.

Alcalá Galiano, Álvaro. *The Fall of a Throne.* London: Thornton Butterworth, 1933.

Armiñan, José Manuel, and Armiñan, Luis. *Epistolario del dictador.* Madrid: Javier Morata, 1930.

Aunós y Peréz, Eduardo. *España en crisis 1874–1936.* Buenos Aires: Librería del Colegio, 1942.

———. *Primo de Rivera/Soldado y gobernante.* Madrid: Editorial Alhambra, 1944.

———. *Semblanza política del General Primo de Rivera.* Madrid: Gráfica Minerva, 1947.

Avilés Fernández, Miguel; Madrazo Madrazo, Santos; Mitre Fernández, Emilio; Palacios Martín, Bonifacio; and Redondo Castro, Isabel. *El siglo XX/Los primeros treinta años.* Madrid: EDAF, 1974.

Blanco, Carlos. *La dictadura y los procesos militares.* Madrid: Javier Morata, 1931.

Blasco Ibáñez, Vicente. *Por España y contra el rey.* Paris: Editorial Excelsior, 1925.

Bordiu, José. *Los municipios y los seguros sociales.* Madrid: Imprenta Municipal, 1927.

Bravo Morata, Federico. *La dictadura,* Vol. 1, *1924 a 1927.* Madrid: Fenicia, 1973.

———. *La dictadura.* Vol. 2, *1927 a 1930.* Madrid: Fenicia, 1973.

———. *El golpe de estado de Primo de Rivera.* Madrid: Fenicia, 1973.

Brenan, Gerald. *The Spanish Labyrinth.* London: Cambridge University Press, 1974.

Burgos y Mazo, Manuel. *La dictadura y los constitucionalistas.* 4 Vols. Madrid: Javier Morata, 1934.

Calvo Sotelo, José. *La voz de un perseguido.* Vol. 1. Madrid: Galo Sáez, 1933. Vol. 2. Madrid: Librería de San Martin, 1933.

———. *Mis servicios al estado.* Madrid: Clásica Española, 1931.

Cambó, Francisco. *Primo de Rivera.* Madrid: Editorial Reus, 1946.

Cánovas Cervantes, S. *Apuntes históricos de "Solidaridad Obrera."* Barcelona: Ediciones C.R.T., n.d.

Capella, Jacinto. *La verdad de Primo de Rivera.* Madrid: Hijos de T. Minuesa, 1933.

Carr, Raymond. *Spain 1808–1939.* Oxford: Clarendon Press, 1966.

Castillo, Juan José. *Propietarios muy pobres.* Madrid: Servicio de Publicaciones Agrarias, 1979.

Castrillo Santos, Juan. *¿Se ha redimido España?* Madrid: Zoila Ascasíbar, 1930.

Ciges Aparicio, Manuel. *España bajo la dinastía de los Borbones.* Madrid: Aguilar, 1932.

Cimadevilla, Francisco. *El General Primo de Rivera.* Madrid: Afrodisio Agudo, 1944.

Cortes Cavanillas, Julián. *Alfonso XIII.* Barcelona: Editorial Juventud, 1973.

———. *La dictadura y el dictador.* Madrid: Velasco, 1929.

Díaz-Plaja, Fernando. *La España política del siglo xx.* Vol. 2, *De la dictadura a la guerra civil.* Barcelona: Plaza & Janes, 1972.

———. *El siglo xx.* Madrid: Instituto de Estudios Políticos, 1965.

Duarte, Fernando C. *España: Miguel Primo de Rivera y Orbaneja.* Madrid: Julián Espinosa, 1923.

Durán, J. A. *Historia de caciques, bandos e ideologias en la Galicia no urbana.* Madrid: Siglo Veintiuno de España, 1972.

Fernández Almagro, Melchor. *Historia del reinado de Alfonso XIII.* Barcelona: Montaner y Simón, 1934.

Finat Rojas, Hopólito. *¿Caul es el horizonte político de España?* Madrid: Francisco Beltrán, 1929.

Gandarias, Manuel. *Perfiles psíquicos del dictador Primo de Rivera y bosquejo razonado de su obra.* Cadiz: Escuelas Profesionales Salesianas, 1929.

García-Nieto, María Carmen; Donézar, Javier M.; and López Puerta, Luis. *La dictadura.* Madrid: Guadiana de Publicaciones, 1973.

García Venero, Maximiano. *Historia del nacionalismo catalan,* 2 Vols. Madrid: Editora Nacional, 1967.

García Venero, Maximiano. *Santiago Alba*. Madrid: Aguilar, 1963.
González Ruano, César. *El General Primo de Rivera*. Madrid: Ediciones del Movimiento, 1954.
———. *Miguel Primo de Rivera*. Madrid: Ediciones Nuestra Raza, n.d.
Guzman, Eduardo de. *1930*. Madrid: Tebas, 1973.
Haroc, Lewis. *General Primo de Rivera*. Madrid: Editorial Dólar, n.d.
las Heras Marín, Enrique. *Auxiliar indicador de la legislación española*. Madrid: Editorial Reus, 1929.
Herr, Richard. *Spain*. Englewood Cliffs, N.J.: Prentice-Hall, 1974.
Herrero García, Miguel. *Primo de Rivera*. Madrid: Editorial Purcalla, 1947.
de Hoyos y Vinent, Antonio. *El primer estado*. Madrid: Compañía Ibero-Americana de Publicaciones, 1930.
Iglesia, Caledonio de la. *La censura por dentro*. Madrid: Compañía Ibero-Americana de Publicaciones, 1930.
Iglesias, Dalmacio. *Política de la dictadura*. Barcelona: Espasa-Calpe, 1930.
Información Comercial Española. *Economía política de la dictadura de Primo de Rivera, Cuadernos Económicos de I.C.E.* Madrid: Ministerio de Comercio y Turismo, 1979.
Jellinek, Frank. *The Civil War in Spain*. New York: Howard Fertig, 1969.
López de Ochoa, General Eduardo. *De la dictadura a la republica*. Madrid: Zeus, 1930.
Marco Miranda, Vicente. *Las conspiraciones contra la dictadura*. Madrid: Tebas, 1975.
Maura Gamazo, Gabriel. *Bosquejo histórico de la dictadura*. 2 Vols. Madrid: Tipografía de Archivos, 1930.
Maura Gamazo, Gabriel, and Fernández Almagro, Melchor. *Por qué cayó Alfonso XIII*. Madrid: Ambos Mundos, 1948.
Maurín, Joaquín. *Los hombres de la dictadura*. Barcelona: Editorial Anagrama, 1977.
Oliveros, Antonio L. *Asturias en el resurgimiento español*. Madrid: Juan Bravo, 1935.
Oller Piñol, J. *Martínez Anido*. Madrid: Librería General de Victoriano Suárez, 1943.
Ortega y Gasset, Eduardo. *España encadenada: La verdad sobre la dictadura*. Paris: Juan Dura, 1925.
Ossorio y Gallardo, Ángel. *Mis memorias*. Buenos Aires: Editorial Losada, 1946.
Pabón, Jesús. *Cambó*. 3 Vols. Barcelona: Editorial Alpha, 1952, 1969.
Payne, Stanley G. *Politics and the Military in Modern Spain*. Stanford: Stanford University Press, 1967.
Pemartín Sanjuan, José. *Los valores históricos en la dictadura española*. Madrid: Publicaciones de la Junta de Propaganda Patriótica y Ciudadana, 1929.

Pérez, Dionisio. *La dictadura a través de sus notas oficiosas.* Madrid: Compañía Ibero-Americana de Publicaciones, 1930.

Petrie, Charles. *King Alfonso XIII and His Age.* London: Chapman & Hall, 1963.

Pilapil, Vicente R. *Alfonso XIII.* New York: Twayne, 1969.

Preston, Paul. *The Coming of the Spanish Civil War.* New York: Barnes & Noble, 1978.

Prieto, Indalecio. *Convulsiones de España.* 3 Vols. Mexico City: Ediciones Oasds, 1967, 1968, and 1969.

Primo de Rivera, Miguel. *Intervenciones en la Asamblea Nacional del General Primo de Rivera.* Madrid: Sáez Hermanos, 1930.

———. *La obra de la dictadura.* Madrid: Sáez Hermanos, 1930.

Ramírez, Manuel, ed. *Estudios sobre la segunda republica española.* Madrid: Editorial Tecnos, 1975.

Ramos Oliveira, Antonio. *Historia de España.* Vol. 2. Mexico City: Compañía General de Ediciones, n.d.

———. *Politics, Economics and Men of Modern Spain.* London: Victor Gollancz, 1946.

Ratcliff, Dillwyn F. *Prelude to Franco.* New York: Las Americas Publishing Company, 1957.

Reparaz, Gonzalo de. *Las responsibilidades políticas de la dictadura.* Madrid: Galo Sáez, 1933.

Revesz, Andrés. *Frente al dictador.* Madrid: Biblioteca Internacional, 1926.

Robinson, Richard A. H. *The Origins of Franco's Spain.* Pittsburgh: University of Pittsburgh Press, 1971.

Rubio Cabeza, Manuel. *Crónica de la dictadura.* Barcelona: Ediciones Nauta, 1974.

Saldaña y García Rubio, Quintiliano. *Al servicio de la justicia: La orgía áurea de la dictadura.* Madrid: Javier Morata, 1930.

Tarduchy, Emilio R. *Psicología del dictador.* Madrid: Sáez Hermanos, 1929.

Tuñón de Lara, Manuel. *La España del siglo xx.* Paris: Librería Española, 1966.

———. *Historia y realidad del poder.* Madrid: Edicusa, 1973.

Tusell Gómez, Xavier. *La España del siglo xx.* Barcelona: Dopesa, 1975.

Articles and Periodicals

Beals, Carleton. "Alfonso and Rivera in Joint Dictatorship." *Current History* 30 (July 1929): 633–40.

Beals, Carleton. "Modern Spain." *The Nation* 128 (26 June 1926): 760–62.

———. "Modern Spain." *The Nation* 129 (3 July 1929): 11–13.

———. "Modern Spain." *The Nation* 129 (17 July 1929): 74–76.

Ben-Ami, Shlomo. "The Dictatorship of Primo de Rivera." *Journal of Contemporary History* 12 (1977): 65–84.

Bledsoe, Gerie B. "The Quest for *Permanencia:* Spain's Role in the League Crisis of 1926." *Iberian Studies* 4, no. 1 (1975): 14–21.

Brinon, Fernand de. "An Interviewer in Spain: A Study of Dictatorship." *The Living Age* 324 (21 March 1925): 633–40.

Brooks, John. "Annals of Finance: Privateer." *New Yorker,* 21 May 1979, pp. 42–102, and 28 May 1979, pp. 42–91.

Carter, W. Horsefall. "Spain under Her Dictator." *The Contemporary Review* 134 (August 1928): 201–8.

Chandler, J. A. "Spain and her Moroccan Protectorate." *Journal of Contemporary History* 10, no. 2 (1975): 301–22.

Colectivo de Historia. "La dictadura de Primo de Rivera y la bloque de poder en España." *Cuadernos Económicos de I.C.E.* 6 (1978): 178–216.

Desmond, R. T. "The Aftermath of the Spanish Dictatorship." *Foreign Affairs* 9 (January 1931): 297–307.

———. "The New Regime in Spain." *Foreign Affairs* 2 (15 March 1924): 457–73.

Fleming, Shannon E.; and Fleming, Ann K. "Primo de Rivera and Spain's Moroccan Problem, 1923–1927." *Journal of Contemporary History* 12, no. 1 (1977): 85–99.

George, R. E. Gordon. "Spain's New Domestic and Foreign Policies." *Current History* 23 (December 1925): 345–53.

Harrison, Joseph. "Big Business and the Failure of Right Wing Catalan Nationalism, 1901–1923." *The Historical Journal* 19, no. 4 (1976): 901–18.

———. "Big Business and the Rise of Basque Nationalism." *European Studies Review* 7 (1977): 371–91.

Heathcote, Dudley. "Primo de Rivera and the New Spain." *The Fortnightly Review* 120 (November 1926): 593–603.

Lugan, Alphonse. "The Dictatorship in Spain." *Current History* 22 (June 1925): 345–54.

Malerbe, Pierre. "La dictadura de Primo de Rivera." *Historia 16,* extra 3 (June 1977): 76–87.

"The New Spanish Government." *European Economic and Political Survey* 1 (31 December 1925): 10–12.

Payne, Stanley G. "Spanish Fascism in Comparative Perspective." *Iberian Studies* 2 (Spring 1973): 3–12.

"Pillars of Government." *The Living Age* 325 (23 May 1925): 405–10.

Poynter, J. W. "Spain and Its Problems." *The Contemporary Review,* November 1923, pp. 611–18.

Primo de Rivera, Miguel. "Spain on the Road to Prosperity." *Current History* 23 (March 1926): 822–23.

Salazar, Rafael. "Perfil humano de Primo de Rivera." *Historia y Vida* 3 (January 1970): 58–63.

Saldaña y García Rubio, Quintiliano. "El famoso 'affaire' de la Compañía Santander-Mediterraneo." *Revista Nacional de Economía* 30 (March–April 1930): 177–214.

Sánchez, F. "Bibliographical List Relative to the Dictatorship of Primo de Rivera." *The Hispanic American Historical Review* (1931): 551–54.

"Spain under the Military Directory." *The Economic Review* 10 (22 August 1924): 169–70.

Waddell, Agnes S. "Spain under the Dictatorship." *Foreign Policy Association Service* 5 (4 September 1929): 221–38.

Unpublished Sources

Archivo Histórico Nacional (Madrid), Sección de la Presidencia.

Archivo General de Alcalá de Henares, Archivo de la Presidencia del Gobierno.

Boyd, Carolyn Patricia. "The Army and the Breakdown of Parliamentary Government in Spain, 1917–1923." Ph.D. diss., University of Washington, 1974.

Fleming, Shannon E. "Primo de Rivera and Abd-el-Krim: The Spanish Struggle in Morocco, 1921–1927." Ph.D. diss., University of Wisconsin, 1975.

Helmbold, Robert W. "A Study of the Role of the Military in Politics in Japan and Spain during the Interwar Period." Master's thesis, University of Chicago, 1951.

Malefakis, Edward E. "Why Reform Failed in Spain." Paper presented at the meeting of the American Historical Association, Boston, December 1970.

POLITICAL REFORM

Government Publications

Asamblea Nacional Consultiva. *Anteproyecto de constitución de la monarquía española y otras leyes complementarias.* Madrid: Nueva Imprenta Radio, 1929.

Instituto de Estudios de Administración Local. *Cincuentenario del Estatuto Municipal.* Madrid: Instituto de Estudios de Administración Local, 1975.

———. *Estudios y estadísticos sobre la vida local de España.* Madrid: Instituto de Estudios de Administración Local, 1943.

———. *La hacienda en el municipio rural español.* Madrid: Instituto de Estudios de Administración Local, 1949.

Books

American Universities Field Staff, Center for Mediterranean Studies. *The Identification of Pre-Fascist Elements in Certain Modern Societies.* Rome, 1971.

Balcells, Albert. *Historia del nacionalismo catalán, 1900–1939.* Madrid: Siglo Veintiuno, 1976.

Ben-Ami, Shlomo. *The Origins of the Second Republic in Spain.* Oxford: Oxford University Press, 1978.

Bullón Ramírez, Antonio. *Historia del secretariado de la administración local.* Madrid: El Consultor de los Ayuntamientos y de los Juzgados, 1968.

E.T.L. *Por pueblos y aldeas.* N.p.: Editorial Católica Toledana, 1928.

Elorza, Antonio. *Ideologías del nacionalismo vasco.* San Sebastián: L. Haranburu, 1978.

Felice, Renzo de. *Mussolini il duce.* Turin: Giulio Einaudi editore, 1974.

Fraile, Manuel. *El problema de la hacienda en los municipios rurales.* Madrid: Unión de los Municipios Españoles, 1928.

García Canales, Mariano. *La teoría de la representación en la España del siglo XX.* Murcia: Publicaciones del Departamento de Derecho Político, 1977.

García Cortes, Mariano. *Memoria.* Madrid: Unión de Municipios Españoles, 1928.

García de Enterría, Eduardo. *La administración española.* Madrid: Alianza Editorial, 1972.

Hansen, Edward C. *Rural Catalonia under the Franco Regime.* Cambridge: Cambridge University Press, 1977.

Kern, Robert W. *Liberals, Reformers and Caciques in Restoration Spain, 1875-1909.* Albuquerque: University of New Mexico Press, 1974.

Medhurst, Kenneth. *Government in Spain.* Oxford: Pergamon Press, 1973.

Moral, Joaquín del. *Oligarquía y "enchufismo."* Madrid: Galo Sáez, 1933.

Morillo-Velarde Pérez, José I. *El alcalde en la administración española.* Seville: Universidad de Sevilla, 1977.

Nicanor Puga, E.; Pí y Suñer, José María; and Cuesta, Fernando. *Informe sobre las haciendas locales.* Madrid: Unión de los Municipios Españoles, 1927.

Pemán, José María. *El hecho y la idea de la Unión Patriótica.* Madrid, 1929.

Reglá, Juan. *Historia de Cataluña.* Madrid: Alianza Editorial, 1978.

Ribé, Manuel. *Memorias de un funcionario.* Barcelona: Marte Ediciones, 1963.

Saura Pacheco, Antonio. *Presupuestos de las entidades locales.* Madrid: Instituto de Estudios de Administración Local, 1948.

———. *Principios y sistemas de haciendas locales.* Madrid: Instituto de Estudios de Administración Local, 1949.

Soldevilla, Fernando. *El año político.* Madrid: Julio Cosano, 1923-28.

Tusell, Javier. *La crisis del caciquismo andaluz (1923-1931).* Madrid: Cupsa Editorial, 1977.

———. *Oligarquía y caciquismo en Andalucía.* Barcelona: Editorial Planeta, 1976.

Tusell Gómez, Javier; and Chacón Ortiz, Diego. *La reforma de la administración local en España 1900-1936.* Madrid: Instituto de Estudios Administrativos, 1973.

Unión de los Municipios Españoles. *Memoria.* Madrid: Unión de los Municipios Españoles, 1927.

Valverde, José Tomás. *Memorias de un alcalde.* Madrid: Talleres Gráficos Escelier, 1961.

Varela Ortega, José. *Los amigos políticos.* Madrid: Alianza Editorial, 1977.

Wheeler, Douglas L. *Republican Portugal.* Madison: University of Wisconsin Press, 1978.

Articles and Periodicals

Ben-Ami, Shlomo. "The Forerunners of Spanish Fascism: Unión Patriótica and Unión Monárquica." *European Studies Review* 9 (January 1979): 49–79.

Corominas, Pedro; Vidal y Guardiola, Miguel; Tallarda, José María; Bausili, Andrés; Massó, Cristobal; Plana, Aljandro; Estragués, José; Caralt y Roca, J; de Nadal, Joaquín M.; Gay de Montella, Rafael; and Valdellos, José A. "La revisión de la obra económica de nuestras corporaciones locales durante la dictadura." *Revista Nacional de Económia* 30 (January–February 1930): 113–16.

García Hernández, José. "Hacienda estatal y hacienda local." *Revista de Estudios de la Vida Local* 13 (1954): 3–50.

George, R. E. Gordon. "Political Reform in Spain." *The Edinburgh Review* 242 (July 1925): 138–51.

Graham, Malbone W., Jr. "The New Spanish Constitution." *Current History* 28 (July 1928): 644–47.

Heraldo del Panadés (Villafranca del Panadés), 1929–30.

Historia 16, extra 5 (April 1978), "Autonomías: un siglo de lucha."

Hojas Libres (Hendaye), 1927–29.

Jiménez, Lombardo M. "El Estatuto Municipal y las contribuciones especiales." *Revista de Obras Públicas* 74 (1 January 1926): 16–18.

Linz, Juan J. "The Party System of Spain: Past and Future." *Party Systems and Voter Alignments.* Edited by Seymour M. Lipset and Stein Rokkan. New York: Free Press, 1967.

Mandoli-Giro, José María. "El derecho provincial." *San Jorge* 8 (1952): 61–63.

Martín-Retortillo, Cirilio. "Maura, municipalista." *Revista de Estudios de la Vida Local* 13 (1954): 51–60.

Medhurst, Kenneth M. "The Central-Local Axis in Spain." *Iberian Studies* 2 (Autumn 1973): 81–87.

Payne, Stanley. "Catalan and Basque Nationalism." *Journal of Contemporary History* 6 (1971): 15–51.

———. "Spanish Conservatism 1824–1923." *Journal of Contemporary History* 13 (1978): 765–89.

Tusell Gómez, Javier. "Abogados catalanes contra la dictadura." *Historia 16* 4 (October 1979): 46–54.

———. "The Functioning of the Cacique System in Andalusia." *Politics and Society in Twentieth Century Spain.* Edited by Stanley Payne. New York: New Viewpoints, Franklin Watts, 1976.

Ucelay, José de. "Las obras municipales y el servicio hidráulico." *Revista de Obras Púlicas* 74 (1 April 1926): 183–85.

———. "Servicios municipales." *Revista de Obras Públicas* 74 (1 January 1926): 28–32.

Unión Patriótica (Madrid), 1926–29.

Unpublished Sources

Dal Cal, Enrique Ucelay. "Estat Catala: The Strategies of Separation and Revolution of Radical Catalan Nationalism (1919–1933)." Ph.D. diss., Columbia University, 1979.

Linz, Juan J. "Spanish Cabinet and Parliamentary Elites: From the Restoration (1874) to Franco (1970)." Paper presented at Bellagio, August 1970.

ECONOMIC REFORM

Government Publications

Bernard, A. *Taxation of Incomes, Corporation, and Inheritances in Canada, Great Britain, France, Italy, Belgium, and Spain.* U.S. Senate. Document 186, 8:8400. Washington, D.C.: U.S. Government Printing Office, 1925.

Consejo de Economía Nacional. *La renta nacional de España.* 2 Vols. Madrid: Consejo de Economía Nacional, 1945 and 1947.

Great Britain. Department of Overseas Trade. *Economic Conditions in Spain.* London: His Majesty's Stationery Office, 1930.

———. *Report on Economic Conditions in Spain.* London: His Majesty's Stationery Office, 1928.

Instituto Nacional de Estadística. *Comercio exterior de España 1901–1956.* Madrid: Instituto Nacional de Estadística, 1958.

League of Nations. Economic Intelligence Service. *Statistical Yearbook of the League of Nations, 1930–1931.* Geneva: League of Nations, 1931.

Books

Banco Central. *Estudio económico 1956.* Madrid: Banco Central, 1956.

Banco Urquijo/Servicio de Estudios en Barcelona. *Las fuentes de financiación de la empresa en España.* Madrid: Editorial Moneda y Crédito, 1968.

Benavides, Leandro. *La política económica en la II república española.* Madrid: Guadiana de Publicaciones, 1973.

Benítez de Lugo, Felix. *Obra económica, financiera, y monetaria de la dictadura.* Madrid, 1930.

Bernis, Francisco. *Consecuencias económicas de la guerra.* Madrid: Estanislao Maestre, 1923.

Calvo Sotelo, José. *La contribución y la riqueza territorial en España.* Madrid: Servicio de Catastro de Rústica, 1926.

Cambó, Francisco. *La valoración de la peseta.* Madrid: Aguilar, n.d.

Campillo, Manuel. *Las inversiones extranjeras en España 1850–1950.* Madrid: Gráficas Manfer, 1963.

Campo, Isidro del. *Lo que no ha dicho Romanones: La hacienda en el antiguo régimen.* Madrid: Juan Pueyo, 1925.

Canals, Salvador. *La cuestión ferroviaria.* Madrid: Alrededor del Mundo, 1923.

Canosa, Ramón. *Un siglo de banca privada 1845–1945.* Madrid: Nuevas Gráficas, 1945.

Ceballos Teresi, José G. *Historia económica, financiera y política de España en el siglo xx.* 7 Vols. Madrid: Editorial El Financiero, 1931.

———. *Política y economía.* Madrid: Editorial El Financiero, 1934.

Chilcote, Ronald H. *Spain's Iron and Steel Industry.* Austin: University of Texas, 1968.

Fuentes Quintana, Enrique. *Sistema fiscal español y comparado.* Madrid: Burotel, 1967.

Gual Villabi, Pedro. *Política del comercio de los transportes.* Barcelona: Editorial Juventud, 1950.

Harrison, Joseph. *An Economic History of Modern Spain.* New York: Holmes & Meier, 1978.

Hertz, Frederick. *The Economic Problem of the Danubian States.* London: Victor Gollancz, 1947.

Lacomba, Juan Antonio. *Introducción a la historia económica de la España contemporanea.* Madrid: Guadiana de Publicaciones, 1969.

Lindner, Elli. *El derecho arancelario español.* Barcelona: Bosch, 1934.

Miguel, Antonio de. *El potencial económico de España.* Madrid: Gráfica Administrativa, 1935.

Moore, Wilbert E. *Economic Demography of Eastern and Southern Europe.* Geneva: League of Nations, 1945.

Muñoz, Juan. *El poder de la banca en España.* Madrid: ZYX, 1969.

Olariaga, Luis. *La política monetaria en España.* Madrid: Librería General de Victoriano Suárez, 1933.

Paris Eguilaz, Higinio. *El movimiento de precios en España.* Madrid: Consejo Superior de Investigaciones Científicas, 1943.

Perpiñá Grau, Román. *De economía hispana, infraestructura, historia.* Barcelona: Ediciones Ariel, 1972.

El problema de los ferrocarriles españoles. Madrid: Gráfica Administrativa, 1933.

Ramos Oliveira, Antonio. *El capitalismo español al desnudo.* Madrid: Librería Enrique Prieto, 1934.

Roldan, Santiago; García Delgado, José Luis; Muñoz, Juan. *La formación de la sociedad capitalista en España 1914–1920.* Madrid: Confederación de Cajas de Ahorro, 1973.

Sarda, Juan. *La intervención monetaria y el comercio de divisas en España.* Barcelona: Bosch, 1936.

Sevillano Carbajal, Virgilio. *¿La España . . . de quien?* Madrid: Gráficas Sánchez, 1936.

Sintes Olives, F. F.; and Vidal Burdils, F. *La industria eléctrica en España.* Barcelona: Montaner y Simón, 1933.

Solé Villalonga, Gabriel. *La deuda pública española y el mercado de capitales.* Madrid: Instituto de Estudios Fiscales, 1964.

Tamames, Ramón. *Estructura económica de España.* Madrid: Sociedad de Estudios y Publicaciones, 3d ed., 1965; 5th ed., 1970; 6th ed., 1971.

Torres, Manuel de. *El problema triguero y otras cuestiones fundamentales de la agricultura española.* Madrid: Consejo de Investigaciones Científicas, 1944.

Tortella Casares, Gabriel. *Banking, Railroads and Industry in Spain 1829–1874.* New York: Arno Press, 1977.

Trave, Federico. *Estudio sobre la peseta y los cambios 1898–1935.* Madrid: Editorial Reus, 1935.

Velarde Fuertes, Juan. *Flores de Lemus ante la economía española.* Madrid: Instituto de Estudios Políticos. 1961.

———. *Política económica de la dictadura.* Madrid: Guadiana de Publicaciones, 1968.

———. *Sobre la decadencia económica de España.* Madrid: Editorial Tecnos, 1969.

———, ed. *Lecturas de economía española.* Madrid: Editorial Gredos, 1969.

Wais San Martín, Francisco. *Historia general de los ferrocarriles españoles 1830–1941.* Madrid: Editora Nacional, 1967.

Articles and Periodicals

Aguilar, Manuel. "La actividad en la constucción de obras públicas y la valoración de la peseta." *Revista de Obras Públicas* 77 (1 March 1929): 92–96.

Andrés Álvarez, Valentín. "Historia y crítica de los valores de nuestra balanza de comercio." *Moneda y Crédito* 4 (March 1943): 11–25.

Aracil, Rafael, and García Bonafé, M. "Contemporary Spanish Economic History." *Journal of European Economic History* 9 (1979): 463–78.

Arespacochaga, Juan. "La política hidráulica en la decadencia económica española." *De Economía* 7: 146–213.

Ballesteros, Pío. "Medio siglo de hacienda española." *Anales de Economía* 8 (October–December 1948): 371–432.

Barreiro, Luis. "La industria minero-siderurgica española." *Revista Nacional de Economía* 3 (January–February 1930): 69–78.

Bermúdez Canete, Antonio. "Los presupuestos de la estabilización." *Revista Nacional de Economía* 31 (September–December 1930): 443–516.

Copp, Philip. "Spain: An Agricultural and a Growing Industrial Power." *Commerce Reports* 52 (29 December 1930): 771–74.

Cuesta Garrigos, Ildefonso. "Los grandes bancos españoles. Su evolución (1922–1943)." *Moneda y Crédito* 2 (December 1944): 36–65.

"Crónicas regionales." *Revista Nacional de Economía* 30 (March–April 1930): 303–18.

"Dictamen de la comisión nombrada por real orden de 9 enero de 1929, para el estudio de la implantación de patrón oro." *Lecturas de economía española.* Edited by Juan Velarde Fuertes. Madrid: Editorial Gredos, 1969.

Durán, F. "Algo sobre ferrocarriles." *Revista de Obras Públicas* 78 (15 May 1930): 262–67.

―――. "Transportes por carretera." *Revista de Obras Públicas* 78 (1 September 1930): 404–6.

"Economic Conditions in Spain." *The Economic Review* 14 (6 August 1926): 116–18.

Economic Tendencies in Spain." *The Economist* 105 (26 November 1927): 919–20.

Escario, José Luis. "Politíca de obras públicas." *Economía Española* 1 (1933): 15–24.

Fernández Díez, Gregorio. "La economía castellana ante la dictadura." *Revista Nacional de Economía* 30 (1930): 121–26.

Ferrari, Egidia. "Irrigation in Spain: A New Type of Institution." *International Review of Agricultural Economics* 4 (1926): 297–414.

Fontana, Josep, and Nadal, Jordi. "Spain 1914–1970." *Contemporary Economies-2.* Edited by Carlo M. Cipolla. New York: Barnes & Noble, 1977.

Houston, J. M. "Irrigation as a Solution to the Agrarian Problem of Spain." *Geographical Journal* 16 (1950): 55–63.

"Información." *Revista Nacional de Economía* 30 (March–April 1930): 281–94.

Las Finanzas, 1923–30.

Livengood, Charles. "Spain to Promote Consumption of National Products." *Commerce Reports* 41 (14 October 1929): 82.

Machimbarrena, Vicente. "La mejora y ampliación de la red ferroviaria española." *Revista de Obras Públicas* 128 (15 April 1930): 157–59.

Martin, Percy F. "Roads of Spain." *Roads and Road Construction* 7 (1 July 1929): 275–76.

Martín-Retortillo Baquer, Sabastián. "Trayectoria y significación de las confederaciones hidrográficas." *Revista de Administración Pública* 9 (January–April 1958): 85–126.

Martínez de Bujanda, E. "The Spanish National Irrigation Plan." *International Review of Agriculture* 25 (June 1934): 237–43.

Massó, Cristóbal. "La política monetaria española: 1868–1928." *Revista Nacional de Economía* 83 (January–February 1929): 17–37.

McGee, John S. "Government Intervention in the Spanish Sugar Industry." *The Journal of Law and Economics* 7 (October 1964): 121–74.

Muñoz, Juan. "La expansión bancaria entre 1919 y 1926: La formación de una banca nacional." *Cuadernos Económicos de I.C.E.* 6 (1978): 98–162.

Nadal Oller Jordi. "The Failure of the Industrial Revolution in Spain 1830–1914." *The Emergence of Industrial Societies-2*. Edited by Carlo M. Cipolla. London: Collins, Fontana Books, 1973.

Nadal Oller, Jorge. "La economía española 1829–1931." *Una historia económica*. Edited by Bano de España. Madrid: Banco de España, 1970.

Naylon, John. "An Appraisement of Spanish Irrigation and Land Settlement Policy since 1939." *Iberian Studies* (Spring 1973): 12–18.

Ortega Grau, Carlos, and Rafart Febrer, Juan. "Estudio sobre la deuda del estado español." *Cuadernos de Información Económica y Sociológica* 5 (December 1957): 134–85.

Paris Eguilaz, Higinio. "Comercio exterior, presupuestos y desarrollo económico en España." *Anales de Economía* 16 (April 1956): 53–125.

———. "Problemas de la expansión siderurgica en España." *Anales de Economía* 12 (July–December 1952): 271–384.

Perpiña Grau, Román. "Notas históricas de la economía carbonera española." *Lecturas de economía española*. Edited by Juan Velarde Fuertes. Madrid: Editorial Gredos, 1969.

Reparaz, Federico. "Las obras públicas y la cotización de la peseta." *Revista de Obras Públicas* 79 (15 February 1931): 66–71.

Rodríguez Spiteri, J. "Las carreteras españolas vistas por un inglés." *Revista de Obras Públicas* 77 (15 September 1929): 360–61.

Sánchez Cuervo, L. "El problema de la energía eléctrica en España." *Revista de Obras Públicas* 74 (15 October 1926): 450–53.

Sebastián, Mariano. "La presión tributaria en España y sus efectos sobre el ahorro y la capitalización." *Revista de Derecho Privado* 5 (1955): 197–215.

Serrano, César. "La racionalización de la industria de producción de energía eléctrica." *Revista Nacional de Economía* 30 (July–August 1930): pp. 3–16.

"Spain." *The Economic Review* 15 (15 March 1927): 126–28.

"Spain." *The Economic Review* 15 (15 June 1927): 274–76.

"Spain." *The Economic Review* 15 (15 December 1927): 506–7.

"Spain: Finance." *The Economic Review* 12 (4 September 1925): 208–10.

"Spain: Political and General." *The Economic Review* 13 (12 February 1926): 135–38.

"Spanish Economic Reconstruction." *European Economic and Political Survey* 3 (31 March 1928): 445–50.

Tyng, F. Edmond, Jr. "The Gold Standard for Spain." *The Foreign Securities Investor* 2 (9 June 1926): 3–4.

Vicens Vives, Jaime. "La industrialización y el desarrollo económico de España de 1800 a 1936." *Revista de Economía Política* 40 (January–July 1960): 138–47.

SOCIAL REFORM

Government Publications

"Asociación constituída por los vocales de representación patronal en el Instituto de Reformas Sociales. *El "control" obrero.* Madrid: Instituto de Reformas Sociales, 1923.

Instituto Nacional de Previsión. *Caja nacional contra el paro forzoso.* Madrid: Instituto Nacional de Previsión, 1934.

———. *Caja nacional contra el paro forzoso.* Madrid: Instituto Nacional de Previsión, 1935.

———. *Compilación de disposiciones legislativas.* Madrid: Instituto Nacional de Previsión, 1932.

———. *Compilación de disposiciones vigentes sobre seguros sociales.* Madrid: Instituto Nacional Previsión, 1956.

———. *Comunicación del instituto sobre la próxima discusión internacional del seguro contra el paro.* Madrid: Instituto Nacional de Previsión, 1934.

———. *Medalla del trabajo.* Madrid: Instituto Nacional de Previsión, 1930.

———. *Memoria 1934.* Madrid: Instituto Nacional de Previsión, 1935.

———. *Previsión contra el paro forzoso.* Madrid: Instituto Nacional de Previsión, 1928.

———. *¿Qué es el Instituto Nacional de Previsión?* Madrid: Instituto Nacional de Previsión, 1927.

———. *Régimen obligatorio de retiros obreros.* Madrid: Instituto Nacional de Previsión, 1925.

Instituto de Reformas Sociales. *Avance estadístico de huelgas: Correspondiente al primer semestre de 1922.* Madrid: Instituto de Reformas Sociales, 1922.

———. *Avance estadístico de huelgas: Correspondiente al segundo semestre de 1922.* Madrid: Instituto de Reformas Sociales, 1923.

———. *Avance estadístico de huelgas: Correspondiente al primer semestre de 1923.* Madrid: Instituto de Reformas Sociales, 1924.

———. *Movimiento de los precios al por menor en España durante la guerra y la postguerra 1914–1922.* Madrid: Instituto de Reformas Sociales, 1923.

Jiménez, Inocencio. *El Instituto Nacional de Previsión.* Madrid: Instituto Nacional de Previsión, 1930.

Ministerio de Trabajo. *Boletín Oficial del Ministerio Trabajo.*

———. *Estadística de los accidentes de trabajo.* Madrid: Instituto Nacional de Trabajo, 1924–1931/32.

———. *Estadística de las huelgas.* Madrid: Ministerio de Trabajo, 1925–34.

———. *Salarios y jornadas de trabajo 1914–1930.* Madrid: Ministerio de Trabajo, 1931.

Books

Alonso, Bruno. *El proletariado militante: Memorias de un provinciano.* Mexico City: Casa Ramírez Editores, 1957.

Amsden, Jon. *Collective Bargaining and Class Conflict in Spain.* London: Weidenfield & Nicolson, 1972.

Andrés-Gallego, José. *El socialismo durante la dictadura 1923–1930.* Madrid: Tebas, 1977.

Aunós y Pérez, Eduardo. *La política social de la dictadura.* Madrid: Real Academia de Ciencias Morales y Políticas, 1944.

Bello, Luis. *Viaje por las escuelas de España.* 4 Vols. Madrid: Magisterio Español, 1926, 1927, 1928, and Compañía Ibero-Americana de Publicaciones, 1929.

Bookchin, Murray. *The Spanish Anarchists.* New York: Free Life Editions, 1977.

Canals, Salvador. *Cuestiones económicas: El Comite Oficial de Seguros y el reaseguro obligatorio en el estado.* Madrid: Alrededor del Mundo, 1923.

Carazony de las Roda, Miguel; Granados Aguirre, Mariano; Maeso Enguídanos, Alfonso; Segovia Burillo, Ángel; and Peces-Barba del Brio, Gregorio. *Legislación española: Leyes sociales.* Madrid: Editorial Lex, 1934.

Castro, Cristóbal. *Al servicio de los campesinos.* Madrid: Javier Morata, 1931.

Comes, Simone. *L'Organisation Corporative de l'Industrie en Espagne.* Paris: Librairie de Jurisprudence Ancienne et Moderne, 1937.

Cotorruelo Sendagorta, Agustín. *La política económica de la vivienda en España.* Madrid: Consejo Superior de Investigaciones Científicas, 1960.

Domingo, Marcelino. *La escuela en la república.* Madrid: M. Aguilar, 1932.

Dottrens, Roberto. *El problema de la inspección y la educación nueva.* Madrid: Espasa-Calpe, 1935.

Fernández-Díaz-Faes, José María. *Lo social en la Asturias del siglo xx.* Oviedo: Diputacion de Asturias, Instituto de Estudios Asturianos, 1966.

Gallart Folch, Alejandro. *Derecho español del trabajo.* Barcelona: Editorial Labor, 1936.

García-Nieto Paris, Juan N. *El sindicalismo cristiano en España.* Bilbao: Universidad de Deusto, Instituto de Estudios Económico-Sociales, 1960.

Gascón y Miramón, Antonio. *Hacia una ley de cooperativos.* Madrid: Servicio de Publicaciones Agrícolas, 1927.

González, Anabel; López, Amalia; Mendoza, Ana; and Urueña, Isabel. *Los orígenes del feminismo en España.* Madrid: Editorial Zero, 1980.

González, Regino. *Las cooperativas.* Madrid: Imprenta Torrent, n.d.

González-Rothvoss, Mariano. *Anuario español de política social 1934–1935.* Madrid: Sucesores de Rivadeneyra, 1934.

Grijalba, Alfonso R. *El contrato de labor.* Madrid: Francisco Beltrán, 1922.

Guichot, Joaquín; and Ruiz Almansa, Javier. *El paro involuntario y estadística del mismo.* Madrid: Consejo Superior de Trabajo, Comercio e Industria, 1925.

Jordana de Pozas, Luis. *La previsión contra el paro forzoso.* Madrid: Sobrinos de Sucesora de Minuesa de los Ríos, 1928.

Llopis, Rodolfo. *La revolución en la escuela.* Madrid: M. Aguilar, 1933.

López de Sebastián, José. *Política agraria en España 1920–1970.* Madrid: Guadiana de Publicaciones, 1970.

Malefakis, Edward E. *Agrarian Reform and Peasant Revolution in Spain.* New Haven: Yale University Press, 1970.

Martínez Sierra, María. *La mujer ante la república.* Madrid: Tipografía Artística, 1931.

Maura Gamazo, Gabriel. *Jurados mixtos para dirmir las diferencias entre patronos y obreros y para prevenir o remediar las huelgas.* Madrid: Asilo de Huérfanos del S. C. de Jesús, 1901.

Meaker, Gerald H. *The Revolutionary Left in Spain.* Stanford: Stanford University Press, 1974.

Nadal, Jordi. *La población española.* Barcelona: Ediciones Ariel, 1971.

Novoa, Emilio. *Comités paritarios.* Madrid: Editorial Reus, 1931.

Payne, Stanley G. *The Spanish Revolution.* New York: W. W. Norton, 1970.

Pestaña, Ángel. *Terrorismo en Barcelona.* Barcelona: Editorial Planeta, 1979.

Posada, Carlos G. *Los seguros sociales obligatorios en España.* Madrid: Revista de Derecho Privado, 1943.

Redonet y López Dóriaga, Luis. *Crédito agrícola: Historia, bases y organización.* Madrid: Calpe, 1924.

Rico-Avello, Carlos. *Notas para la historia de la sanidad española.* Madrid: Dirección General de Sanidad, 1955.

Royo Martínez, Miguel. *El problema de la vivienda.* Seville: Editorial Edelce, 1953.

Ruiz González, David. *El movimiento obrero en Asturias.* Oviedo: Amigos de Asturias, 1968.

Sangro y Ros de Olano, Pedro. *Crónica del movimiento de reforma social en España.* Madrid: Sobrinos de la Sucesor de M. Minuesa de los Ríos, 1925.

———. *Principios y realizaciones del servicio social.* Madrid: Sobrinos de la Sucesora de M. Minuesa de los Ríos, 1934.

Santiago, Enrique. *La Unión General de Trabajadores ante la revolución.* Madrid: Sáez Hermanos, 1932.

Tuñón de Lara, Manuel. *El movimiento obrero en la historia de España.* Madrid: Taurus Ediciones, 1972.

———. *Variaciones del nivel de vida en España.* Madrid: Ediciones Península, 1965.

Articles

Altea, Conde de. "National Corporative Organization in Spanish Industry." *International Labour Review* 15 (June 1927): 828–41.

Aranguren, José Luis. "La mujer de 1923 a 1963." *Revista de Occidente* 1, segunda época (1963): 31–43.

Caamaño, Carlos. "El problema del paro obrero." *Blanco y Negro* 45 (2 June 1935).

Cano Rodríguez, José María. "La actual legislación sanitaria y sus modificaciones convenientes." *Revista de Obras Públicas* 77 (15 October 1929): 390–91; 67 (15 November 1929): 431–36; 78 (15 April): 159–64; 128 (1 July 1930): 323–26.

"Cooperative Movement in Spain." *Monthly Labor Review* 25 (October 1927): 788–91.

Giner, Salvador. "The Structure of Spanish Society and the Processes of Modernization." *Iberian Studies* 1 (Fall 1972): 53–68.

Harrison, R. Joseph. "The Beginnings of Social Legislation in Spain 1900–1919." *Iberian Studies* 3 (Spring 1974): 3–8.

Kaplan, Temma. "Spanish Anarchism and Women's Liberation." *Journal of Contemporary History* 6 (1971): 101–10.

Linz, Juan; and Miguel, Amando de. "Within Nation Differences and Comparisons: the Eight Spains." *Comparing Nations*. Edited by Richard Merritt and Stein Rokkan. New Haven: Yale University Press, 1966.

Sánchez López, Francisco. "Movilidad social en España." *Revista de Estudios Políticos* 119 (1961): 29–65.

"Social and Labor Conditions." *The Economic Review* 8 (9 November 1923): 404–5.

"Spanish Housing Law and Provisional Regulations of the Law." *Monthly Labor Review* 17 (July 1923): 188–91.

Unpublished Sources

Feldman, Harry. "The Socialist Movement in Spain 1917–1930." Master's Thesis, Columbia University, 1958.

Waggoner, Glen A. "Engineering Social Change: The *Comisión* and *Instituto* for Social Reforms, 1883–1923." Paper presented at the meeting of the American Historical Association, Boston, December 1970.

Index

Abd el-Krim, 38, 58
Accounts Tribunal of the Kingdom, 133
Acha, General, 124
Agrarian reform, 64, 179–80
Agriculture, 25, 28, 175–81; credit for, 104, 178
Aguilera, General Francisco, 48, 63
Aizpuru, General, 50
Alba, duke of, 113–14
Alba, Santiago, 21, 29, 30, 46, 58, 72 n.50, 103, 119, 143
Alcalá Zamora, Niceto, 21, 55, 82
Alfonso XII (king of Spain), 17
Alfonso XIII (king of Spain), 49–50, 56, 61, 63–64, 71 n.25, 108, 112–14, 118–21, 124, 140, 157, 167 n.18, 219
Álvarez, Melquiades, 55
Amoral familism, 135
Amortization department, 144–45
Anarchosyndicalism, 32, 43 n.60, 47, 55, 57, 68, 69, 94, 191, 210, 226–27
Andes, count of, 59, 121, 172–73
Anticlericalism, 24
Anual, 38, 46
Apprentices, 196
Ardanaz Crespo, General Julio, 59
Argüelles, Manuel, 89
Arlegui, General Juan, 54, 94
Army. *See* Military
Arnus Bank, 139
Artillery corps. *See* Military
Ascaso, Francisco, 227
Association of Producers and Distributors of Electricity, 164
Aunós y Perez, Eduardo, 53–54, 57, 59, 60, 191–93, 197, 205–6, 208–11, 219
Azaña, Manuel, 37, 55, 233

Azcárate, Gumersindo de, 52

Banking, 26, 30, 41 n.30, 42 n.51, 64–65, 67, 74 n.101, 136, 138–46, 149, 151 n.28, 159–60, 166 n.1, 167 n.4
Bank of Catalonia, 89, 94
Bank of Spain, 30, 138–39, 145, 148
Barrera, General Emilio, 53, 159
Basque provinces, 22, 29, 39 n.3, 98, 99 n.29, 108, 160
Belgium, 206
Benjumea, Rafael. *See* Guadalhorce, count of
Bermúdez de Castro, General Luis, 54, 58
Budget, 30, 42 n.45, 42 n.48, 138–46, 149 n.6, 150 n.8
Burguete, General, 124
Business, 61, 64–65, 67, 74 n.101, 108, 134–36, 159, 170, 174, 176

Cabia, marquis of, 148
Cabriñana, marquis of, 133
Caciquismo, 19, 22, 37, 38, 39 n.8, 80–84, 90, 92, 124–26, 232
Callejo, Eduardo, 59, 120, 215–21
Calvo Sotelo, José, 33, 52, 53, 54, 57, 59, 60, 61, 83–87, 95–96, 109–10, 120–21, 124, 135–38, 143, 146, 148–49, 160, 166, 172
Cambó, Francesco, 29, 47, 53
CAMPSA, 140, 151–52 n.34, 165–66, 174
Carlists, 22, 66, 106
Carr, Raymond, 34
Carrión, Pascual, 36–37
Cars, 223
Castellanos, Mercedes, 66
Catalonia, 18, 22, 23, 24, 29, 34, 37, 53, 55,

252

62, 63, 65, 67, 70n.15, 79, 92–98, 100n.46, 101n.56, 108, 110, 146, 151n.28, 160, 171–72, 176, 209, 210, 218
Catholic Action, 62
Catholic trade unions, 62, 191, 227
Cavalcanti, General José, 48–49, 52
Chacón Ortiz, Diego, 22
Child laor, 195–96
Church, 24, 32, 34–35, 61, 62, 74nn. 86 and 87, 107, 218, 220. *See also* Anticlericalism
Civil governor, 58–61, 84, 91, 95–96, 105
Clases medias, 21, 66–68, 105–7, 111, 118, 233
CNT (National Confederation of Labor). *See* Anarchosyndicalism
Coal, 25, 42n.42, 164–65, 172
Combined Olive Oil Commission, 129
Combustible Fuel Funding Agency, 165, 191
Comillas, marquis of, 48, 93
Commission for the Protection of National Production, 5
Commodity Committee, 176
Communists, 57, 68, 191, 226–27
Conflicts of interest, 55, 65–66
Conservative party, 17, 20, 21, 22, 23, 24, 29, 37, 46, 49, 65, 115, 139, 210
Constitutional draft of 1929, 117–19
Constitution of 1876, 17, 79, 103, 108, 111, 120, 123, 125
Cornejo, Admiral, 58
Corporatism, 84–85, 118, 169–70, 191, 192, 205–11
Correa, General, 124
Cortina, marquis of, 57
Costa, Joaquín, 66
Cotorruelo Sendagorta, Agustín, 197
Cotton Junta, 124

Debt, governmental, 60, 143–45
Delegates. *See* Governmental delegates
Deterding, Henri, 147
Domingo, Marcelino, 233
Durruti, Buenaventura, 227

Ebro Hydrographic Confederation, 145, 163, 177–78
Education, 18, 60, 62, 214–21

Eight-hour day, 57
El Debate, 55, 62, 97, 103, 110, 113
El Día Gráfico, 92
Electric power, 25–26, 30, 161–64
El Sol, 97
Energy, 161–66. *See also* CAMPSA; Coal; Electric power
Epoca, La, 97
Exchange rate, 67, 146–49
Exterior Bank of Spain, 94, 142
Eza, viscount of, 33

Flores de Lemus, Antonio, 52, 83, 86–87, 147
Foreign investment, 26, 40–41n.28, 173–74
Foreign trade, 28, 41n.29, 164
Foro, 25, 40n.22
France, 216
Franco, Francisco, 146, 177, 233–34
Free syndicates, 191
Fuel Council, 124

García de los Reyes, Admiral Mateo, 59
García Prieto, Manuel, 38, 46, 50, 55
General Intervention Agency of the State, 133
General Office of Commerce, Industry, and Insurance, 164
General Office of Railroads and Tramways, 157
Germany, 216
Gil Robles, José María, 53, 83
Gimeno, count of, 97
Goded, General Manuel, 121
Goicoechea, Antonio, 115, 116
Gómez Jordana, General Francisco, 71n.37, 124
Gómez Nuñez, General, 124
Gónzales Oliveros, Wenceslao, 220
Governmental delegates, 58, 79–83, 199
Guadalhorce, count of, 59, 60, 120–21, 124, 156, 160, 163–65
Guad el Jelu, marquis of, 211
Gual Villabi, Pedro, 230
Güell, count of, 48, 93

Hermosa y Kith, General Luis, 71n.37, 124
Herrera, Ángel, 62, 103
Herrero, Ignacio, 65

Hertz, Frederick, 181–82
Highways, 18, 160–61
Hitler, Adolf, 62
Hojas Libres, 112, 138, 148, 162
Housing, 33, 196–98

Industrial Credit Bank, 142, 169
Industrialists. *See* Business
Industry, 28, 145–46, 169–75, 176
Intellectuals, 22, 67
International Labor Office, 191, 194–95, 201, 223
International Telegraph and Telephone, 93, 139, 174
Irrigation, 177–78
Isabella II (queen of Spain), 56
Italy, 20, 56, 121–22

Jordana, General, 123
Jordana de Pozas, Luis, 83
Jover, Grigorio, 227
Junta for Further Study, 218

Labor legislation, 192–93
la Cierva, Juan de, 115, 116
Landowners, 21, 61, 64, 108, 135–36, 170, 177, 180
Largo Caballero, Francisco, 69, 115, 191–92
Latifundia, 25, 31
League for the Development of National Production, 93
Liberal party, 17, 20, 21, 22, 23, 24, 29, 37–39, 46–47, 49, 115, 139, 210
Llaneza, Manuel, 69, 115
Lliga party, 23, 29, 34, 36, 47, 53, 93–94
Local Credit Bank, 57, 87–89, 94, 142, 145
Local government, 17–19, 79–102, 104. *See also* Municipal government; Provincial government
Lorenzo Pardo, Manuel, 59, 60, 163

Macià, Francesc, 97
Madariaga, César de, 59
Madrid Mercantile and Industrial Directorate, 67
Madrid Mercantile Union, 136
Maeztu, Ramiro de, 115, 116
Magaz, marquis of, 71 n.37
Magaz y Pers, Antonio. *See* Magaz, marquis of
Malefakis, Edward E., 25, 179–80
March, Juan, 138, 160
Martínez Anido, General Severiano, 54, 57, 58, 72 n.54, 94, 115, 124, 142, 191, 198–99
Maura, Antonio, 29, 52, 66, 83
Maura, Gabriel, 115, 116
Maurism, 106
Mayandía y Gómez, General Antonio, 71 n.37, 124, 155
Medhurst, Kenneth, 89–90
Milans del Bosch, General, 124
Military, 23, 35–36, 38–39, 46, 48, 60, 62–63, 72 n.53, 82, 94, 121, 124–25
Minifundia, 25
Moreno Zulueta, Francisco. *See* Andes, count of
Morocco, 24, 34–36, 38, 46, 47, 58, 63, 70 n.21, 104, 146, 206
Municipal government, 18–19, 95. *See also* Local government; Municipal Statute
Municipal secretary, 85, 90–91
Municipal Statute, 56–57, 80, 83–91, 113, 162, 193, 218
Murillo Palacios, Francisco, 199
Muslera Planés, General Mario, 71 n.37
Mussolini, Benito, 56, 62, 112, 121–22, 147, 175, 206

Nación, La, 60
National Agronomy Institute, 179
National Assembly, 61, 66, 108, 111–19, 194, 226–27, 230
National Catholic Agrarian Confederation (CNCA), 66, 177
National Catholic Association of Propagandists, 62
National Council for Combustible Fuels, 165
National Economic Council, 57, 66, 124, 170, 172–73, 176, 179, 191
National Highway Authority, 160
National Insurance Institute, 87, 200–201
National Touring Foundation, 145
Navarro, General Luis, 71 n.37
Neutra masa, 23, 58, 66, 79, 106, 126, 139, 231
Nobility, 64
Nouvilas, General Godofredo, 63

Index 255

Nuñez, Juan, 140

O'Donnell, General. *See* Tetuan, duke of
Official Motor Transport and Automobile Commission, 124
Orange Junta, 179
Ortega y Gasset, José, 37
Ossorio, Ángel, 36, 57, 82, 115

Palanca, José Alberto, 199
Patriotic Union, 56–57, 58, 59, 66, 67, 103–15, 122–23, 126, 140, 177, 194, 216, 230–31, 233
Payne, Stanley, 34
Pemán Pemartín, José María, 109, 116
People's party, 22, 37, 53
Permanent Spanish Electrical Commission, 164
Pestaña, Ángel, 227
Plebiscite of 1926, 61, 108, 112–13
Poland, 9
Ponte, Galo, 53–54
Portugal, 9
Pradera, Victor, 110, 116
Prieto, Indalecio, 68, 233
Primo de Rivera, José Antonio, 65, 75 n.108, 139
Primo de Rivera y Orbaneja, Miguel, 9, 39, 45–69, 79–83, 91–98, 103–16, 118–26, 133–34, 136–37, 139–40, 148–49, 155–57, 159–60, 169–80, 191–96, 201–2, 210, 215–16, 218–21, 226, 230–34
Provincial government, 17–19
Provincial Statute, 57, 91–98, 113, 218
Public health, 18, 198–200

Radical party, 37
Railroads, 25, 27, 30–31, 104, 145, 155–61, 165, 167 n.14
Railroad Statute, 156
Railway Funding Agency, 156, 161
Ramos Oliveira, Antonio, 27–28
Reforestation, 178–79
Reformist party, 22, 37
Regulating Committee for Industrial Production, 170
Republicans, 24, 67, 126
Resin consortium, 179
Revesz, Andrés, 111–12
Ríos, Fernando de los, 68

Rio Tinto Company, 147
Rist, Charles, 143, 153 n.50
Rodríguez Mourelo, General, 113–14
Rodríguez Pedré, General Dalmiro, 71 n.37
Romania, 9
Romanones, count of, 55, 112
Ruiz del Portal, General Francisco, 71 n.37

Salazar, Antonio de Oliviera, 9–11
Sánchez Guerra, José, 65, 82, 110, 112–14
Sangro y Ros de Olano, Pedro, 59
Sarda, Juan, 146
Savings Bank for the Development of Small Properties, 140, 142
Sbert, José María, 220
Secretary. *See* Municipal secretary
Seguí, Salvador, 33, 47
Segura, Cardinal, 62
Seton-Watson, Hugh, 183
Shipbuilding, 30
Shipping, 158–60
Silió, César, 115, 116
Sindicatos libres. *See* Free syndicates
Social insurance, 200–201
Socialists (Spanish Socialist Workers Party or *PSOE*), 22, 37, 55, 68–68, 75 nn. 118 and 119, 126, 138, 191–92, 210, 226
Social Reform Institute, 36, 191–93, 205–6
Society of Industrial Assemblies, 164
Soldevila, Cardinal, 33
Somatén, 55, 66–67, 80, 110–11, 159, 231
Soriano, Rodrigo, 45–46
Spanish Coal Consortium, 164
State Mortgage Bank, 145
Steel, 30, 158
Strikes, 32–33, 37, 43 n.72, 209, 227–28
Students, 61–62
Superior Banking Council, 140, 148
Superior Labor Council, 191
Superior Railroad Council, 124, 156, 157, 191

Tariffs, 27–28, 31, 41 nn. 31 and 32, 64, 93–94, 104, 171–73
Tartiere banking interest, 65
Taxation, 18, 26–27, 29, 54, 60, 64, 86–87, 96, 133–38, 177
Technical Construction Company, 142
Telephones, 223
Tetuan, duke of, 58–59, 162

Torres Mendoza, marquis of, 113–14
Tourism, 26, 160
Traditionalism, 110, 116, 126
Transatlantic Corporation, 145, 159
Tusell Gómez, Javier, 22

UGT (General Union of Workers), 33, 62, 68–69, 191–92, 210, 226
Unamuno, Miguel de, 57, 115, 218
Unemployment, 227–28
United Kingdom, 191, 216, 219
United Mining Credit Bank, 140
Urquijo, marquis of, 64–65, 93, 139–40, 176

Valencia, 47
Vallellano, Count of, 53, 83
Vallespinosa y Vior, General Adolfo, 71 n.37
Vergara, Carlos, 146
Viver, baron of, 88

Wages, 32–33, 43 n.67, 223–25
Welfare, 18
Weyler, General Valeriano, 63
Women's rights, 84, 193–95, 223
World War I, 24, 28, 30, 33, 37, 110, 139, 146, 155, 169

Yanguas Messía, José María, 59, 116
Yugoslavia, 9

Zabalza, General, 49